THE GOD WITHIN
Kant, Schelling, and Historicity

Emil Fackenheim
Edited by John Burbidge

For nineteenth-century thinkers, the central problem of religious consciousness in the modern West was the tension between prevailing concepts of individual autonomy and the traditional Judaeo-Christian claim for divine revelation. *The God Within* brings together ten of Professor Emil Fackenheim's essays on the German Idealists who struggled to resolve this tension.

This philosophic preoccupation found its most searching and comprehensive expression when the traditional notion of 'God as Transcendent' was reconceptualized as 'the God within.' The internalization of God's 'otherness' reached its climax with Hegel, the subject of Fackenheim's earlier work, *The Religious Dimension in Hegel's Thought.* This long-awaited companion to that volume examines the earlier stages of the process, beginning with its initiator, Kant, then considering Schelling in both his earlier and later phases, and, finally, looking once more at Hegel. The investigation of this movement, together with the related themes of history and the literary arts, leads to reflection on the significance of taking historicity seriously. Included is the classic, much-cited article 'Metaphysics and Historicity,' which connects the philosophy of German Idealists to twentieth-century questions of historicity and existential thought in particular. The previously unpublished essay 'Schelling in 1800–1801: Art as Revelation,' provides an overview of philosophical history from Kant through Fichte and Schleiermacher, to the later Schelling.

All the essays gathered here are concerned with the radical singularity of history and existence on the one hand and the demands of philosophical truth on the other. They are informed by Professor Fackenheim's engagement with the profound philosophical challenges of our day – particularly his efforts, as a Jewish theologian, to confront the horrors of the Holocaust. We see, through Fackenheim's exposition, how these thinkers sought to come to terms with the presence of radical evil, a problem whose modern relevance is explored in this volume's epilogue, the 1988 essay 'Holocaust and *Weltanschauung*: Philosophical Reflections on Why They Did It.'

EMIL FACKENHEIM was Professor of Philosophy Emeritus, University of Toronto, and Professor of Philosophy at the Hebrew University, Jerusalem. He was the author of numerous books, including *To Mend the World* and *Encounters between Judaism and Modern Philosophy*.

JOHN W. BURBIDGE is a professor in the Department of Philosophy at Trent University. He is the author of *On Hegel's Logic, Hegel on Logic* and *Religion, and Real Process: How Logic and Chemistry Combine in Hegel's Philosophy of Nature.*

Emil L. Fackenheim

THE GOD WITHIN

Kant, Schelling, and Historicity

Edited by John Burbidge

UNIVERSITY OF TORONTO PRESS
Toronto Buffalo London

Toronto Buffalo London
Reprinted 2017
ISBN 978-0-8020-0697-4 (cloth)
ISBN 978-1-4875-8721-5 (paper)

Printed on acid-free paper

Toronto Studies in Philosophy
Editors: James R. Brown and Calvin Normore

Canadian Cataloguing in Publication Data

Fackenheim, Emil L., 1916–
The God within : Kant, Schelling, and historicity

(Toronto studies in philosophy)
Includes bibliographical references and index.
ISBN 978-0-8020-0697-4 (bound). – ISBN 978-1-4875-8721-5 (pbk.)

1. Kant, Immanuel, 1724–1804 – Religion. 2. Schelling, Friedrich Wilhelm Joseph von, 1775–1854 – Religion. 3. Religion – Philosophy. I. Burbidge, John, 1936– . II. Title. III. Series.

BL51.F33 1996 200.1 C95-932625-1

The author, the editor, and University of Toronto Press acknowledge the assistance of Howard Ganz in the publication of this volume.

University of Toronto Press acknowledges the financial assistance to its publishing program of the Canada Council and the Ontario Arts Council.

Dedicated to the memory of Fulton H. Anderson

Contents

Preface

Around 1950, Emil Fackenheim turned his scholarly attention to German philosophy. Having earned his doctorate at the University of Toronto in medieval philosophy during the war, he was now a junior member in its Department of Philosophy, encouraged by its head, Fulton H. Anderson, to prove his mettle. Essays began to appear on Schelling's philosophy of the literary arts (chapter 5), Kant's philosophy of history (chapter 3), and Schelling's late philosophy (chapters 6 and 7). It was an early interest in Kierkegaard that directed his attention to Schelling's philosophy of revelation, and a comment of Schelling's about Kant that raised the question of what German idealism had to say about radical evil (see chapter 2). By a happy coincidence, several of these pieces served to mark the 150th anniversary of Kant's death and the centenary of Schelling's, just as a later paper on Hegel's epigram 'On the Actuality of the Rational and the Rationality of the Actual' (chapter 10) marked the bicentenary of Hegel's birth.

By the middle of the decade, this interest in German idealism crystallized around a project on the philosophy of religion from Kant to Kierkegaard. For this was a period, as Fackenheim notes in chapter 4, when a significant shift occurred in the philosophical understanding of God. The Transcendent became the God Within, a development that opened up, as time went on, the spectre of the human becoming more (and less) than human. The late Schelling and Kierkegaard reinvoked revelation to counter this development, but with little success.

Part one of *From Kant to Kierkegaard* was in the main completed, and was published much later as the first entry in the Cambridge University Press anthology *Nineteenth Century Religious Thought in the West*, edited by Ninian Smart, John Clayton, Stephen Katz, and Patrick Sherry (chapter 1). Part three became *The Religious Dimension in Hegel's Thought* when the chapters on Hegel outgrew their preordained limits. Part four, on the later Schelling and Kierkegaard, would have expanded an early essay, 'Schelling's Philosophy of Religion,' that had appeared in 1952 (chapter 7). 'But,' writes Fackenheim, 'of the planned part two, on Fichte, Schleiermacher and Schelling in the years 1794–1800, only a chapter on Schelling's *System of Transcendental Idealism* of 1800 was written, back in 1958, and, in the hope of once integrating it into a whole, then left unpublished.' With that hope now given up, a gap remained between the discussion of Kant in chapter 1 and that of the young Schelling in chapter 4, now revised for publication. So for this volume Fackenheim added to that latter chapter an introductory overview of the years 1792 to 1800 to provide a bridge. 'I might add,' he notes, 'that it has not been easy for me to integrate that overview, written in 1994, with a manuscript written thirty-five years earlier.'

The publication of *The Religious Dimension in Hegel's Thought* required a change in the earlier plan. *From Kant to Kierkegaard* became *The God Within*, a companion to the Hegel volume that would provide the background in Kant, Fichte, Schleiermacher, and Schelling to Hegel's rethinking of the philosophy of religion.

The Religious Dimension in Hegel's Thought appeared in print in 1967. As Fackenheim recounts in his Introduction to this volume, in that very year an event occurred that changed the focus of his academic interest. The threat to Israel's survival implied by Nasser's expulsion of the UN peace-keeping force and closure of the Gulf of Aqaba to Israeli shipping not only triggered the Six-Day War but also aroused Jewish consciousness throughout the world to the fearsome possibility that the Holocaust could recur. It became necessary to rethink the recent past and reappropriate it into Jewish memory, enabling not only Jews but also all those with whom they were in dialogue to respond authentically to the world after Auschwitz.

Emil Fackenheim became a leading figure within this movement because his own thought and development reflected and anticipated the life and experiences of his community. *God's Presence in History* (1970), *Encounters between Judaism and Modern Philosophy* (1973), *The Jewish Return into History* (1978), *To Mend the World* (1982, 1989, and 1994), and *The Jewish Bible after the Holocaust – A Rereading* (1990) are a few of the many works that came from his pen. When each was finished and off to the publisher, Fackenheim thought of returning to the earlier work on the philosophy of religion. But it was not to be. The existential focus on questions of Jewish self-definition continued to take precedence over the reflective discussion of philosophical theories.

During the years that he was working on *From Kant to Kierkegaard*, however, Fackenheim was also developing his own philosophical position. In accordance with the conventions of the day, his philosophy was to be universal: open to, and designed to convince, any reasonable person. It bore no mark of a distinctively Jewish commitment. While it drew on his analysis of the Kantian and Schellingian philosophy of religion, and increasingly was marked by Hegelian themes, it was equally influenced by the thought and writing of the early Heidegger.

An invitation from Marquette University to give the Aquinas Lecture in 1961 offered Fackenheim an opportunity to define his own position, not only vis-à-vis German idealism, but also with respect to Heidegger. *Metaphysics and Historicity* opened the possibility of a radical limit to historical relativity in the encounter with a hidden God. The argument there sketched was further developed as a lecture he gave to the Inter-American Congress of Philosophy, held at Laval University in 1967, entitled 'The Historicity and Transcendence of Philosophical Truth.' In the published version of this lecture, Fackenheim added an introduction, which is here reprinted in full.

All the chapters in this collection, then, stem from a time when, as Fackenheim himself says, the two parts of his academic interests were kept separate.[1] On the one hand he was exploring Jewish thought, and in particular German-Jewish philosophy. (The latter essays are currently being republished by Indiana University Press in *Jewish Philosophers and Jewish Philosophy*, edited by Michael Morgan.) On the other he concentrated on a 'universal' perspective, more appropriate, as it was then thought, to a secular department of philosophy. That separation collapsed after 1967. In *Encounters* there is no longer an attempt to explicate Kant, Hegel, and Heidegger on their own terms. They are made to dialogue with the Jewish tradition, and are thereby shown to be limited and partial. Hegelian motifs become interwoven with Rabbinic anecdotes; Heidegger is challenged as an advocate of an ahistorical paganism.

For all that these works represent a stage of Fackenheim's development before that integration into a single Jewish philosophy, they have nonetheless contributed to it. And they anticipate it. For Fackenheim's exposition of Kant, Schelling, and Hegel are all characterized by a particular motif. None of these philosophers are talking about abstractions. In their philosophies of religion they are coming to terms with life, a life that has to cope with, and overcome, radical evil. All of them, in one way or another, anticipate the existentialism of Kierkegaard. At the same time they do so with intellectual integrity. At each stage Fackenheim sets up a dilemma that a particular combination of concerns would pose, and then shows that Kant, Schelling, or Hegel not only recognized the dilemma, but had subtly introduced concepts that grasp both horns and offer a more comprehensive, and more satisfactory, intellectual solution. In Fackenheim's interpretation of these philosophers of German Idealism, thought and life were integrated. That is why, in the last analysis, he could neither remain with a divided focus for his academic activities, nor accept the lived consequences of Heidegger's philosophy.

It is Fackenheim's sense that Kant, Schelling, and Hegel were grappling with living issues that makes the articles collected in this volume of continuing interest for the study of both German idealism and historicity. All of them are concerned with the relation between the radical singularity of history and existence on the one hand and the demands of philosophical truth on the other. Aware of the dilemma involved in this polarity, Fackenheim sees more clearly than most the inner logic that unifies all of Kant's thought, including his essays on history and religion, as well as the necessity that drove Schelling beyond transcendental idealism to the later philosophies of freedom and of revelation. The current revival of interest in Schelling's thought will benefit from contact with Fackenheim's perceptive analysis, just as treatments of Kant's philosophy of history continue to refer to his discussion as one of the few to fit the occasional essay on the 'Conjectural Beginning of Human History' into the context of the critical philosophy.

Because Fackenheim has been schooled at the feet of Kant, Schelling, and Hegel, his own venture into the questions of historicity – of the intersection of singular existence with a universal metaphysics – is all the more penetrating. Few have stated the challenge to traditional philosophy more effectively, while yet building on its most significant achievements.

For Fackenheim, the debate between Hegel on the one hand (who pushed the project of internalizing the God of revelation to profound limits) and the late Schelling on the other (who, together with Kierkegaard, attempted to recover the transcendent God) continues to be of contemporary importance. It overshadows all subsequent dismissals of revealed religion by such as Marx and Nietzsche, and is more profound than the deepest of Heidegger's thought. To stand against a world impregnated with evil, one must not only understand how the modern world at its best sought to domesticate the transcendent God, but also explore the ways revelation may still be understood to break through human defences, offering both judgment and hope.

As an example of how this challenge continues into the present, we conclude the volume with an essay published in 1988: 'Holocaust and *Weltanschauung*: Philosophical Reflections on Why They Did It.'

This volume is dedicated to the memory of Fulton H. Anderson, who, as Head of the Department of Philosophy at the University of Toronto, was prepared to appoint a rabbi at a time when Jewish appointments were rare at the university, and whose musings about the need for publications stimulated a junior lecturer to produce these essays on Kant and Schelling. Anderson, too, once stopped me on Queen's Park Crescent to suggest in his gruff manner that I apply for a Woodrow Wilson Fellowship, even though I had made little impression in his undergraduate course on Plato.

In preparing these essays for republication I have without comment updated footnote references by including English translations of texts, many of which were published since the 1950s, and the recent critical edition of Hegel's collected works. Similarly, cross-references direct the reader's attention to the appropriate chapter in this volume, rather than to the original publication (details of which can be found in the Permissions and Acknowledgments at the end of the book). Quotations that were in German in the original have also been translated. The only exceptions are two passages from Heidegger (pp. 217 and 230) where the meaning is contained in plays on German words. While on occasion the standard English version is used, in most cases either the author or the editor has made his own translation. Other editorial comments are noted by square brackets. The index has been prepared by Kir Kuiken.

John Burbidge
Trent University

Author's Acknowledgments

Since most of this book was written a good many years ago it seems fitting for me, in expressing thanks, to reminisce a bit, and to mention friends, colleagues, and supporters of the past as well as of the present.

On 15 December 1941 I appeared in the office of the late Dean G.S. Brett, to apply for admission to the PhD program in philosophy. Late in the year as it was, although through no fault of mine, I said that I could not expect credit for the year. He replied never mind, I could show what I could do. There was a further problem, I went on: a refugee from Nazi Germany, I had no academic degree but only a rabbinic diploma; but this had been accepted as equivalent by the University of Aberdeen. 'What is good enough for Aberdeen,' the dean replied, 'is good enough for us.' And then, seemingly glad to be done with this stuff and nonsense, he launched into a discussion of Aristotle, making me feel that I had never left home.

The University of Toronto philosophy department was home in my years on the staff from 1948 until my retirement in 1981. The personal aspect was important: nobody ever had better colleagues. But the philosophical was the crucial aspect, and in this the central figure was F.H. Anderson. (This book is dedicated to his memory.) Schelling was not exactly popular in English-speaking universities at the time, and when I joined the staff there was no graduate course even on Hegel. One day I took my courage into my hands and told F.H. that I wanted to teach a course on Hegel. (The courage was needed because of two formidable figures, Hegel and F.H. himself.) 'Do you understand Hegel?' he asked. The question was more like an assault. 'Yes,' I lied, and went on to teach Kant, Fichte, Schelling, and Hegel in all the years ahead. Anderson's philosophical principle (by which the department was run) was that, by dint of their greatness, the great philosophers of the past are crucial for the philosophical present, and whatever he may have thought of Schelling, or even Hegel, he never denied their greatness. Many are not at home in a department run on that principle. For me it was perfect.

Among the present, I have expressed thanks elsewhere to John Burbidge: without his labours this volume would not have seen the light of day. And special thanks are due to Howard Ganz of Willowdale. A long-time supporter of my work, he has once again shown his generosity.

Emil L. Fackenheim
Jerusalem, September 1995

Introduction

I

In 1957–8 I held a Guggenheim fellowship. I still remember the trepidation that preceded my decision to apply; how, even after filling in the form, I postponed mailing my application until the last moment; how, late that last Saturday night, I drove to the main Toronto Post Office and sent it by special delivery, half hoping that it would get to New York by the Monday deadline, half hoping that it wouldn't.

It was not so much that, if given the fellowship, I would have to write a book – something I had not ventured before. Indeed, that was the least of it. Far more serious was that in *From Kant to Kierkegaard* I would deal with philosophers of towering stature. Even Fichte, Schleiermacher, and Schelling – to say nothing of Kant and Hegel – would be giants if they lived in our own, philosophically meagre age: theirs is rightly considered the 'golden' one in German philosophy. Much could be said about my interest in that age while, myself, living in one that, putting it mildly, has not been golden in Germany, not in life and, also, not in philosophy.

But even that was far from all. My interest in *From Kant to Kierkegaard*, to be sure, was objective and scholarly, albeit mixed with not a little nostalgia. But I would be less than forthright if I pretended that mine was then – or ever – scholarship for its own sake alone. I was also gripped personally, for I had an inkling that the deepest concern of these thinkers, then and there, was not all that different from my own, here and now.

That 'here and now' of mine had its origin way back in 1935–8, when I was a student of Judaism in Berlin. A century earlier Soren Kierkegaard had come to the same city, there to hear the sixty-six-year-old Schelling lecture on the subject of divine Revelation, on the God of the

Scriptures. What could be thought and believed about these in the modern world? It was an apt time for these two Christians to have that concern, for both held that the challenge of modernity to their traditional verities was most profoundly expressed in the philosophy from Kant to Hegel that had just run its course in Germany.

Back in 1841, that concern brought these two thinkers to Berlin, the one from Munich, the other from Copenhagen. Both were, or tried to be, Christians. What brought young German Jews such as myself, in 1935–8, to a very different Berlin? Why study Judaism at all, at that of all times and, of all places, in the capital of Nazism? The answer is that Nazi Berlin was both the most absurd and the most appropriate place for just that study. That was the view of my friends and myself at the time; and it is my view still, almost sixty years later.

As for the absurdity, we knew far less than the full truth, for had we known we would have abandoned our books and hurried from one consulate to the next, in an attempt to flee for our lives. Still, we knew a great deal. The Berlin of 1935–8 *was* an absurd place for young Jews to study anything, to say nothing of studying Judaism. But Nazi Berlin as an *appropriate* place?

Probity of mind and heart once brought two great Christians to Berlin, even a sense of urgency. But that Christian urgency of theirs, in 1841, can in no way compare with our Jewish urgency in 1935–8, when our whole world could colllapse at any moment. (In the so-called *Kristallnacht* of 9 November 1938, it did.) As for what brought us to Berlin, it was mind and heart, to be sure, but not these alone, for encompassed was our whole existence. Our parents and grandparents had been German Jews, but who were *we* now? Indeed, who were *Jews* now? Our quest, then, was for our Jewish past and future, *all* of it. Climactically, however, it was – if such was still possible in our modern, enlightened, catastrophic age – for the God of Israel.

Once during those hectic years my cousin Lisa asked me how I could study at a time like this. I replied that we knew that we were sitting on a powder keg, but had to be calm enough to smoke cigars while sitting on it. During the Gulf War the Scud missiles were falling on Israel, without our knowing where they would fall or what they contained. At the height of it a neighbour asked me why I did not run from Jerusalem as I once had from Berlin. I told her that Berlin story of mine, but added that two things were different now. I was no longer smoking cigars, and I had no intention to run from Jerusalem.

From Kant to Kierkegaard was never completed. Hegel's philosophy proved to be immensely thought- and time-consuming, and my work on it became, instead of just part of a book, *The Religious Dimension in Hegel's Thought.*

The book appeared in 1967. The Six-Day War happened in the same year. In the three weeks of dread that preceded it, Jews all over the world feared, and had reason to fear, that Israel would be destroyed. This threat of a second Jewish Holocaust forced me to face the first, the one that has happened.

Prior to 1967 I had thought about the catastrophe only indirectly and, moreover, had been protected in such thought by much philosophical and theological armour. Now – and increasingly as the years wore on – I had no choice but to shed the armour, to become vulnerable, even close to naked. There is really no way for a thinker to expose his thought to the Holocaust, and then to return to business – philosophical or theological – as usual.

So I never got to the remainder of the original project, promised as *The God Within* in the Hegel book.

II

Only at one other time in my life did I apply for, and receive, a major fellowship, and my Killam years (1977–8) too were marked by trepidation, but this time it was of a different order. In the nearly ten years since 1967 I had reached the conclusion – to cite Theodor Adorno – that the 'metaphysical capacity is paralyzed' by the Holocaust, while yet insisting – to amplify on my own very first, but never abandoned statement, made in 1967 – that a posthumous victory for Hitler is as fully forbidden in philosophy or theology as in any other sphere of life or thought. Given this paradoxical stance, it was certain from the start that my new project, post-Holocaust Jewish and philosophical thought, could be no more than a fragment. Hence my trepidation, this time, the second time.

Such as it is, *To Mend the World*, begun in the Killam years, is my *magnum opus.* It was first published in 1982. Over a decade has passed since then. The Holocaust ended half a century ago. Most of the survivors are gone. Holocaust literature has become a vast library. Quite a few theologians and some philosophers have written. Yet now I wonder whether the truly *radical* response required in either discipline is not still largely missing – whether it either is yet to come or will never come at all.

But reflections such as these belong elsewhere. What belongs here is the fact that, while the year 1967 marks a caesura in my thought, I did not abandon the golden age in German philosophy even after. In *Encounters between Judaism and Modern Philosophy* (1973), Kant, Hegel, and Kierkegaard are indispensable: I find this noteworthy. To my mind, more noteworthy still is the fact that, while in the first, destructive part of *To Mend the World* the paralysis of which Adorno has written is shown to spread among philosophers, among them Spinoza, Kant, Hegel, and Heidegger, in the second, 'mending' part of the book there is a post-Holocaust reappearance of sorts of thinkers harking back to the golden age, among them Kant, Hegel, Schelling, and even Fichte. Heidegger does not reappear.

Thus I find the publication of this volume, composed of essays mostly written prior to 1967, welcome and meaningful, and am grateful to my colleague, friend, and former student, Professor John Burbidge, for having edited it. The 'former student' part is the most important, and John is one of several who have gone on in the field, sometimes understanding me better than I have understood myself.

It is a joy for a teacher to be able to say that about his former students.

III

Only once in my forty-odd years of teaching was I overcome in mid-lecture, needing several minutes before I could control my feelings and carry on.

At the University of Toronto my favourite course was the golden age in German philosophy. At Jerusalem's Hebrew University I continued with this period, but now the emphasis was on Jews and Judaism, and for these the age was not golden, for the people still lived under repressive laws, and the religion had yet to emerge from the Ghetto. The struggle for the emancipation of Jews, and for a modern renewal of Jewish faith – these are the themes of Jewish history in that period.

One day I was lecturing on a remarkable friendship. He was Daniel Friedrich Schleiermacher, a Protestant theologian. She was Henrietta Herz, a brilliant Jewish woman of wide philosophical interests. He was writing his first book, *On Religion*, and kept sending her sections for comment. The two were in almost daily contact.

Then Schleiermacher came to Judaism and, having stated that it once was a living faith, he wrote that it was long dead: 'Those who yet wear its livery are only sitting lamenting beside the imperishable mummy, bewailing its departure and its sad legacy.' Perhaps he convinced Henrietta of the truth of this view. Or, to judge by what she wrote about Judaism in her memoirs, perhaps she convinced him. In any case she eventually became a convert.

At this point in my lecture I lost control, for I thought of Will Herberg and Reinhold Niebuhr. Herberg, an American Jew disillusioned with Marxism and secularism, went to Niebuhr, the great Protestant theologian, and asked to be converted. But Niebuhr sent him back to the study of Judaism, of which Herberg was wholly ignorant, and, having listened to Niebuhr and studied Judaism, Will eventually became a major Jewish theologian. I knew him well, and found him inspiring.

This flashed into my mind in mid-lecture, and with it a tragic flaw of Germany even at her greatest – her philosophy in its golden age. Why did not Schleiermacher do for Henrietta Herz what Niebuhr would one day do for Will Herberg? To be sure, in 1799, the year *On Religion* was completed, Judaism in Germany was at a nadir, but Henrietta might have had an early share in the renewal of it in the next century, one impressive enough to earn Berlin the title of the Jerusalem of Europe.

My friends and I still experienced much of this in the years 1935–8. Indeed, from 1933 on Jewish life in Germany had what can only be called a renaissance. But it was of short duration. The Holocaust, the murder of every available Jew in the Nazi Empire, was yet to come. The end of a flourishing Judaism came in a single night of terror. Schleiermacher was mistaken in his view that Judaism was long dead. But during the night of 9 November 1938, the *Kristallnacht*, German Judaism was murdered.

E.L.F.
Jerusalem, October 1994

THE GOD WITHIN

Kant, Schelling, and Historicity

1 Kant's Philosophy of Religion

Kant wrote extensively on the subject of religion. Although a child of the Age of Enlightenment and as such suspicious of, if not hostile to, all religious orthodoxies, he could not leave religion alone, whether 'within the bounds of reason' or even beyond it, touching on (if not actually dealing with) the Christian revelation. His three *Critiques* all end with religious questions, and one work – *Religion within the Bounds of Reason Alone* – deals with nothing else.

Despite an air of deceptive obviousness, the religious issues in question, as dealt with by Kant, almost all raise complex questions for the interpreter. Among these are the relation between ritual and morality, between political and religious authority, and – most obscure but surely also most important – the room, if any, left by 'reason only' for the Christian revelation.

However, one problem in Kant's philosophy of religion surpasses all others in significance. In Kant's view, morality is the highest sphere of rationally accessible truth. It also must be autonomous, i.e., unlimited in scope and authority by a sphere beyond it. Despite all this he asserts the necessity of a 'transition' from 'morality' to 'religion.' Kant must explain and justify the necessity of this 'transition.' In case he fails, his philosophy of religion fails as a whole. His 'moral religion' – as well as any other form of supposedly justified religion – reduces itself, in that case, to morality pure and simple. As for religion – all religion as such and in principle – it is, in that case, at best useful humbug. Such, however, was not Kant's view.

I

On frequent occasions Kant defines religion as the interpretation of our moral duties as divine commandments. This definition, while authoritative, is not without difficulties. For if the religious interpretation adds grounds or motives to the moral ones already present in the concept of duty, it threatens moral autonomy; and if it does not, it threatens to make religion itself into a redundancy. It would seem that these difficulties can be removed only if one turns from this first definition to a second and considers this latter as the more fundamental. Kant asserts that 'morality necessarily leads to religion.'[1] An inspection of Kant's first definition, already referred to, would have to ask how this transition is possible. An inspection of Kant's second, more fundamental definition must ask why the transition is necessary. This second definition identifies religion as justified hope.

In a celebrated passage in the Critique of Pure Reason Kant writes: 'All the interests of my reason, speculative as well as practical, combine in the following three questions: (i) What can I know? (ii) What ought I to do? (iii) What may I hope?'[2] The third question is answered by religion. It does so not by exercise of an additional capacity, over and above the capacities for knowledge and moral action, but rather by somehow conjoining these two, and by recognizing a limitation in their conjunction.

'Reason' is not 'interested' in religious hopes which men happen to have but only in such as are justified. The justification itself cannot consist in the demonstration of a human tendency to hope, for this could be mere wishful thinking even if it were more or less or even altogether universal. Nor is it sufficient to demonstrate that the religious hope in question does not contradict the laws of logic or morality. To be sure, a restriction of this sort is necessary. (In Kant's view there can be no rationally justified religious hopes for supernatural events which would shatter the laws of nature, or for divine acts of Grace which would shatter the laws of morality.)[3] It is not, however, sufficient. Since Kant has confined knowledge to the realm of appearance, it is quite possible to have non-contradictory opinions about whatever may transcend appearance; but the mere logical tenability of such opinions is not enough to make them part of a rational hope. Again, it is equally possible to find examples of religious hopes which are morally unobjectionable. Such could include even the crude kind of religious thought which expects of heaven no more than just rewards for earthly virtue. But once more the fact that such hoping may be morally unobjectionable does not mean that it is rationally justified.

How then *can* the religious hope be rationally justified? Not by a theoretical necessity, for knowledge is confined to the phenomenal world.

Nor is there a moral necessity for religious hoping.[4] For while it may be morally necessary *for us* to mete out reward in accordance with moral desert, no such necessity exists for believing that the universe will do the same. Indeed a religious hope which springs from nothing more than a cosmic projection of the idea of justice simply begs the question. But if the religious hope cannot spring from either a theoretical or a moral necessity how can it nevertheless be rationally justified? For according to Kant, reason has no more than these two functions.

With this question, we have come upon the most critical and most profound aspect of Kant's religious thought. It is the most critical, because on his ability to answer this question the transition from Kantian morality to religion wholly depends. It is the most profound, because his answer revolutionizes religious thought, substituting as it does 'moral theology' for the traditional 'natural theology' which Kant has seen himself compelled to discard. Unfortunately, this aspect of his thought is also one of the most obscure parts of Kant's teaching. Indeed, it is only fair to confess that a host of critics have dismissed it in despair, and that the following attempt to understand it is not made without trepidation.[5]

II

In view of the importance of the subject, we begin with an extensive summary. Reason in all its functions is unable to rest satisfied with the relative and the conditioned; it seeks the absolute and the unconditioned. In the sphere of the practical, this is the highest Good. The question facing man, as a rational being, is: what is the correct notion of the highest Good?

Two rival views command attention, namely, the Epicurean and the Stoic. For the Epicurean, the highest Good is happiness, while for the Stoic it is the kind of virtue which is acquired by the performance of duty for duty's sake. These two views are mutually exclusive. The Epicurean considers virtue as a mere by-product of happiness, vice being nothing but the result of sickness or unhappiness. For the Stoic, happiness is a mere by-product of virtue; for true happiness consists in the knowledge of duty performed and virtue acquired; to want any other kind of happiness is itself a vice. These views, then, are in sharp contrast. But both are in error, the one because it mistakes man for an animal, the other because it mistakes him for a god.

Epicureanism is in obvious error, for it mistakes all moral autonomy for mere heteronomy. But to act morally is to act because of duty, not for the sake of happiness; and virtue, far from being a mere means to or by-product of happiness, is an absolute Good in its own right. However, the Stoic error, while less obvious, is no less significant. Virtue, while the supreme Good, cannot be the complete Good. Man is a *product* of nature. As such he needs happiness, and this need is not evil but innocent.[6] Hence to consummate human destiny the highest Good must contain happiness as well as virtue; and to consummate it in one synthesis it must contain, not any and all happiness, but happiness in exact proportion to virtue.

Appearances to the contrary notwithstanding, the concept arrived at is in far more radical contrast with the Stoic and Epicurean concepts than these two are with each other. If Stoic or Epicurean *is* right, man can wholly fulfil the meaning of his destiny.[7] But the ideal now arrived at implies that man cannot do so, at least within the span of earthly life and without the help of God.

According to the Epicurean, to be sure, man cannot hope to attain absolute happiness. But he can accept as his ideal something less because he is not *obligated* to attain absolute happiness: indeed, he is not obligated at all. In the Stoic view, in contrast, man is obligated to attain absolute virtue. However, he is capable of attaining it, and to the extent to which he fails he can blame only himself. But if the view now arrived at is correct, man is obligated to attain a Good which he is incapable of attaining. He is obligated to attain it because it is implied in the categorical imperative; yet he is incapable of attaining it. The one component of the highest Good – absolute virtue or holiness – he can aim at but never wholly reach; the other component – happiness in proportion to virtue – he can advance only haphazardly but not systematically. The latter he could do only if 'the maxim of virtue [were] ... the efficient cause of happiness.'[8] But since happiness is wholly unlike virtue, this is not the case. In short, 'to realize the highest Good is (i) to aim at moral perfection (ii) to reach it (iii) thereby to merit happiness and (iv) to acquire it, as a necessary consequence of perfect virtue.'[9] But while man even at his best can achieve only the first of these goals he is obligated to achieve all four.

But what man is obligated to achieve he must be able to achieve. It is therefore necessary that the conditions exist by virtue of which he can fulfil his obligation. These conditions are man's immortality and the existence of God.

Absolute virtue or holiness is not a state of successful struggle against conflicting inclination, but a state in which there remains no conflicting obligation and hence no need for struggle. As a moral being, man is obligated to attain this state; but as a finite being, he can only approximate it. This contradiction can be removed only if the approximation can be infinite. But this presupposes man's immortality.

But immortality, by itself, enables man only to achieve absolute virtue, not happiness in proportion to virtue. This is because happiness is wholly unlike virtue, the former belonging to the world of nature, the latter to the moral world; and these two worlds, so far as finite understanding is concerned, are wholly separate. How then can man, by being virtuous, bring about deserved happiness? This is possible only if the two worlds, though apparently separate, are nevertheless ultimately connected; if the same Being is the author of moral law and the natural world: that is, if there is a God who is omniscient, omnipotent, and, above all, holy.

Kant concludes that 'morality necessarily leads to religion' because moral obligation necessarily leads to the belief in the conditions without which it cannot be fulfilled. Religion is, on the one hand, the interpretation of moral duties as divine commandments; as such it adds to autonomous morality the belief that moral duties can be fulfilled, because the author of moral law is also the author of nature.[10] On the other hand, religion is the hope for the chance to attain holiness, and for the gift of deserved happiness; as such it is rationally justified because moral reason demands that that can be realized which ought to be realized.

III

This may suffice as a summary of Kant's teaching. We must now consider its significance. And we may begin by stating a number of formidable criticisms which have been directed against it ever since his views first appeared in print:

(i) The argument for immortality rests on mutually exclusive premises. The one asserts that what we are obligated to attain we must be able to attain; the other asserts that we are obligated to attain something which we cannot attain, namely, holiness. Yet if, for the sake of consistency, either of these premises is dropped the argument vanishes.[11]

(ii) The decisive premise in the argument for God is an alien and indeed insufferable intruder into Kant's moral thought. We cannot be morally obligated to bring about the deserved happiness of others, nor morally will to acquire our own; not the former because it is not always within our power; not the latter because we exist in order to do our duty, not in order to become happy. Thus while Kant requires a notion of the highest Good, as the ultimate object of the moral will, this object cannot include happiness.[12] 'The principle of personality alone is the object looked for. Any additional object is not only unnecessary but even detrimental.'[13] But with this conclusion the argument for God loses its force.

(iii) The arguments for immortality and God (provided one is prepared to take them seriously, the above difficulties notwithstanding) are mutually exclusive. Each solves the problem (assuming that there is a problem) in a way which precludes the solution provided by the other. For if (as the argument for immortality asserts) we are able infinitely to approximate holiness, provided only we are given the 'time' to do it, we approximate a state in which we can no longer stand in need of happiness, and the need for a God who dispenses deserved happiness disappears. And if (as the argument for God asserts) the dualism between virtue and the need for happiness persists even in infinity, then immortality is needed, not in order to provide us with a chance to achieve holiness, but merely in order that we might receive the rewards of our earthly goodness.[14]

(iv) The concepts of immortality and God are incompatible with the conclusions of Kant's most fundamental philosophical doctrines. For if temporality and sensuality can belong only to phenomena, they cannot belong to the soul in a non-phenomenal existence. Yet without time and sensual desire how can there be moral struggle and moral progress? But it is precisely the need for infinite moral struggle and progress which gives rise to the belief in immortality to begin with. Again, categories such as causality can apply only to phenomena. How then can they apply to God, who is not a phenomenon? Yet if they do not apply to Him how can He be the author of nature and moral law? But it is precisely the need for a cause, linking the worlds of nature and morality, which gives rise to the belief in God at all.[15]

(v) So much for the essence of God and immortality. What about their existence? Do God and immortality exist? But 'existence,' for Kant, has meaning only in a phenomenal context. Are they, then, mere ideas produced by our reason? But the problems for the solution of which they are needed are precisely such as cannot be solved by *our* powers of production; and if there are no such problems God and immortality are not needed at all. But perhaps they are ideas to which we – necessarily but mistakenly – ascribe existence, that is, necessary fictions? But then if it *is* true that morality is possible only if God and immortality exist, morality is *itself* a fiction. And if this is *not* true even the fictions are not necessary.[16]

What is one to make of this formidable list of difficulties – a list which, incidentally, could easily be expanded? Is one to conclude that Kant's whole teaching concerning God and immortality must be dismissed, as a hopeless mass of confusion?[17] Yet in so doing one would dismiss what, to Kant himself, was the culminating point of his entire philosophy. For it is a mistaken belief that Kant's *Critique of Pure Reason* aims at the elimination of all metaphysics. Rather, it aims at eliminating the old *kind* of metaphysics in order to prepare the ground for a wholly new kind.[18] And the content of this new kind of metaphysics includes, in addition to freedom, immortality and God. Kant writes: 'God, freedom and the immortality of the soul are the problems to the solution of which, as their ultimate and unique goal, all the laborious preparations are directed.'[19]

IV

It is in this last observation that the key to an understanding lies. Kant's 'theology' or 'metaphysics' is a new *kind* of metaphysics, and it appears as confused and inconsistent only so long as it is mistaken for the old kind. Kant destroys the metaphysics which is based on speculation and replaces it with a metaphysics which is based on moral consciousness. He seeks to prove, not immortality and God, but that the belief in immortality and God is implicit in finite moral consciousness. He seeks to develop, not philosophical concepts of God and immortality, but the concepts of God and immortality which are implicit in finite moral consciousness. If these beliefs are, by certain standards, somehow inadequate, it is not because of incompetent philosophizing on Kant's part, but because of certain characteristics of finite moral consciousness. The task of philosophy is not to change or reject these beliefs, but to show what they are, and why they are implicit in finite moral consciousness. This raises, to be sure, the question why such a philosophical enterprise should be regarded as metaphysics, rather than a mere analysis of the structure of finite moral consciousness. But the answer to this question, while complex in its details, is quite simple in principle: the philosopher too is a finite moral agent; and it is in his latter rather than his former capacity that he is in touch with ultimate moral reality: and as a philosopher he recognizes this fact. This, we contend, is the innermost secret of Kant's 'practical' metaphysics.

V

These contentions must now be demonstrated in detail. And we begin by stressing that they are not wholly unfamiliar to anyone acquainted with Kant's moral thought, even if his religious thought is as yet unknown territory. For he has already come upon Kant's doctrine of freedom, the first part of his 'practical' metaphysics and the indispensable basis for all that is to come. Here Kant has proved, not freedom, but that the belief in freedom is implicit in moral consciousness. He has tried to show, not how freedom can be philosophically understood, but that moral consciousness alone can understand it, to the extent to which it can be understood at all. And freedom turns into a metaphysical truth (rather than being a pseudo-moral illusion) through the demonstration that the philosopher *can* accept it as a reality because it does not contradict causality, and that he *must* accept it as a reality because he, too, is a moral agent.

But as we now turn from freedom to God and immortality a new element makes its appearance. The belief in freedom is implicit in moral consciousness in so far as it is moral. The belief in God and immortality is implicit in it in so far as it is *finite* as well as moral.[20] It is implicit in it because the structure of finite morality has certain inner contradictions. The beliefs in God and immortality can resolve these contradictions only by reflecting them. Philosophy must explicate these beliefs, along with their contradictions; but it must culminate by defining the sense in which the philosopher – who recognizes these contradictions – can nevertheless accept the beliefs which contain them. It is only with the accomplishments of this last task that Kant's 'practical metaphysics' is established.

VI

We begin with Kant's analysis of the structure of finite morality. An infinite moral being would have the notion of moral law but no notion of duty or obligation. Moral law would be the law of its very being; it would necessarily act out of the sheer love of goodness and could not act otherwise.[21] But to a finite moral being – which does not produce itself but is a natural product and as such endowed with natural inclinations[22] – moral law is not the law of its very being. It is not something that *is* but something that *ought to be*. It is present only in the form of obligation; what ought to be can be, in this case, only through obedience and self-constraint.[23] Finite moral existence is struggle and must always remain struggle. Such an existence can achieve virtue, that is, victory in the struggle. But the victory can never reach holiness, that is, a state in which all constraint ceases because nothing remains that needs to be constrained.[24]

But while there is no point at which finite moral existence could cease struggling it is nevertheless obligated to attain a state in which it not only *could* but *would have to* cease struggling because all struggling has become meaningless. This is for three interrelated reasons. Virtue has degrees. Increasing virtue consists of an increasing strength of moral character and a corresponding decrease or transformation of conflicting inclination. Finally, there is no highest degree of possible virtue short of the degree at which the strength of moral character is absolute, and conflicting inclination either vanquished or transformed; that is, short of the point at which virtue passes into holiness.[25]

The contradiction of finite moral existence may therefore be formulated as follows. The more intense a finite agent's moral awareness and effort are, the smaller is his *actual* distance from what he ought to be – and the more acute is his *awareness* of his distance from what he ought to be. If ever his moral awareness and moral effort reaches absoluteness, there would no longer *be* a distance, and obligation *as* obligation would vanish; yet if at any state, including the last, he shook off obligation, as *having* vanished, he would, instead of being above the state of moral struggle, forthwith tumble below it.[26]

This contradiction could be avoided only if it could be believed, either that at some conceivable stage obligation could be shaken off, holiness having been achieved, or that there is a degree of virtue short of holiness at which moral reason could rest content. However, both these alternatives represent morally impossible forms of escapism. Moreover, this is not only because they involve illusions about some distant future moment but, more importantly, because they are capable of perverting finite moral existence at any present moment. His own empirical nature can never be wholly transparent to any finite being,[27] hence if it could be believed at *some* moment that holiness is achieved (and the stage of moral struggle superseded) it could be believed at *any actual* present moment. So much for the first above alternative. As for the second, any degree of virtue short of holiness which one may choose to be sufficient is chosen arbitrarily; hence, once such a choice is allowed, what already *is* may be considered sufficient, and the distinction between 'is' and 'ought' evaporates.

The upshot is that, provided he takes his moral situation seriously, the finite moral agent is forced to believe in his own immortality, understanding this latter as an infinite duration making possible through struggle an infinite approximation of holiness. He need not be *conscious* of this belief. Nor need he actually *hold* it while not morally engaged. *But while he is in actual moral engagement this belief is necessarily implied in his engagement.*

VII

We must now turn to the aspect of the structure of finite moral existence by virtue of which it implies belief in God. This concerns the relationship between moral willing, moral acting, and moral ends. An infinite moral being would not, strictly speaking, aim at ends. For there would be, to such a being, no aims as yet unachieved. Since moral law would be the law of its very being, its willing would not be an aiming at something, but identical with its acting. There could be, in the case of such a being, no distinction between its willing – its self-determination – and its acting – its belabouring of an independent external reality. For to such a being there would *be* no independent external reality. In willing it would produce *ex nihilo* what it willed.[28]

The structure of finite moral existence is altogether different. In the first place, all *finite* willing must aim at *ends*. To be sure, if it is moral it is determined not by a desire for ends but by the moral law; but this means, not that finite moral willing can be without ends, but that it aims at these because of duty rather than desire.[29] A finite moral willing which did not aim at ends would not be willing at all.

In the second place, finite *willing* can never be identical with *acting*. *The finite moral being, while productive of its moral willing, is not productive of its own being.* It is a being which has not made itself, existing in a world which it has not made. Hence its willing, if it is moral willing, is a self-determining; but its acting is a belabouring of a reality independent of it. The dualism between willing and acting, non-existent in the case of an infinite moral being, is, in the case of finite moral beings, inescapable.

This dualism implies a distinction between two kinds of possible ends, namely, those which can be achieved by willing alone, and those which can be achieved only by the kind of overt acting which transforms the world. The question arises whether only the former kind of end, or the latter as well, can be included among moral ends, that is, among such as the finite moral agent can be obligated to realize. The former ends would all come under the heading of promoting his own virtue, the latter, under the head of advancing other people's happiness.[30]

But any attempt to confine moral ends to the former kind would distort the characteristics of finite moral existence. Indeed, to eliminate other people's happiness, as a morally *necessary* end, is in the end to destroy one's own virtue, as a morally *possible* end. A person who attempts, as a matter of duty, to advance the happiness of others succeeds, even if his attempt fails, in strengthening his own virtue. This would not be true if he sought to advance other people's happiness *in order to* strengthen his own virtue. In that case, his willing, instead of being geared to action, would have degenerated into mere self-absorption. Finite willing, while distinct from acting, is not a complete reality devolving upon itself. All serious finite willing is a willing-to-act. And a finite moral willing which does not will-to-act is a mere vague 'meaning well,' not serious willing at all.[31]

It follows that the two kinds of end stand or fall together.[32] To be sure, they are distinct kinds of end. But unless the kind of end which can be realized only by acting can be taken morally seriously, the kind of end which can be attained by willing alone becomes unattainable; for in that case willing (which in the case of finite beings can be serious only if it is willing-to-act) degenerates into a mere concern with self. The conclusion is that the highest Good, as the complex of all moral ends, must contain not only virtue but also happiness; and if the highest Good is to be one whole, this must be happiness in proportion to virtue.

But at this point there arises a problem of the utmost significance. The finite moral agent is always in control of his moral willing, for in this he determines himself. But he is never wholly in control of his acting, for in this he belabours an independent world. Indeed, radically considered – if the consequences of the acting as well as the acting itself are taken into account – he is never in control at all. This is obvious to anyone who has ever tried to predict all the consequences of his acting prior to acting.

The question is not how the finite moral agent can be responsible for consequences of his acting which he cannot foresee or control. He cannot be responsible for such consequences. The problem is rather how, since the consequences of his acting are ultimately beyond his control, and since all his serious willing is willing-to-act, it is possible for him *even to will*. This would certainly be impossible if external reality were *known* to be systematically obstructive of the finite moral agent's moral purposes, or even if it were indifferent to them. For no one can seriously will to realize ends which he knows to be impossible, or even such as he knows to come into being – if they *do* come into being – by the kind of haphazard chance which is wholly unrelated to his actions.[33] The finite agent does not know, to be sure, that the world is hostile or indifferent. But neither does he have conclusive evidence to the contrary.

So far as the evidence is concerned, the question is open. However, the finite moral agent does not leave it open. He engages in serious moral willing and acting, morally constrained by the categorical imperative, and undeterred by his ignorance of the ultimate consequences of his acting. And this means nothing less than that, whether he knows it or not, he believes in God. He may *be* an agnostic or atheist while not morally engaged; and he may *think* that he is an agnostic or atheist while he *is* morally engaged. But his *actual* moral engagement implies the belief that that which moral law bids him realize in nature can be realized in it because there is a 'common author' of both.[34]

VIII

We have now considered the aspects in the structure of finite moral existence which necessitate the beliefs in immortality and God. We must now consider their relation. This relation is one of contradiction. This contradiction finite moral existence cannot ignore or remove but only accept. Its acceptance – together with the belief that it is not ultimate – is religion.

The contradiction is between two ultimate syntheses required by finite moral existence, the one being holiness, the other, a totality which unites virtue with happiness.[35] This contradiction exists because the finite moral agent cannot, and yet must, take his own need for happiness morally seriously. On the one hand, he cannot take it seriously, for if he regards it as fixed and definable he assumes that there is a fixed degree of virtue which he cannot and hence need not transcend; and if he does not regard it as fixed and definable it is a need destined to gradual elimination. On the other hand, he must take morally seriously at least the need of happiness found in others. For if he does not, he cannot seriously act and will-to-act at all. But how can he accept that *others* need the synthesis of virtue and happiness and yet believe *himself* to be capable of the synthesis of holiness?

The religion of finite moral existence does not supersede but reflects this contradiction. We considered above briefly Kant's definition of religion as the interpretation of our moral duties as divine commandments, along with its difficulties. These difficulties can now be removed. Religion, as so defined, does not add either to the finite agent's moral knowledge or to his moral motivation. It *does* add the belief that the ends which he is obligated to realize in the world *can* be realized in it. However, religion as considered in this aspect only is one-sided, and, if made absolute, self-contradictory. For this reason religion is not only the interpretation of our moral duties as divine commandments (and with it the implied synthesis of holiness). It is also the hope for deserved happiness. But this aspect, too, if made into an absolute, is one-sided and self-contradictory. A *direct* expectation even of deserved happiness would not merely freeze into absolutes arbitrarily chosen degrees of virtue; it also makes impossible all genuine virtue, and hence, all deserved happiness. For genuine virtue can be acquired only if it is sought for its own sake, not for the sake of the reward of happiness; but if the hope for deserved happiness is the ultimate synthesis this is impossible. In short, to make the first aspect of religion absolute (the synthesis of holiness) would be to fall back into the Stoic error, to make the second aspect absolute (the synthesis of virtue and deserved happiness), into the Epicurean error; and all the efforts made to avoid them would be in vain.

Religion in its totality, then, includes both these aspects, without yet resolving the contradiction which exists between them. As such it is a focusing, not on the hope for deserved happiness, but on achieving a moral stature which is worthy of happiness. In this focusing, the aim of achieving moral stature is quite independent of whether there is or will be happiness according to moral worth; because of this independence it implies the need for the synthesis of holiness. Yet the hope is inevitably in the background,[36] implying the need for the synthesis of virtue and happiness. Religion culminates at the point at which the finite moral agent recognizes his radical inability to understand the relation between that which must be achieved by himself and that which can be expected only from God.[37]

IX

Kant has now completed his analysis of the structure of finite moral existence, and of the religious beliefs implied in it. But this analysis is not, by itself, 'practical metaphysics.' It turns into the latter only by virtue of the thesis that the *engaged* standpoint of finite moral existence is *metaphysically ultimate, for the philosopher no less than for the man in the street.* Kant has already asserted that freedom – which appears as a reality in the moment of moral engagement – is *in fact* a reality rather than a useful or necessary fiction. He now makes the same assertion concerning immortality and God.

But the latter assertion involves far greater difficulties than the former, and indeed can be made only if it is decisively qualified. The belief in freedom was philosophically acceptable (albeit unprovable and even unintelligible) because it was found to be free from contradiction. But the beliefs in God and immortality are *not* free from contradiction, and cannot be made so by a process of philosophical purification. For they necessarily reflect the contradictions of finite moral existence which alone give rise to them. How can these beliefs nevertheless be philosophically acceptable? They are acceptable, Kant replies, if they are regarded as 'symbolic anthropomorphisms.'[38]

The finite-moral concepts of immortality and God are, in the first place, clear anthropomorphisms. Whatever the characteristics of the self apart from its phenomenal existence, temporality and sensibility cannot be among them. And whatever the nature of God – if there *is* a God – will and reason, as we can alone conceive them, cannot be among His attributes.[39]

But, in the second place, to recognize a belief as anthropomorphic is not necessarily to reject it. Only a 'dogmatic anthropomorphism' – which mistakes anthropomorphic beliefs for literal truth – is unacceptable. A 'symbolic anthropomorphism' is not.[40] This latter is an anthropomorphism which is recognized as such and yet not abandoned, first, because it contains truth in however inadequate a form; second, because this truth is inaccessible in a more adequate form.

That the first of these two conditions applies here is understood if some Kantian fundamentals are remembered. Kant teaches a dualism between the empirical and the intelligible-moral self, and between the empirical-natural and the intelligible-moral world. He does not teach that there are two selves and two worlds, but that to our finite standpoint there appear to be two selves and two worlds. The one self and world (which we know) are only appearance; and the other (which are more than appearance) we do not know; they are disclosed to us only in the experience of moral obligation. To an absolute standpoint there would be, not two selves but one self, and not two worlds but one world; and these would somehow contain both our selves and our worlds: for – this is the crucial point – 'appearance' is not illusion;[41] whatever it may be to an absolute standpoint, it would not be sheer nothingness.

It follows that if the standpoint of finite morality is, on the one hand, confined to the dualism of the two selves and the two worlds; and if, on the other hand, it is driven to the belief that this dualism is not ultimate, then it can *represent* this climactic belief only in terms which contain empirical and phenomenal elements. It also follows that, if it is the case that philosophical criticism can *recognize but not transcend* the limitations of the standpoint of finite morality, then it cannot *replace* the beliefs of that standpoint with truth in a higher form; it can only recognize that these beliefs are 'symbolic anthropomorphisms,' and that their terms are only of 'analogical'[42] significance.

X

But the question still remains *whether* the standpoint of finite morality can be transcended, either by philosophy itself or in some other way. Kant's 'practical metaphysics' culminates in the demonstration that this is impossible.

Philosophy recognizes as finite not only the standpoint of theoretical consciousness but also that of finite morality. Does this mean that, in recognizing their finiteness, it can itself attain to an absolute standpoint? On a number of occasions, Kant considers this possibility. But he invariably rejects it.[43]

Human understanding distinguishes between the possibility and actuality of things. But to a reason freed of the finite aspects of human understanding this distinction could not exist. For it would have neither concepts of the merely possible nor sensual intuitions of the merely actual. Being purely intuitive, it would have only the actual; and since the actual could not be distinguished from the possible, it would be the necessary. An absolute or divine reason, and all it knows, would be absolute necessity.[44]

Again, finite moral reason distinguishes between what ought to be done and what is done. But for a moral reason freed of the conditions of finiteness 'there would be no difference between obligation and act.' 'In an intelligible world ... everything is actual by reason of the simple fact that, being something good, it is possible.'[45] Natural and moral law would coincide. And beings which, being finite, would be under the first law would also be *ipso facto* under the second: they would not merely be capable of conforming to moral law but so constituted as to conform necessarily to it.[46]

This last conclusion is the main reason why the concept of an unconditionally necessary being, while the 'most unavoidable,' is also the 'most inaccessible concept of speculative human reason.'[47] It is unavoidable, not only for ordinary speculation in its search for the 'last bearer of all things,'[48] but also for the Kantian kind of criticism which, in recognizing the human theoretical and moral standpoints to be finite, gives rise to the problematic notion of an absolute standpoint. Yet this 'unavoidable' concept of the unconditionally necessary is also 'most inaccessible' and a 'veritable abyss' which swallows 'the greatest no less than the least perfection,'[49] and among these is the perfection which matters above all, namely, moral perfection. Speculative reason shrinks from the abyss with the assertion that 'God is the Holy One but he cannot create a holy being.'[50] It retreats to the standpoint of finite morality and its symbolic-anthropomorphic truths. The unconditionally necessary is not a reality known from an absolute standpoint, but a problematical concept arising for the finite standpoint. It is a concept by means of which the finite standpoint, becoming philosophical, recognizes its own finiteness.

XI

But perhaps the standpoint of finite morality can be transcended in a non-philosophical way? The claimant which Kant considers is what he calls 'mysticism.' However, for this he reserves some of his sharpest attacks.

It has often been charged that Kant had little or no insight into the nature of religious emotions, and that this failing accounts for the 'narrow moralism' of his religious concepts. But the first charge is manifestly false, and the characterization of his religious concepts as narrowly moralistic reflects obtuseness to the basic Kantian religious problematic. Kant repudiates, not religious feeling and its role in the religious life, but the belief that religious feeling can be speculatively or morally cognitive. And he attacks as 'mysticism' and *Schwärmerei*, not all religious experience, but merely the kind which believes itself in the sort of direct contact with the Deity which would supersede theoretical and moral concepts alike. In its extreme form, mysticism points, as the ultimate Good, to 'a state of absorption in the abyss of the Deity, in which personality is absorbed in the Deity and hence annihilated.'[51] In less extreme forms, it still asserts that the divine essence or the divine will can somehow immediately be felt. However, in the lesser as well as in the more extreme form, 'mysticism' is a dangerous illusion.

In the first place, even if religious experience were cognitive, it could not be *known* to be so. 'Even if God really spoke to man, the latter could never know that it was God who had been speaking. It is radically impossible for man to grasp the Infinite through his senses, to distinguish Him from sensual beings, and thus to recognize Him.'[52] In the second place, if religious experience were cognitive, it could not be autonomously cognitive. 'If such an immediate intuition happened to me ... I would still have to use a concept of God as a standard by which to decide whether the phenomenon in question agreed with the necessary characteristics of a Deity.'[53] Even in his most tolerant mood Kant can at most grant that religious experience corroborates the knowledge which reason already possesses. And the reason in question is finite moral reason. But, in the third place, in his less tolerant (and more authentic) mood

Kant cannot grant even this much. For the concept of God is that of the Transcendent and the Unconditioned. But the Transcendent and the Unconditioned can only be thought. To claim that It can be immanent and experienced is nothing less than to utter a contradiction in terms.[54] This contradiction is not only speculative but moral as well. 'The question is whether wisdom is poured into man from above, through inspiration, or achieved from below, through the power of his practical reason.'[55] But if Kant has made anything clear, it is that only if it is self-legislating can moral reason be moral at all.

Kant concludes that all forms of religious *Schwärmerei*, far from being forms of genuine religion, are on the contrary indicative of a want of religion. Authentic religion consists in the acceptance of the contradictory condition of moral finiteness, an acceptance made possible by the faith that this condition is not ultimate. It is for want of this faith that religious *Schwärmerei* seeks to escape from the condition of moral finiteness. But its attempt is vain. What it seeks is a divine gift immediately felt; but what it finds are the products of its own imagination mistaken for divine.[56] The mystic believes himself to have risen above the stage of mere religious hope; he believes himself to possess God instead of merely hoping for Him. In fact, he has fallen far below the stage of religious hope; and what he possesses is not God but merely his own inflated, deified self.

2 Kant and Radical Evil

In commemoration of the one hundred and fiftieth anniversary of Kant's death, 12 February 1804

In the year 1792 Kant administered a shock to some of his admirers. He published in the *Berlinische Monatsschrift* an essay which bore the ominous title *On the Radical Evil in Human Nature*. The shock was repeated in the following year, when this essay was republished as the first and in many ways the crucial part of Kant's long-awaited work in the philosophy of religion, *Religion within the Bounds of Reason Alone*.

Kant's *Fundamental Principles of the Metaphysics of Morals* had appeared in 1785, and his *Critique of Practical Reason* in 1788. These two works had quickly fired the enthusiasm of the moral and religious humanists of the age. They wholeheartedly agreed with the central teaching of these works concerning man's moral freedom. Kant justified their faith that man was free to raise himself above nature to spiritual self-realization, and that in order to do so he required the help of neither nature below nor God above. The religion of these men was a humanistic religion, whose essential faith was in man's inherent goodness. If they thought of evil at all, they understood it as mere inertia, to be progressively removed by man himself. They rejected a religion which regarded evil in man as somehow essential. Thus if they were Christians, they were Christians of a very unorthodox sort. For they repudiated original sin, and the incarnation required to wipe it out.

Among the admirers of Kant were the great German poets. Schiller regarded the Kantian 'determine thyself' as one of the greatest words ever spoken by man. Goethe, though less favourably inclined toward Kant, was nevertheless able to write under his influence the telling sentence: 'God is the objectivation of the feeling of human dignity.'[1] The great German poets regarded Kant as an ally in their battle for the dignity of man.

And now Kant suddenly spoke of radical evil! Moreover, he treated it as if it were an essential part of religion! He seemed to have turned traitor to his own gospel of man's moral freedom, and to have gone over to the enemy, to the detractors of man. True, Kant had spoken of evil before. But he had not spoken of radical evil. Evil had been merely the 'incomplete development of the capacity for good.'[2] It was an imperfection which man himself could conquer. Indeed, he was actually in the process of conquering it.[3] Now Kant spoke of an evil somehow inherent in human nature itself. Little wonder that Schiller regarded the essay as 'scandalous.'[4] And little wonder that Goethe went so far as to cast aspersions on Kant's motives in writing it. Only some ulterior motive, he thought, could account for his defection. In a well-known letter to Herder he wrote: 'Kant required a long lifetime to purify his philosophical mantle of many impurities and prejudices. And now he has wantonly tainted it with the shameful stain of radical evil, in order that Christians too might be attracted to kiss its hem.'[5]

Were these criticisms justified? This paper will seek to show that they were not. The essay on radical evil certainly represents a shift in doctrine. But this shift is not due to political considerations of any kind, to a desire to appease intolerant theologians or the Prussian censor.[6] Nor is it due to the encroachment of theological upon philosophical principles.[7] Kant's religion is a philosophical religion independent of all revelation; and his 'radical evil' cannot be identified with original sin. Kant's shift to radical evil is made for a strictly philosophical reason; and this reason is, strangely enough, the need to give a full and adequate justification of moral freedom. Kant becomes gradually convinced that moral freedom can have no other meaning than the freedom to choose between good and evil. And he finds it necessary to introduce the doctrine of radical evil so as to make freedom, in this sense, intelligible.

II

In order to understand Kant's doctrine of radical evil, it is necessary to understand the problems which lead to its introduction. We must therefore begin with a summary of his ethical teaching, as stated in the *Fundamental Principles of the Metaphysics of Morals* and the *Critique of Practical Reason.*

Man, according to Kant, belongs at once to two worlds. One is the world of sense, the other the intelligible world. As a member of the former, he is subject to natural inclinations; as a member of the latter, he is subject to a universal moral law. His membership in the two worlds is revealed to man in his moral experience. He alone of all beings has a concept of a moral imperative or duty. None but he can distinguish between 'I want' and 'I ought.'

An animal, wholly determined by its natural inclinations, knows of no such distinction. It may find itself torn between want and want, but never between want and duty. If it could speak, it might use the expression 'I ought'; but it would always mean by it 'I ought because I want'; the ought would be relative to a want, and thus part of it. But where desire conflicts only with desire, and never with duty or moral law, there can be no good or evil. The animal, which belongs to the world of sense only, is innocent. A man may be good or evil: but he is never innocent.

An animal, then, has no sense of moral duty; but neither has a god. A being wholly belonging to the intelligible world would indeed know the moral law; but it would have no desires which could possibly conflict with that law. Such a being would act in conformity with the moral law, but it would do so as a necessity flowing from its very nature. It would act out of the sheer love of goodness, and could not act otherwise. But the moral law is experienced as duty only where there is a desire which may conflict with it. The 'I ought' is significant only where it can differ from the 'I want.' A being in which this distinction is absent is not good but holy. But while man may do what he ought to do, he never does it merely as a matter of course. A man may be morally good; but he can never be holy.

In order to act morally I must not merely do my duty, I must also do it for duty's sake. The fact that it is my duty must be sufficient reason for my doing it. An action springing from any other motive may be lawful; but since the motive is ulterior, it is, properly speaking, not moral. Thus I may abstain from crime solely because of my fear of punishment; or I may support my aged father solely because I love him. But it would clearly be my duty to abstain from crime even if, contrary to Hollywood legend, it *should* pay; and I should be obligated to support my father even if the Oedipus complex had wrought havoc among my emotions.

It may seem that these two examples differ substantially; for love of one's father is a noble emotion, whereas the fear of punishment is not. But what they have in common is that they are both inclinations which, as such, are not subject to my will. Hence I cannot be obligated to have one inclination rather than another.[8] Only that action is moral which is motivated by reverence for the moral law itself. The inclinations may indeed support what the moral law commands, and it is very pleasant if they do; but they can never constitute the morality of an action.

A good man, therefore, is a man who makes the moral law the sufficient motive of all his morally relevant actions. His principle in life, or, in Kantian language, his maxim, is the moral law itself. This is the celebrated categorical imperative: 'Act as if the maxim of thy action were to become by thy will a universal law of nature.'[9]

Morality, then, lies essentially in the will. The human will may be determined by respect for the moral law, or it may be determined, in part or completely, by the inclinations. Kant calls the former a good or autonomous will; the latter he calls a heteronomous will, a will which yields, in varying degrees, to the commands of inclination.

This account of moral obligation raises the problem of moral freedom. It presupposes that man, while subject to the inclinations of his empirical nature, is yet free to obey the moral law apprehended by his reason. Is there such a freedom? Clearly, all moral obligation disappears if there is not. Kant never wavers in the slightest degree on this fundamental point: only that can be a moral duty which I am free to fulfil; only that can be a moral crime which I am free to avoid. No action is morally relevant which is not the result of a free decision. Hence if moral freedom is an illusion, there is neither good nor evil, but only moral indifference. And all supposed acting from duty alone is a mere self-deception.

Is freedom a reality? Kant's *Critique of Pure Reason* defends the possibility of freedom; whereas the *Critique of Practical Reason* defends its actuality. According to the former of these works, human knowledge understands, not things as they are in themselves, but merely things as they appear to us, or phenomena. Metaphysics, or the knowledge of things in themselves, is impossible. This means that freedom cannot be proven; for freedom, if it exists, is a property, not of man as a phenomenon, but of man as a member of the intelligible world. But it also means that freedom cannot be refuted. Such a refutation would have to show that moral freedom and causal necessity are incompatible. But the causal necessity which we know applies only to phenomena, and hence only to man in so far as he is an empirical being. Causality does not apply to things in themselves. Therefore, while we cannot prove that there is moral freedom, we can at least prove its possibility. It is possible that man, as a phenomenon, should be wholly governed by causal necessity, yet, as a member of the intelligible world, should nevertheless be free.

How then do we know that freedom is an actuality? We have this knowledge, argues the *Critique of Practical Reason*, not in the form of theoretical proof, but in the form of moral faith. We all are conscious of the moral law; we cannot escape the sense of obligation it imposes on us. Yet there can be no moral obligation without moral freedom. We know ourselves as free, because we know ourselves as morally obligated. The categorical imperative speaks to our consciences the words: 'Thou oughtst, hence thou canst.'

III

The foregoing may suffice as an account, of necessity brief and even superficial, of the essentials of Kant's moral doctrine. We must now consider more closely an important ambiguity in this doctrine. Kant wavers between two views of moral freedom. According to the one, man is free in the degree to which he is determined by the moral principle; according to the other, he is free to choose good or evil. The former view predominates in the writings so far considered; Kant adopts it as the only view which is philosophically intelligible. But in the essay on radical evil he emphatically embraces the latter view; and his reason is that it alone is morally defensible. He embraces it at the risk of leaving it philosophically unintelligible.

We begin, then, with the earlier account of freedom. By a free will Kant does not mean an undetermined will. Such a will would be unintelligible; and it certainly would not be a moral will. A moral will is not an undetermined will, but a will determined by the moral principle. The difference between a free and an unfree will lies not in that the latter is determined while the former is not. Rather, the unfree will is determined by an object, while the free will is determined by itself. The unfree or heteronomous will follows whatever inclination commands. The free or autonomous will liberates itself from the domination of inclination, and determines itself toward obedience to the moral law.

Now this clearly means that the will can determine itself in one way only: toward obedience to the moral law. Any other determination is not self-determination, but determination by the object of inclination. Hence a free will can only be a good will. Indeed, a free will and a good will are one and the same thing. Kant recognizes this implication with the utmost clarity. He defines the will as 'a faculty of determining oneself to action in accordance with the conception of certain laws.'[10] He derives from this definition the conclusion that 'the mainspring of the human will ... cannot be anything other than the moral law.'[11] Hence 'a free will and a will under moral laws are one and the same thing.'[12] As forthright perhaps as any is this passage: 'the pure will is good in all men; there can be no such thing as a will contrary to the [moral] law.'[13]

This conclusion may well puzzle a superficial reader. For it may seem to obliterate the distinction between the good and the holy will, which Kant had so carefully drawn. A holy being, Kant had said, is in necessary conformity with the moral law; but a human being is not. The fact that the latter ought to do his duty does not mean that he necessarily does it. Indeed, the very concept of 'ought' implies that he is free to do otherwise. Does not Kant's identification of the free with the good will deny man's freedom to ignore duty? And in so doing, does it not obliterate the distinction between a good and a holy will?

The solution of the puzzle is this: man differs from God, not in that he may will anything other than the moral law, but in that he may not will at all. Or rather: God is morally free absolutely, whereas man always possesses only a degree of such freedom. A pure will would indeed be necessarily good in all men; but will in man is never pure. This amounts to saying that we must distinguish, not between a good and an evil, but between a pure and an impure will. Or, if we prefer, between a will which is strong and a will which is weak. To the degree to which man wills, he wills the good; and to the degree to which he is driven toward anything but the good, he does not will at all. He is the will-less victim of his inclinations.

Kant illustrates this conclusion in a striking passage. 'There is no one, not even the most consummate villain ... who, when we set before him examples of ... steadfastness in following good maxims ... does not wish that he might also possess these qualities. Only on account of his inclinations and impulses he cannot attain this in himself, but at the same time he wishes to be free from such inclinations which are burdensome to himself ... He is [thus] conscious of a good will, which by his own confession constitutes the law for the bad will that he possesses as a member of the world of sense ... '[14] The villain here portrayed is not evil-willed but weak-willed. In so far as he wills at all, he wills the good; and in so far as he follows evil, he acts as determined, not by himself, but by an all-too-powerful inclination.

Now this account of moral freedom is open to so grave an objection that Kant, in the essay on radical evil, abandons it. For the account is compelled to deny that there can be such a thing as an evil will. Along with the evil will, it must deny evil itself. And in denying both, it cannot justify moral responsibility for moral evil.

The inclinations, as such, are neither good nor evil. The animal which is wholly governed by them is not immoral but amoral. This must clearly mean that in man, too, the inclinations are innocent. Good and evil are terms which refer, not to them, but only to free acts of will. 'Moral good or moral evil refer to the actions, not the emotions of a person ... ; they are terms properly applied only ... to maxims of the will.'[15] But, according to Kant, there can be no will which is free and yet evil. What we might loosely call an evil will is merely a heteronomous or weak will. And a weak will is really only imperfectly good; it is not evil. To the extent to which it is will, it is good; and to the extent to which it is not good, it is not will at all. But where will is absent there is only inclination. And inclination is not immoral but amoral, not guilty but innocent. The weakling who yields to it is, qua yielding, not willing; and hence he is not responsible.

Let us once more consider Kant's unfortunate villain. 'Unfortunate' is the exact attribute we should apply to him. Everybody calls him a villain, treating him as if he had willed evil, whereas in fact he has done nothing of the kind. In so far as he wills freely he wills good. His moral failure is due, not to an act of will but to lack of will. And this lack of will cannot, again, be an act of will, a will, as it were, not to will. For, according to Kant, whatever is not will toward good is not free will at all. This means that his moral failure is due to the domination of inclination, pure and simple, and will does not enter into it. It follows, therefore, that the villain is not a villain at all, but an innocent weakling. And he deserves, not our censure, but our pity.

To sum up we may say that Kant has tried to understand moral freedom by viewing man as subject to two laws: the laws of nature governing his inclinations, and the moral law governing his will. In this account, free will threatens to disappear into two necessities: a pure will which qua will, is necessarily good; and the inclinations which are subject to a necessary law of nature, and hence morally indifferent. The possibility of evil has disappeared between divine holiness and animal innocence.

Kant comes to reject this view. Man, to be genuinely free and responsible, must have the choice, not between willing the good and not willing at all, but between good and evil. It must be possible for him to choose freely, i.e., responsibly, and yet choose *against* the moral law. The sole task of the essay on radical evil is to justify this possibility.

IV

'That "the world lieth in evil" is a plaint as old as history, old even as the older art, poetry; indeed, as old as that oldest of all fictions, the religion of priest-craft.'[16] These dramatic words open the essay on radical evil.

Kant begins by quoting age-old wisdom in support of the fact that evil exists. The philosopher must explain it; he cannot explain it away.

Attempts to explain evil away do, of course, abound. Thus evil is often regarded as a kind of abnormal condition requiring no explanation in its own right, and disappearing along with the abnormal circumstances which have produced it. Proceeding in this vein, some blame evil on civilization, others on the lack of it. Kant makes short shrift of all such explanations, without bothering to give a formal refutation. The facts speak too loudly against them. Is civilization the villain in the piece, and is man by nature 'noble'? The savage is anything but noble. He is given, not to mere animal fighting and killing, but to wanton cruelty and murder – to a cruelty which appears to be for cruelty's sake. If there is an innocent state of nature, then man is never in that state. Is then perhaps untamed nature to blame? Is there a latent goodness in man which, given civilization, will come to the fore? Here 'we must listen to a long melancholy litany of indictments against humanity: of secret falsity even in the closest friendship, ... of a propensity to hate him to whom we are indebted ... and of many other vices still concealed under the appearance of virtue, to say nothing of the vices of those who do not conceal them.' And, Kant concludes, if these facts are not sufficient to convince us, we need but look at the relations among nations: a state of perpetual war, hot or cold; a state sufficient to ridicule man's hope for a naturally evolving millennium as a 'wild fantasy.'[17]

Kant takes this impressive factual evidence as sufficient proof that evil is no mere abnormality. It is somehow an essential and universal condition. This does not mean that every man is an out-and-out scoundrel. Kant holds no such gloomy view of human nature. But it does mean that the *possibility* of evil must somehow lie in human nature itself. And by evil we do not mean pain, disease, death, etc. No doubt these abound, but we are not concerned with them. Our concern is solely with moral evil, and 'nothing is morally evil [i.e., capable of being imputed] but that which is our own *act*.'[18] The evil whose possibility we must explain is a free act against good, and nothing else.

With this definition of evil Kant eliminates from the outset, as inadequate, a host of metaphysical theories. Evil cannot be located in a pre-existing cosmic principle, such as matter, the irrational, or non-being. These exist prior to my act of will, and independently of it. I am under their control, not they under mine. If they are the source of an evil, this is not moral evil. Anything which no will has freely chosen is not evil but innocent.

For the same reason, evil cannot lie in a pre-existing and unalterable condition within human nature. It cannot be, say, the limitation placed on human nature by the senses, a limitation distinguishing man from God. Man has not freely chosen this limitation, and is thus not responsible for it. Kant strongly attacks Stoicism, which regards the passions *per se* as evil and defines good in terms of their suppression by reason. The Stoic maligns what is innocent; and he arrogantly – and vainly – strives to escape from his human nature and become God.

Evil cannot lie in the sensible constituent of human nature; but neither can it lie in the other constituent, viz., reason. To explain evil, one might argue that reason in man is innately perverse; that, apprehending the moral law, it acts against it merely *because* it is the moral law, and that it does so necessarily. But in that case man could not help doing evil; to do so would be his very nature. And it would therefore not be his responsibility, but the responsibility of Him who created it.

Moreover, both these explanations fail to characterize evil in man as it really is. Evil is not the mere yielding to passion; it is more than that. But neither is it the sheer diabolic defiance of the moral law simply because it is the moral law; it is less than that. Man may do evil, but he is no demon. The one explanation asserts too little, the other too much. For man is neither animal nor devil.

In what, then, does evil consist? It lies in neither of the fixed constituents of human nature, but in a perversion of their original relation; and this perversion is brought about by man himself. Man is meant to subordinate his inclinations to the rule of the moral law. Wherever he actually does so, he is good, at least in principle. The categorical imperative, in all its purity, will be the maxim of his will. He may, of course, yield to inclination; but he will do so merely out of weakness. He can never wilfully deviate from the moral law. In sharp contrast, man may subordinate, not his inclinations to the moral law, but the moral law to his inclinations. Then he is not merely weak, but evil. For he wills freely, yet in a way involving departure from the moral law. As Kant puts it: 'the proposition "man is evil" can mean only, that he is conscious of the moral law, but has nevertheless adopted into his maxim the (occasional) deviation therefrom.'[19]

Here then we have Kant's new and crucial formula. Man's choice is not between acting on the good as principle and not acting on principle at all. The choice is not between a good will and the absence of will. Man always acts on principle and freely; and he is always responsible. But his principle will be either the moral law, pure and simple, or the deviation therefrom, occasional or otherwise. Man may thus decide freely, and yet against the moral law. In other words, he is free to choose between good and evil.

This new formula undoubtedly gives greater satisfaction to our moral consciousness. But can it be philosophically justified? Kant proceeds to consider its implications.

We have seen that the term 'good' applies, properly, not to an action, but to the maxim of the will from which actions flow. Furthermore, by the term 'maxim' we did not mean the haphazard motive inspiring an individual act, but a rational, over-all principle governing a man's life as a whole. The same considerations must now be applied to evil. 'We call a man evil ... not because he performs actions that are ... contrary to law, but because these actions are of such a nature that we may infer from them the presence in him of evil maxims.'[20] Again, the term 'maxim' must mean an over-all principle. No doubt individual motives inspiring individual actions may be considered in isolation; but since man is a rational being who lives by an over-all principle, this will be a superficial consideration. Thus the motive behind an individual action may be respect for duty; and it may yet flow from an over-all maxim which includes the deviation from duty on other occasions.

But if this be admitted, two startling conclusions follow. The first of these is that a man is either radically good or radically evil; the second, that all men are, in fact, evil.

A man's empirical actions may be partly good, partly evil, partly morally indifferent. But this underlying maxim cannot be partly good partly evil; and it certainly cannot be morally indifferent. For either his over-all principle is to follow the moral law without qualification, wherever it applies; or else he has included deviation from it among his principles. No doubt there are degrees of evil. The principle of one man will be to take but an occasional holiday from the moral law, and to take that with great qualms; whereas the principle of another will be to make the holiday permanent, and without any qualms whatever. Yet this difference in degree does not affect the principle. We are confronted with a radical 'either-or.' Either perversion has entered into a man's principles, or it has not. Man is either good or evil. There is no third alternative. As Kant says: '[man's] disposition in respect to the moral law is never indifferent.'[21]

The second implication is even more startling. There can be no doubt that all men are evil. For even a single evil action presupposes the perversion of principles, and is impossible without it. We may regard our fellow-men sufficiently highly to believe that some of them sin very rarely. But surely we must admit that 'there is no man who liveth and sinneth not.'

At this point Kant is driven to a conclusion which may well seem paradoxical. He must maintain, on the one hand, that evil is innate in human nature and therefore radical; and, on the other hand, that it is nevertheless produced by each man in himself. Both assertions are necessary: the first, in order to explain the occurrence of any evil action; the second, in order to justify us in calling it evil.

If evil is not, in some sense, innate, then we are unable to explain how anyone could ever commit an evil act. A man would then either will the good or else not will. He would follow good maxims, or no maxims at all. In other words, we should be driven back to the original Kantian position which can explain only moral weakness, but not moral evil. Every genuinely evil act, no matter at what point in time we locate it, already presupposes the maxim to deviate from the moral law. It is that maxim, not the action itself, which is evil. And that maxim must, in some sense, be innate.

Yet it must be innate in quite a specific sense. As we have seen, evil cannot be a fixed part of human nature, existing independently of any act of the human will. Thus evil, though 'radical, innate ... in human nature, yet nonetheless is brought upon us by ourselves.' Kant elaborates by affirming that evil is 'termed innate only in this sense, that it is posited as the ground antecedent to every use of freedom in experience (in earliest youth as far back as our birth) and is thus conceived of as present in man at birth – which is not to say that birth is the cause of it.'[22]

Perhaps it is well to give Kant's view a formulation in which the dubious term 'innate' is avoided. A man's empirical and temporal actions are, in so far as they are morally relevant, merely the manifestation of a commitment to principles in which man determines what may be called his character. Such a commitment is the necessary presupposition of all moral life in the temporal and empirical world. But it is itself non-temporal and non-empirical, and known to us only by inference. That commitment consists in a radical decision, freely made, between good and evil. The empirical life lived by us all is of such a nature as to presuppose a decision for evil.

One question remains. Can a ground be discovered for this decision itself? Is there a higher principle determining the will in its decision? Kant's answer must be emphatically in the negative. If man's alternative consists in willing the good or not willing at all, then indeed there is a higher principle determining the will; it is the moral law itself. But if man chooses freely, either for or against the moral law, then there can be no higher determining principle. Then each decision of each man is a metaphysical ultimate; and whichever choice is made, it is an ultimate irrationality.

V

The doctrine of radical evil, as so far presented, has so close a resemblance to the Christian conception of original sin as to be practically indistinguishable from it. Kant himself refers to the biblical account of the fall.[23] Nevertheless, 'radical evil' and 'original sin' cannot be identified.

Original sin is a state in which I am obligated to a law which I am nevertheless unable to obey. It is a paradoxical condition. Man can recognize, but not overcome, this condition; to overcome it requires an act of divine grace. To Kant the state of original sin is a moral and metaphysical impossibility. For he categorically denies the possibility of a situation in which there is a moral obligation without a corresponding moral freedom.

To be sure, man has brought radical evil upon himself. But if it is incradicable ever after, then man's freedom has ceased with the first free act in which he chose evil; and along with his freedom, man's responsibility has disappeared as well. But, says Kant, 'despite the fall, the injunction that we ought to become better men resounds unabatedly in our souls; hence this must be within our power.' Elsewhere he says: 'through no cause in the world can ... [man] cease to be a freely acting being.'[24] Through no cause: that is to say, not even through himself.

Kant's opposition to original sin is further illustrated by his general conception of religion. If sin is original, it follows that man must approach God primarily, not with his moral achievements, none of which are pure, but with the awareness of his sinfulness. And it follows further that God does not reward man according to merit; for man has no merit. God's gift to man is grace which, if and when it comes, is wholly unmerited.

In sharp contrast, Kant regards moral action as the core of the religious life. He defines religion as 'the recognition of all duties as divine commands.' And he denies the religious value of any activity other than moral action. 'Whatever, over and above good conduct in life, man fancies that he can do to become well-pleasing to God is mere illusion and pseudo-service of God.'[25] This pseudo-service presumably includes the sort of meditation and prayer in which man, recognizing his sinfulness, throws himself upon the mercy of God.

To be sure, Kant concedes that man is always imperfect; that he therefore requires divine aid; and that religion is the hope for such aid. But he denies that it is accessible in this life, and considers all supposed experience of it as sheer enthusiasm and illusion. Moreover, he regards it as harmful to think too frequently of God's future aid; such thoughts can only serve to induce moral lassitude. Indeed, our sole concern with God's future aid should be to live in such a way as to be worthy of it. Thus it does not really make any difference to the life we ought to live now whether this future divine aid – of which we can, in any case, form no conception – is fact or fancy. In order to live the good life now, we do not require it.

There is, then, a vast difference between original sin and Kant's radical evil. Both doctrines assert a radical perversion in man as he is now, a perversion brought about by man himself. Both assert that, inasmuch as this perversion is radical, no mere gradual reform can eliminate it. To eliminate it requires a total action of conversion, an act of redemption, the creation of a new man. But whereas, according to Christian doctrine, only God can redeem fallen man, Kant asserts, and must assert, that man can redeem himself.

But surely such an act of self-redemption is, according to Kant's own principles, utterly impossible! For Kant himself declares that 'how it is possible for a naturally evil man to make himself a good man wholly surpasses our comprehension; for how can a bad tree bring forth good fruit?'[26] Kant has introduced radical evil because any empirical evil act already presupposes a perversion of principles in a man's intelligible character. How then can any empirical good action restore the original goodness of character? Indeed, how is any unqualifiedly good action possible? We seem here driven to a ludicrous conclusion: Kant has adopted radical evil in order to account for man's freedom for evil; yet this very doctrine now seems to leave freedom for good inexplicable. Are we to say that the philosopher can explain either man's freedom to do good, or to do evil, but not both?

Kant denies this fateful dilemma. True, man cannot wipe out radical evil in himself by gradual reform, by deviating in his actions less and less from the moral law. It is the maxim to deviate at all which must be abandoned, and this requires, not reform, but revolution, not growth, but rebirth, the creation, as it were, of a new man. But man himself can put on the new man. 'A man [can] reverse ... , by a single unchangeable decision, that highest ground of his maxims whereby he was an evil man (and thus put on the new man).'[27]

How this act of self-conversion is possible is utterly unintelligible. For no higher determining ground can be discovered for it. The ground is not the moral law; for this is not in itself a determining principle; nor is the ground man's previous character, for this is exactly what is evil and what he puts away. This revolution, then, is a sort of *creatio ex nihilo*. But then, in this regard the conversion toward good is exactly parallel to the original perversion toward evil. It too is an ultimate act of decision for which there is no higher ground.

Kant's doctrine of the possibility of conversion thus sheds a final light on his doctrine of radical evil. Evil is radical only in the sense that at each moment we find that we have already committed evil; and we had to be evil in order to do it. But evil is not radical in the sense that we are not now responsible. On the contrary, in each empirical action, at every here and now, our whole being is at stake, and we are wholly responsible. 'In the search for the rational origin of evil actions, every such action must be regarded as though the individual had fallen into it directly from a state of innocence.'[28]

Kant thus places man in a cosmic position which is at once majestic and frightening. Everything in the universe is finished, from the lowliest plant to God Himself: everything but man. For what matters about man is not the finished constituents of his nature, but his character. And his character is not ready-made. Each man must make his own.

Finally the task confronting each man is not the comparatively harmless one of climbing up a ladder, as high as he is able. For his character will be not more or less developed, more or less pure, more or less good. His is the grim and radical choice between good and evil. No degrees of any sort soften the harshness of this 'either-or.' And even though man's temporal life is, as such, mere appearance, nevertheless any here and now may be the expression of a decision in his intelligible nature; and thus in any here and now eternity itself may be at stake. Nothing in heaven or earth is more important than the moment in which a man – any man – makes himself good or bad. And whenever a man makes such a decision, the universe, so to speak, holds its breath.

3 Kant's Concept of History

'The greatest concern of man is to know how he may properly fulfil his place in creation and may rightly understand what one must be to be a man.' Kant

I

Many expositors treat Kant's philosophy of history; but few treat it seriously.[1] Many treat it, for it is popular and attractive; few treat it seriously, for it seems unconnected, and indeed incompatible with the main body of his thought.

Kant views history as in necessary development toward rationality and freedom. It is a plot whose aim is the establishment of a perfect constitution, governing the relations of both individuals and nations. History aims at a social order which renders compatible the freedom of each with that of all; an order therefore which vouchsafes perpetual peace.

Such a view is certainly attractive. The expositor can point to Kant as a humanist, internationalist, and prophet of the United Nations. At the same time, he finds it difficult to take Kant seriously. For in at least three points his view of history seems incompatible with the substance of his philosophy. Kant sets up an exhaustive division between the realms of nature and morality: how then can he allow a special realm for history? He teaches a doctrine of unqualified moral freedom: how then can he also teach an historical determinism? Finally, Kant's philosophy as a whole reflects critical caution; but his philosophy of history seems to be the result of bold, not to say reckless, speculation. How is it possible that the author of the first, or even the second *Critique*, is also the author of Messianic prophecies?

In answer to these questions, some would dismiss Kant's philosophy of history, as deserving no serious attention. They point out that while Kant was profoundly acquainted with natural science he was, after all, quite remote from the study of history; that his writings on the subject are a mere half-dozen short pieces; and that these pieces are written in a popular, non-technical style. They conclude that in these writings speaks, not Kant the philosopher, but the intellectual child of Lessing or Rousseau, or in general the child of his age.

But great philosophers are not intellectual children. And if they have parents at all, they are in the habit of choosing these themselves. It is always possible, and often fashionable, to view philosophical doctrines in a non-philosophical perspective, by treating them as the mere product of the views of others, or of the social needs of the age, or even of the philospher's own unconscious mind. But this is always a risky procedure; for it involves dismissing the philosophy in question *as philosophy*. No doubt such a dismissal can be justified in a number of cases; but that Kant's philosophy of history is among them is, to say the least, not evident without further inquiry. In the first place, it may be true that Kant was an amateur in the field of history; but what matters is that he was very well aware of this fact.[2] If a thinker of his native caution nevertheless ventured into this field, we must at least suspect that he did so for the most serious philosophical reasons, and with the greatest of caution and care. In the second place, if there are glaring contradictions between Kant's system as a whole and his philosophy of history, it is, to put it mildly, unlikely that he was unaware of them. This would be unlikely in any case. What makes it beyond belief is the fact that he wrote his main pieces on history at the precise time when he wrote two of his greatest works.[3] Finally, it is an erroneous belief that Kant is superficial or 'popular' when he uses a non-technical style. Kant regarded a technical style as justified only when the doctrine made it necessary; but some of his most serious doctrines do not require it.

We are obliged, then, to take Kant's philosophy of history seriously after all. To do so is to treat it as a systematic whole, and as systematic part of a larger systematic whole – the Kantian system. Such a treatment cannot, and must not, deny inconsistencies. Whether there are such, and what they are, only the actual investigation can show. But it must attempt to understand inconsistencies, too, in philosophical terms, i.e., as resulting from conflicting or contradictory philosophical requirements. Only when systematic treatment breaks down is it legitimate to introduce for explanation non-philosophic factors, such as irrational changes of mind, a mere yielding to environmental influence, or the weakness of old age. The central obligation which a great philosopher's expositor owes to his subject is to treat him – as a philosopher.[4]

II

We must begin with a brief reminder of some Kantian essentials. Nature, for Kant, is 'the existence of things in so far as they are determined by general laws.'[5] If things were not so determined there would be no nature at all, nor objects of possible knowledge. Among these objects is man himself. He too is part of nature; his existence, also, is determined by general laws.

But man is not only determined; he is also able to determine himself. He is determined by desires implanted by nature; but he can determine himself in accordance with moral law. Moral law is apprehended by human reason, in the form of an absolute command. When man obeys this command he acts freely. To act freely is, at any time, in each rational man's power; hence every rational man is, at all times, responsible.

But how can man be wholly determined by laws of nature and yet be unqualifiedly free? This would indeed be impossible were it not for the fact that nature, as a whole, is only appearance. The world, as observed and known, is only the world as it must appear to us; and man himself, as observed and known, is part of it. But in moral experience and moral action man does not observe and know himself; he knows what he ought to do, not what he is. Hence moral knowledge can reveal more than appearance.

Man, then, belongs at once to two worlds, the world of nature and a supersensible world. This is possible because the former which is known is only appearance, and the latter which is more than appearance is not known; it is revealed only in the moral command to action. Man as an object of knowledge must appear as determined; but in moral experience and action he is revealed as free.

This may be a superficial summary. But it suffices to show that Kant seems compelled to reduce history to a mere part of nature. For while he grants freedom and appearance he denies that freedom can appear. To be sure, the effects of freedom must appear in nature; but they appear as determined according to laws, and what is so determined is nature. Hence there cannot be a separate sphere of history.

Nor can there be a genuine science of history. For all explanation of man must be in terms of laws, belonging to such sciences as discover these laws; and all treatment of man as free is not explanation at all, but judgment, especially moral judgment. Whatever its practical uses, theoretically history lives off the combined charity of two wealthy donors. But the donations are grudgingly given, and the living is not respectable.

III

In view of this conclusion, it is surprising that Kant nevertheless draws a sharp distinction between nature and history, and that he does so on the grounds that history is marked by the appearance of freedom. He expounds this view in an essay entitled *Conjectural Beginning of Human History*.[6]

It is of course possible to dismiss this work, a mere essay of some twenty pages. Those who would do so might find further encouragement in the fact that it is written, oddly enough, in the form of a commentary to the beginning of the book of Genesis. But formidable supporting evidence makes such a cavalier attitude indefensible. We cannot dismiss the content of Kant's essay; we shall be compelled to take seriously even its form.

If it were really Kant's final view that man, as a natural being, is wholly subject to natural laws, we should expect him to tell us what sciences can discover these laws. But on one of these – psychology – Kant casts serious doubts; and the other – anthropology – is in its most important sense no law-discovering science at all.

Kant's position toward psychology is not wholly conclusive. His doubts concern for the most part the methodological capacity of that science to discover laws, though he also seems to doubt whether there are laws to discover.[7] But his conception of anthropology removes all ambiguity as to where he stands. Kant distinguishes between theoretical, moral, and pragmatic anthropology.[8] One is tempted to interpret this distinction as follows: theoretical anthropology explains empirical man in terms of laws; moral anthropology does not explain at all, but applies moral principles to situations of life; finally pragmatic anthropology – presumably the least important of the three – is confined to observations and rules useful for living.[9] But the fact that, of the three, Kant wrote only a pragmatic anthropology would in itself be sufficient to make this interpretation suspect; and, indeed, it is wholly mistaken. Kant's distinction between theoretical and pragmatic anthropology is quite different. He writes: 'The physiological study of man investigates what nature makes of man, while the pragmatic investigates what man makes, can make, or should[10] make of himself.'[11] Theoretical anthropology, then, does not explain all human fact in terms of laws, but merely that part of it which can be so explained; hence it turns out to be merely 'physiological'[12] anthropology. Correspondingly, pragmatic anthropology is not confined to the giving of useful rules; it too deals with human fact – the part which does not fall under laws. And this part is freedom in its appearance.

We must conclude, then, that Kant is serious when, in the essay under consideration, he separates history from nature, as in some sense a special sphere. And from this follows that historiography is a respectable discipline after all. For if pragmatic anthropology investigates what man makes, can make, and should make of himself, then *historiography investigates what he has made of himself.* The past achievements of freedom, as much as its present possibilities and actualities, escape the reach of natural laws.

We might ask whether this conclusion is compatible with the central Kantian position. But to this difficult question we can give only passing attention. We must confine ourselves to observing that if an object of knowledge, to be such an object, must fall under laws, it is doubtful whether freedom, as dealt with by history and pragmatic anthropology, is an object. Kant himself states that while the 'physiological' anthropologist must be a spectator, his pragmatic colleague must be, in some sense, a participant.[13] This, to be sure, would raise the question as to the sort of knowledge obtained in these two disciplines. But this is a question to which Kant never gives explicit attention. His interest in history does not include the epistemology of historiography.[14] Its status, as a form of knowledge, remains obscure.

IV

If freedom can appear in nature; and if consequently history is a sphere which is in some sense separate from nature, we must ask what sort of sphere it is. Kant seeks to answer this question in his essay *Conjectural Beginning of Human History.* To that essay we must now turn.

We may conveniently begin with a summary. Man, like the rest of living nature, was ruled by instinct when first created. He differed from other animals only in having a disposition to rationality. But nothing compelled him to actualize this disposition. He might have remained, like the animals, under the rule of instinct and in a state of innocence.

But man did in fact actualize his disposition. He did so by desiring knowledge. Instead of being satisfied with the food which his instinct desired, he turned to food which his instinct did not desire. What turned him to it was curiosity.

The effects of this seemingly inconsequential step were momentous. For it resulted, all at once, in man's self-discovery as a rational being; as a being, that is to say, capable of choosing his own way of life. For better or worse, man had become independent of the bondage of nature, able to modify, infinitely extend, or even pervert, natural desire. This was his step into history: a step of infinite nobility, but also fraught with infinite dangers. For with the guiding hand of nature gone, man had to guide himself. And as he began to do so, a world of evil as well as good had come within his reach. Little wonder that man shrank from this world, as from an abyss, anxious to return into nature's womb. But such a return was impossible. The one choice which his step into history had made impossible was the choice to renounce all choice.

Hence other steps of reason quickly followed. Next came the transformation of sexual desire. Animal desire seeks immediate and finite satisfaction; and having found it, it falls into dormancy. But man, having become free, began to mix with desire the freedom of imagination. He began to seek satisfaction which is imagined and distant, rather than such as is real and present. Desire became desire for its own sake, wilfully postponing, or even denying itself, satisfaction. It thereby became infinite and insatiable. Having become insatiable, it threatened men with wholesale mutual destruction. To avoid such destruction, men began to create rules of conduct and good manners. Nature made animals sociable; but man, having torn himself loose from nature, had to create the conditions of his sociability himself. Having ceased to be a being of nature, he had to become a being of culture.

Man's third step was the experience of care. The animal seeks food when it is hungry and meets dangers as they come. But man had acquired foresight. Hence he began to worry about the dangers of tomorrow. And the tomorrow extended itself, reaching the point at which man can no longer care and prepare but only fear and wait. Care turned into the fear of death. From death indeed no creature can escape. But, alone of all creatures, man fears it before it comes.

But there was yet a fourth step in the development of freedom; and this, Kant significantly asserts, was the final step. It was the discovery of moral law. The first time man ever took a sheep's skin for his own use, he recognized that while the animal was a means to his ends, he was an end in himself. And this implied, however obscurely, that every man is an end in himself; that what man may do to animals he may not do to such as himself.

This may suffice as a summary of Kant's essay, in so far as it concerns our present purpose.[15] We must now consider its significance. And we may begin by asking why Kant should use this extraordinary form of presentation. He certainly does not mean to give an exercise in speculative history. The writing of history is the office of the historian. Kant describes, not history, but the beginning of history, i.e., those conditions without which history is not possible, and which all actual history already presupposes.[16] Kant gives the a priori of history.

But if this is true, then why this form of a quasi-history? That the choice of this form is deliberate Kant himself strongly hints.[17] What is its purpose?

Kant seeks to state a serious doctrine. But it is a doctrine which it is difficult to state in precise terms, or at any rate in precise Kantian terms. On the other hand, it is easy to state it in the form of a quasi-history; indeed, it can almost be said that such a form is required by the doctrine. The doctrine in question is the appearance, and development, of freedom.

Kant's distinction between nature and freedom had enabled him to understand change and development in terms of antecedent natural conditions, and freedom without them. But now he must deal with the appearance of freedom; and this involves the relating of freedom to antecedent conditions, natural or social. There must be such a relation, if there is to be a development of freedom at all – and this Kant emphatically asserts.[18] Yet the relation must be such as not to destroy what is to develop. Development in history must be quite other than development in nature.

Natural development is understood wholly in terms of the pre-existing being which develops, plus such environmental conditions as may enter. But the development of reason and freedom cannot be so understood; for by their very nature they cannot exist prior to their exercise. They must be self-given, not nature-given. Man, Kant says elsewhere, is not an animal rationale, but an animal rationabile.[19] One might go so far as to say that the term *animal rationale* is, for Kant, a contradiction in terms.[20] A disposition may (and indeed must) pre-exist; but man himself must actualize it. The development of freedom and rationality must be self-development.

But this doctrine has the air of paradox. For the act which actualizes the disposition to freedom and rationality already presupposes their actuality. It is, to be sure, not impossible to remove this air of paradox. But to do so would require the drastic revision of certain Kantian terms.[21] And there is nothing to indicate that Kant is ready for this.

But how, in the absence of such a revision, is the doctrine to be stated? Here we must clearly see what it is that Kant asserts. He does not merely hold the relatively trivial doctrine that man in history can act freely and rationally. This would be quite compatible with the view that freedom and reason are part of the human substance, given by nature. The core and revolutionary part of the Kantian view is that freedom and reason are not part of the human substance, and not given by nature. They are self-given, in an act which tears man loose from nature. And this means that *the conditions which make history possible are themselves quasi-historical.* Hence, in the absence of adequate technical terms, Kant's doctrine concerning the a priori of history is most naturally stated in the form of a quasi-history.

But what is the freedom to be found in, and, indeed, constitutive of history? No doubt there is moral freedom, and this Kant symbolizes by the fourth step of original man. But this is not his only or even his main concern, for there can be (and is) history without moral freedom. The first three steps of original man, in Kant's presentation, symbolize quite another kind of freedom. This is, to be sure self-determination of a sort, but it is not in accordance with moral law. And it is rational only in the sense that it is determined by self-given inventions, and that the range of these is infinite. Moreover – and this fact will assume crucial importance for us later on – this freedom is only partly, but by no means wholly, independent of natural desires. It may enlarge, transform, or even pervert them; but it does not emancipate itself from them.

Freedom, in this sense, we shall term cultural freedom. For it is essentially social in significance. The inventions of one are accepted by the other, and one's example kindles another's imagination. Cultural freedom produces institutions and forms of government, and it is the source of tradition. Its expressions are the substance of history.

We may sum up, then, that Kant establishes history as a special sphere by showing two things: that freedom can appear and develop; and that there is cultural as well as moral freedom.

And this, it may seem, is all Kant can say on the subject of history. He has not asserted any necessary connection between cultural and moral freedom. Nor has he asserted a necessary direction in the development of cultural freedom; indeed, its possibilities are irrational and infinite. Hence the forms in which freedom expresses itself can be investigated only after the fact; and the discipline which must do so is history, not philosophy. Philosophy can give the a priori of history, but it can do no more.

But Kant, as we know, seeks to do a great deal more. He seeks to give nothing less than a construction of all history, past and future. To understand this attempt requires of us an entirely new point of departure.[22] Thus far, Kant has made a division between nature and history, over and above his main division between nature and moral freedom. It will become evident shortly that his main problem now concerns the relation between these two divisions.

V

In order to understand Kant's separation of history from nature it was sufficient to keep in mind his *Critique of Pure Reason* and his *Critique of Practical Reason*. In order to understand his construction of the historical process it is necessary to keep in mind his *Critique of Judgment* as well.

Kant's *Critique of Judgment* is an extremely difficult work; and it is hard to say what its central function is within the Kantian system, if indeed it has any one central function.[23] But perhaps it can be said without distortion that it seeks to join together what the first two *Critiques* have put asunder. The first *Critique* has established the world of appearance, which is, as an object of theoretical knowledge. The second *Critique* has established a supersensible world which ought to be, as revealed in moral consciousness. The third *Critique* attempts to discover traces, of what ought to be, in the world which is.[24]

By way of preliminary orientation we may consider the case which Kant most fully argues. This concerns the science of biology. This certainly seems odd. Biology, like all science, is solely concerned with the explanation of fact; it has no truck with moral purposes. Why then does Kant treat biology in the third *Critique*?[25] To this question we can risk a fuller answer only later on. For the present we can say this much. To view what is in terms of what ought to be is to view it teleologically. Biology may have no concern with moral purposes; but it too must make use of teleological concepts.

Living beings are not only organized; they are self-organizing. Whole and part seem to cause each other, and the end of an organic process seems, in some sense, to determine its beginning. But mechanical explanation explains the whole in terms of the parts, and the end in terms of the beginning. Hence to explain organisms in mechanical terms alone is impossible. Nor does biology in fact try to do so. It proceeds as if there were a purposiveness in the life of the organism, analogous to that found in conscious human activity.

But how can the use of the teleological concept be justified? We do not derive it from observation, for we read purposiveness into nature rather than find it there. It is, then, an a priori concept; but it is one which is not justified. For the first *Critique* has justified mechanical, but not teleological, causality. Kant's solution to the problem is to assign to the teleological concept in biology a heuristic, not an explanatory, function. We use it as a mere guide, with the help of which we explain as far as we can. And all genuine explanation is mechanical.

This solution implies that while purposiveness is a concept necessary to biology, its use does not prove the existence of purposiveness in nature. It proves something, not about nature, but merely about human knowledge. In investigating certain parts of nature, we must proceed as if a concept necessarily formed by us were applicable to nature without.[26]

This, in brief, is Kant's treatment of biology. But it does not help us much in understanding what we have called the fundamental purpose of the third *Critique*: the linking of what is with what ought to be. For the teleological concept in biology is merely a formal tool for the discovery of fact. We have therefore yet to ask why Kant seeks to link the world of nature with that of morality; and how, if at all, biology fits into this attempt.

That Kant makes this attempt is undeniable. Consider the following argument. Not only organisms, but nature as a whole must be regarded as purposive. Water and minerals may be viewed as means to plants, plants to animals, and animals to men.[27] If Kant meant to make human needs the end which all else subserves his case would, to say the least, be dubious. It is too painfully obvious that while man feeds on chickens and cows, he is in turn fed on by fleas, lice, and rats. But Kant does not make human needs a final end. And he seeks to unite teleologically, not the parts of nature with each other, but nature as a whole with morality. Nature, he argues, must be shown to be a means to something which is an end in itself; and human needs are not such an end. The only end-in-itself known to us is man as a moral, not as a natural being. And unless nature as a whole can be shown to be, directly or indirectly, a means to the realization of morality, it is a mere fact without value.[28]

But it is difficult to understand how, within the Kantian system, this can be shown. We know only the world of appearance which is; of the supersensible world we know only that it ought to be. Surely in order to understand what is as a means to what ought to be we should require theoretical knowledge of the supersensible world; and if Kant has made anything clear, it is that such knowledge exceeds our human powers.

If it is difficult to see how such a link between nature and morality is possible, it is no less difficult to understand why it is necessary. This necessity cannot be theoretical, for to theory the question of a moral 'ought' does not arise. Nor can it, strictly speaking, be moral. To understand this latter point we must make an important distinction.

In the second *Critique*, Kant argues that moral consciousness must postulate that nature is ultimately harmonious with moral purposes. But this must not be taken to mean that moral consciousness requires, or even looks for, *evidence* of such a harmony in the empirical world. Nothing could be further from Kant's intention. In order to do my duty, I require no evidence to the effect that crime does not pay, or even that, in a Messianic age, it will pay no more.[29]

The second *Critique*, then, postulates a link between morality and nature, but it accepts it on faith, and apart from all evidence. But the third *Critique* attempts to find *evidence* of moral purposiveness in the empirical world. And for such an attempt there can be, within the Kantian system, no necessity, be it theoretical or moral.

The problem, then, is formidable. Indeed, in terms of one of the current interpretations, it is insoluble. We have seen that the biologist must treat organisms 'as if' they were purposive. This 'as if' is understood by some as signifying a useful fiction. This interpretation may seem plausible so long as biology is considered in itself; but it can explain neither Kant's moral teleology nor his connection of biology with it. To what purpose do we require the useful fiction that nature as a whole has moral value? Since (as we have seen) it is required for neither theoretical nor moral purposes the fiction is useless.[30]

But the text makes it quite clear that the genuine meaning of the Kantian 'as if' is quite different. It signifies, not a useful fiction, but a gap in our knowledge. We cannot derive the teleological concept from the supersensible root which unites nature and morality. But Kant clearly believes both in the existence of that root and in the validity of the teleological concept. He merely denies that we can prove the existence of the former, or the validity of the latter.

And with this clarification the problem is solved. According to Kant, the teleological concept, as the biologist must use it, lacks theoretical justification. Hence it is merely a heuristic, not an explanatory principle. But though *we* cannot connect it with the supersensible root of nature and morality, Kant clearly believes that it *is* connected with that root.[31] Consequently, he can regard organic nature as evidence of a sort – evidence which is, to be sure, theoretically insufficient and morally unnecessary – of what he can loosely call providence. Regarding it in this light, he can ask whether it is reasonable to assume purposiveness in some parts of nature, but none in nature as a whole. In other words, he can connect biological with moral purposiveness. And he must then concentrate on that sphere which alone can directly link nature as a whole with morality, thus giving it value. That sphere is history. Thus a teleological biology can encourage a teleogical history.[32]

But the latter poses far more formidable problems than the former. Here too purposiveness must be the heuristic, and mechanism the explanatory principle. But teleology, in the case of history, is moral teleology; which is to say that the end which all must subserve is moral freedom. And this may well seem to pose a fatal dilemma. Either moral freedom is independent of teleologico-mechanical necessity, in which case the connection between nature and morality breaks down; or else freedom is necessitated, in which case it is no longer freedom. In either case nature (and history) are mere facts without value. Whether this dilemma is indeed fatal depends on whether mechanism, teleology, and moral freedom can all be brought together.[33] Can nature (or history) compel man to be free? To answer this paradoxical question is the task of Kant's construction of history.

VI

Kant gives his construction of history mainly in his *Idea for a Universal History* ... and chapter 83 of the *Critique of Judgment*; but additional material is found in his *Concerning the Common Saying* ..., *Perpetual Peace*, and other minor writings. Since he nowhere pretends to give more than a sketch it is easily summarized.

Nature wants all her creatures to fulfil their destinies. To realize this aim causes her difficulty in only one case: that of man. For man's destiny is the realization of reason and freedom; but they *are* reason and freedom only if man develops them by himself. Hence it might seem that nature can do nothing toward the fulfilment of human destiny. For if she interferes she destroys the very destiny which is to be fulfilled; and if she looks on she is impotent.

But nature is cunning as well as wise. She reveals her cunning in making man, at once, social and anti-social. If he were simply social he would live with his fellows as do ants and bees. And if he were simply anti-social he would live by himself. In neither case would he be compelled to leave behind that dependence on instinct which he desires; his capacity for reason and freedom would remain asleep.

But his instincts permit man to live neither with his fellows nor without them. Hence he must seek to escape from this contradiction and its intolerable consequences. To do so he must make himself rational and free.

But man wants to satisfy his desires, not to develop his reason. Compelled to develop that latter, he wants to use it as a mere means to the satisfaction of the former. But this attempt is progressively thwarted. For so long as reason is a mere means to the satisfaction of man's contradictory instincts it does nothing to alleviate their contradictoriness. On the contrary, since it augments human power, it merely serves to increase the range and fury of human conflict. In the end human power may extend over the whole earth; but this may only mean that there is no place on earth which is safe.

There is only one escape from this fearful development. This consists in the use of reason, not to serve instinct but to master it. Man is progressively compelled to move on this avenue of escape. He is in the end forced to found a society which 'combines with the greatest possible freedom and, in consequence, antagonism of its members, the most rigid determination and guarantee of the limits of this freedom, in such a way that the freedom of each may co-exist with that of others.'[34] Man may not desire the discipline imposed by such an order. But he does not wish self-destruction. Hence he must create this order, and freely accept its discipline.

What happens among individuals must also happen among nations. Nations want security and material wealth. To attain both they wage war upon other nations.

But wars are one thing in the intention of man, quite another in the intention of nature. For they never attain the ends for the sake of which they are waged. There never is a victor who for long enjoys the fruits of his victory. War breeds counter-war; and its effect is not security and plenty, but insecurity, toil, and sacrifice. And since the range of wars must be ever-widening, nations in the end face the same alternative as individuals. They must either use reason to restrain desire, rather than to serve it, or else destroy themselves. But they do not wish self-destruction. Hence they must found an international order which restrains each nation to make all secure: an order which vouchsafes perpetual peace.

This may suffice as a summary of Kant's construction of history. We must now consider its significance.

If there is to be freedom in history, nature cannot compel man to be what he ought to be. She can at best compel him to *make himself* what he ought to be. Furthermore, nature manifestly does not so compel the individual; for many a man dies a crook and a scoundrel, and none a saint. Hence it follows that if there is to be purposiveness in history at all, it can lie only in its *direction*, and that this direction must be that of history as a whole. Nature may necessarily *be* what it ought to be; because it is the sphere of freedom, history can at best necessarily *tend* toward what it ought to be.

But how can necessity and freedom coexist at all? How can nature compel man to be free? It may seem that necessary direction in history is impossible. For either history is governed by necessity, in which case it has no direction; or else it is a sphere of freedom, in which case the direction is not necessary.

We have already seen that Kant has a concept of cultural as well as moral freedom. And we have stressed the fact that while this is the freedom to enlarge, transform, or even pervert natural desires, it is not the freedom to escape from them. This fact now assumes crucial importance.

If all historical freedom were cultural freedom, history as a whole would be irrational and without direction; irrational, because the choice of possible means is infinite; without direction, because the ends would remain those of nature.

But because cultural freedom is subservient to natural ends nature has power over it. And she uses this power, not blindly but to a purpose. This purpose is evident from the contradictoriness of human desires. Nature drives man, not from one expression of cultural freedom to another; she compels man to transcend the state of cultural freedom. Having used reason as the servant of natural desires, man is gradually compelled to make it their master.

But how can nature compel man without destroying his freedom? This is possible because nature confines herself to posing the problem to be solved; she does not solve it. Man himself both must and can give the solution. He must give it, because nature does not give it, and because the problem, unless solved, will destroy him. He can give it because, already free in the choice of means, he can free himself from the despotism of natural ends.

It is obvious, then, that yet another concept of freedom has made its appearance in Kant's philosophy of history. This we may term the freedom of discipline. In the *Critique of Judgment* Kant distinguishes between culture in general, a state in which man is free in general, and the culture of discipline, which 'consists in the liberation of the will from the despotism of desires.'[35] Cultural freedom is the freedom to transform nature; but the freedom of discipline consists in the emancipation from nature. History is a process which begins with cultural freedom and in the ideal future ends with the freedom of discipline. It begins with man's partial and ends with his total transcendence of nature.

VII

But we have yet to ask the decisive question. In the *Critique of Judgment*

Kant sets himself the task to 'seek out what nature can supply for the purpose of preparing (man) for what he himself must do in order to be an end in himself.'[36] This, it will be remembered, is necessary if nature is to be shown to have value; to show that it has is the sole task of Kant's construction of history.

But it is a task which so far has not been accomplished. For even the freedom of discipline is not an end in itself. It is a state in which men discipline their desires, but for motives no nobler than enlightened self-interest. It is a state of legality, not morality. And legality may be a preparation for morality; it is not itself morality. How then can the freedom of discipline prepare for morality, which alone can be an end in itself?

Astonishingly enough, to this decisive question Kant has no clear answer. On some occasions he suggests that the step to law and order, though not a moral step, is a step to morality;[37] and he leaves us wondering whether the first step necessitates the second, or the second presupposes the first. On other occasions (but rare occasions indeed) he seems to suggest that legality will in the end enforce morality as well.[38] And on other occasions again (and these are more frequent) he suggests the radical opposite. A lawful order forces the individual merely to hide his evil motives, not to abandon them, causing him to add hypocrisy to his other vices.[39] Even the most law-abiding society is mere 'glittering misery'[40] without morality; but no society can legislate a good will. Even devils, one of the strongest passages asserts, would be compelled to establish a society of law and order;[41] but while you can make devils law-abiding you surely cannot make them good. When we ask Kant the decisive question we are dramatically left without answer.[42]

But this is not really astonishing, after all. For at this crucial point it becomes evident that Kant's attempt to show a link between nature and morality is in inescapable conflict with his concept of morality itself. According to Kant, a rational man – any rational man – is morally responsible without qualification; he is therefore, in the decisive respect, free without qualification. But the attempt to show that what ought to be necessarily will be requires that freedom be historically qualified, and that the free achievements of some are means to the freer achievements of others. This may be unobjectionable so long as the freedom so qualified is merely cultural freedom or the freedom of discipline.[43] But the qualification of these alone does not solve the problem. For if these freedoms are themselves linked to moral freedom, then the latter too is historically qualified; and if they are not so linked then nature and morality fall apart. History, despite whatever progress it may exhibit, is merely 'glittering misery,' fact without value.

But if the link between nature and morality is broken, then the entire historical construction must suffer collapse. It must not be forgotten for a moment that the teleology which gives rise to it is moral teleology. Teleology in biology may be merely formal, and it may be required for the explanation of facts. But teleology in history is not merely formal; and to explain the facts of history it is not required. If it were, all historiography would have to be teleological; but this Kant explicitly denies.[44] Kant requires teleology in history, not in order to explain historical facts, but in order to show that they have value. But if this cannot be shown – and only a necessary link between history and morality could show it[45] – then the entire enterprise lies in shambles.

VIII

We must conclude, then, that while Kant's analysis of historicity is profound and of lasting value, his construction of the historical process is a failure. And not even Kant's most ardent followers could judge otherwise.

But perhaps we can learn more from Kant's failure than from the successes of those who came after him. These succeeded better in their historical constructions. History emerged as the march of God through time. This march captured the imagination of men, and today it seems to hold millions in its spell. But if Kant failed in his construction of history, it was because he recognized the true nature of this march. It is the death-march of human freedom.

4 Schelling in 1800–1801: Art as Revelation

1 Introduction

Friedrich Wilhelm Joseph Schelling (1775–1854) has earned the title of an always-changing 'Proteus' in philosophy, perhaps the only philosopher ever to produce – depending on the periodization given his literary work by scholars – four, five, or even six philosophical systems in his lifetime. The Kantian philosophy inspired, with breath-taking speed, a succession of major philosophies: Fichte's ethical idealism in 1794, Schleiermacher's religious 'higher realism' in 1799, Schelling's aesthetic 'real-idealism' in 1800, the whole process climaxing with Hegel's absolute idealism. Schelling may be viewed as a veritable embodiment of that process, and in particular, of that speed. Like other people, philosophers change their views. He was perhaps the only philosopher, ever, who did not simply abandon once-held positions but found it necessary forever to go beyond them. And this necessity did not end even when, in Hegel, the process initiated by Kant reached its completion, with Schelling widely seen by others – and, of course, by Hegel himself – as belonging among all the other superseded philosophers.

Hegel died in 1831, in Berlin, then the centre of German philosophy, at age sixty-one. Schelling survived him by twenty-three years; and, having been nearly forgotten in the philosophical backwater of Munich, made a dramatic appearance in Berlin in 1841, for the purpose of one more going-beyond-operation, this time final, and beyond idealism as a whole, his own as well as Hegel's. The perfected – that is, absolute – idealism, he now held, had been but a merely 'negative' philosophy of mere 'Essence,' a phase of philosophy necessary, to be sure, but only in foundation of a 'positive' philosophy of 'Existence' for which the time had now, at long last, arrived.

Because of the 'Protean' nature of his philosophizing, Schelling's writings are extremely uneven. (Hegel, a one-time close friend and ally but subsequent rival, once remarked, unkindly but not altogether incorrectly, that Schelling published his drafts.)[1] Some Schellingian works are obscure and cumbersome, but others have a lucidity – nay, beauty – that has rarely been rivalled and never surpassed. And while at times he is prey to external influence, to the point of seeming to lack all originality, he is indisputably the originator of two of the most powerful and influential modern philosophies: absolute idealism and existentialism. Yet – perhaps just by dint of that originality – precisely these two are expressed in writings obscure in style and method, and unclear if not confused in content. Thus it has come to pass that the credit for absolute idealism has gone to Hegel, and that for existentialism to Kierkegaard. Schelling is widely forgotten.

That this is unjust we shall try to show by examining two stages in his career, these two chosen because they focus on religion, and because of the contrast between them. Just this contrast in the sphere of religion was the main objective of my once-planned *From Kant to Kierkegaard*, which, for reasons stated above in the Introduction, was never completed. That contrast would have permeated that whole book, had it been completed: in the two stages to be examined in the present volume, it appears in Schelling himself. Chapters 6 and more especially 7 will deal with what – with reservations – may be called the aged Schelling's post-idealistic 'return' to the 'divine Other' of revealed religion, what with the idealistic impulse to internalize divine otherness having been (as Schelling and his followers held) superseded, or (as was held by Hegel's posthumous disciples) abandoned and betrayed. In the present chapter we turn to the young Schelling, in whose thought the internalized God of idealism finds His most confident, nay, triumphant – if, as we shall see, startlingly short-lived – manifestation. It was the golden age in German philosophy, and its secret was the close bond between poetry and philosophy. More perhaps than any other work, Schelling's *System of Transcendental Idealism* of 1800 is the apotheosis of that bond.[2]

Two extant pictures of Schelling give an inkling of the contrast just referred to, the first a painting of the young man, the second the only existing photograph of him in old age. What the aged Schelling sees we can see in his eyes.[3] These are the eyes of a man who has been struck, almost physically, by brute facticity: facts that resist idealization. And, as a philosopher, what has struck him is not this or that fact but facticity as such, its bruteness as such, so that, if he is an empiricist of sorts, his is, as he himself on occasion calls it, a 'metaphysical empiricism.' 'Why does anything exist at all, rather than nothing?' he asks, and discovers that between 'to-be' and 'not-to-be' there is a chasm. With this chasm once encountered, others follow. There is, to be sure, a rational proof of God, but it is of His essence only: His existence is beyond reason, requiring it to make a leap. The human too has its facticity: a chasm exists between potential and actual freedom, for to act freely is not to be compelled by a higher law, an a priori necessity, but a choice between good and evil, an a posteriori fact. At least one more metaphysical fact needs to be confronted, and this, for an idealist, is hardest of all: evil. On this Schelling began to brood as early as in 1804, when he could view evil no longer as a negative phase in a harmonizing process, but only as a fall, a rupture, a break. And, on the road to his final – 'positive' – philosophy Schelling writes: 'The Deity reigns over a world of horrors.'[4]

So much for the old man portrayed in the one picture. The young man portrayed in the other could never have written any such passage. A youth just a decade beyond adolescence, this Schelling exudes joy, hope, confidence, as well as no little self-confidence: he is on top of the world. And why not? He resides in Jena, then the centre of philosophy; and great poets and critics, among them Goethe, Schiller, Novalis, and the brothers Schlegel, either reside in nearby Weimar or are frequent visitors, and so is he. As for his philosophical friends and acquaintances, great ones and promising young ones, they include Fichte, Schleiermacher, Hegel, all differing among themselves but all inspired by Kant. And as for the great Kant himself, the *Alleszermalmer*, while residing in far-away Königsberg, he is, *mirabile dictu*, still alive. And then there is that close, brooding friend, Friedrich Hölderlin, long wavering between philosophy and poetry but eventually to become a great poet himself. Exciting things are happening in this young man's world, and this, the world of poets and philosophers, is for him, as for many others at the time, the centre of the universe.

Nor is young Schelling a minor figure in it. If, as could be the case, the picture was painted in 1800, it portrays one who, at age twenty-five, is a celebrated and much-published philosopher, and who, moreover, has just brought out what is widely regarded by scholars as his most important work. The work is, in any case, the most solid philosophical one ever written in endorsement of romanticism. The *System of Transcendental Idealism* of 1800 leads the reader through the things we know and need to know, but the highest knowledge and, indeed, foundation of all is that Truth is Beauty, and Beauty, Truth, for 'Art is Revelation – the only Revelation there is.'[5]

2 From 1794 to 1800

How does German philosophy get to Schelling's 1800? The speed with which work followed work prior to the *System of Transcendental Idealism* creates the impression of superficiality, but this is false. Those were inspired years in philosophy, and the actors in them were men of genius. Just then crucial turns of thought occurred, at least in the one sphere that was to be of the most lasting impact, the internalization of the once-transcendent God. These few years were significant even for subsequent secular history, paving the way as they did for the self-elevation of the human beyond humanity, in such as Feuerbach, Marx, and Nietzsche. As for religious history, their importance cannot be overstated.

The 'breath-taking' movement begins with Fichte, but to understand why there is *movement* at all, a close look must first be taken at the relation between him and the *Alleszermalmer*, who is his great – nay, sole – inspiration. Kant inspires Fichte because, on the one hand, he has *zermalmt* – 'destroyed' – much, but because, on the other hand, he has not destroyed *alles* – 'everything.' Kant earned and deserves the radical *alles* because, while prior critics have destroyed this or that metaphysical doctrine, or this or that approach to the time-honoured discipline, his *Critique of Pure Reason* destroys metaphysics radically, that is, as such and in principle: rational access to transcendent objects, such as Kant's contemporary Moses Mendelssohn still considered possible – God, world, human freedom, the soul and its immortality – is in principle impossible. After this there must be a radical change in philosophy.

But – and, to philosophers from Fichte to Hegel and beyond this 'but' is decisive – while Kant destroyed much, he does not destroy everything. *Theoretical* reason is bound to the limits of the empirical world, but '*practical*' reason transcends them, which is why Kant affirms its 'primacy.' To be sure, for his future positivistic disciples Kant is the arch-debunker of metaphysics: to them his primacy of practical reason means nothing. But to his idealistic disciples just this primacy means everything: what genuine philosopher is not concerned, first and foremost, with possibilities of transcendence? For these disciples Kant is not a grave-digger of metaphysics but a revolutionary, a unique pioneer who opens a new page in an age-old enterprise; or – to change metaphors – he is the herald of a new dawn in philosophy, and perhaps in the world.

Kant's gateway to transcendence is freedom. We cannot prove that we are free, or even understand how an act of ours can be caused by our will alone, yet itself cause a chain of effects. But we do know our freedom in action, in the act of exercising it. By itself this 'knowledge' is only a subjective certainty. But it is converted into objective truth by our knowledge of moral duty. We may often be unsure of what our duties are, and still more often shrink from doing them. But that duties exist no rational being can rationally deny, and these – nay, duty as such – would be a vain conceit if we lacked the freedom to choose, and to choose to obey. Freedom, then, is the *ratio essendi* of duty, and duty, the *ratio cognoscendi* of freedom.

Kant's revolution is the impetus of the 'breath-taking' movement from 1794 to 1800 and beyond. But, for thought to *move* at all, three breaks away from Kant are necessary, and all three are carried out by Johann Gottlieb Fichte (1762–1814). This is astonishing, for Fichte believed himself to be the most faithful of all the master's disciples, and indeed insisted for the longest of times – loudly and to one and all – that his own *Science of Knowledge* (1794) was pure Kant and nothing but Kant, admittedly very different in form, but in content only slightly, in that it made explicit much that was only implicit in Kant himself. At length this public insistence of his annoyed Kant, to the point of making him publish a statement saying that if he had meant to write his philosophy differently he would have done so. 'Protect me from my friends,' he asked the public. As for his enemies, he added, he could take care of them himself.

But on his part, Fichte did not give up immediately, even then. The aging master, he rejoined, no longer understood his own philosophy. Fichte was never lacking in boldness, although often in tact.

But the fact is that he broke away from Kant from the start, in his first work, published as *An Essay towards a Critique of All Revelation* in 1792, but first written a year earlier, by way of introducing himself to Kant when he visited the latter in Königsberg.[6] Kant had recommended the manuscript for publication, and when the slim volume appeared, but with the author's name accidentally omitted, it was widely assumed to be Kant's own long-awaited work on the subject, so that, when the truth about the actual author came out, Fichte became famous overnight. Had he done it on purpose, he could not have worked it better. But, of course, he did not: not only his philosophy but also he personally was of strong moral principle.

However, as regards the identity of views of the two thinkers, both the public and Fichte himself were in error; and Kant cannot have more than glanced at the manuscript before endorsing it. Simply by virtue of *being* a Kantian 'critique,' a work entitled *Critique of All Revelation* denies the otherness of Revelation that is of its essence. In contrast, Kant's own work on religion, published in the next year, does nothing of the kind. Each of the four chapters of *Religion within the Bounds of Reason Alone* (1793), all 'within the bounds' of reason, is followed by a 'general remark' that points, if only obliquely, beyond these 'bounds,' and to aspects of the Christian faith. Or so it would seem: 'Revelation in Kant' is an elusive subject. (I once gave up an in-depth inquiry into it as fruitless.) Kant writes with caution; but, whether more because of the awesome subject or because of the Prussian censor, Kant scholars, I think, will never settle.

On his part, the thirty-year-old Fichte casts Kant's life-long caution aside. And, after this beginning of the post-Kantian movement of thought, Revelation disappears from the scene, not to emerge again seriously until Schelling's positive philosophy and, of course, Soren Kierkegaard.

With this first break with Kant we reach Fichte in his own right, and in what follows boldness remains his hallmark, in thought, but also, incidentally, in life. As for Kant, had he taken the time and made the effort to study the intricacies of the *Science of Knowledge*[7] – one of the most difficult works in philosophy – he might have admired its speculations for their subtlety but would surely have considered them reckless.

Boldness moves Fichte from his first to his second break with Kant. The freedom rightly exalted by Kant is not the mere ability to choose this or that, but autonomy, the obedience by the moral will of a law imposed, not by another but by itself. I once found it necessary to inquire whether, in order to be autonomous, Kant's moral will needs *to be* the author of moral law, or merely to *accept* moral law, of which it is *not* the author, *as though* it were that author; and the conclusion I then reached is that Kant opts for the cautious, less radical position.[8]

Not surprisingly, Fichte opts for the bold, radical alternative, and this as if there were no other: the will *creates* the law it obeys.

From his point of view he is right: for him there *is* no alternative. This is because of his third and climactic break with Kant – in the end, the one that really matters. The break is implicit in the very first principle of the *Science of Knowledge* of 1794. (I keep mentioning the year because Fichte went on dealing with the issues of this, his first major work, but the 1794 work remained the influential one and, in the view of most scholars, also his *magnum opus*.) For Kant, human beings are *creatures*: this is so self-evident to him that he never discusses it, confining himself to offhand remarks, to the effect that it is a 'mystery' that one creature, the human, should, qua creature, be created by another yet, qua rational, be capable of autonomy. These remarks may be offhand, but they are not thoughtless, for Kant's whole moral and religious philosophy teaches consistently, even systematically, that human nature is rational *yet finite*. (See chapter 1 above.)

For Kant, then, the 'mystery' of created freedom is ultimate. On his part, Fichte gets rid of the mystery by getting rid of the creatureliness. Simply by virtue of *being* Ego, the Ego is in *no* respect 'posited' by another but in *every* respect – that is, absolutely – posited by itself: 'The Ego posits itself' is the first principle of the *Science of Knowledge*, *ex hypothesi* in reality and, in speculative thought, in conscious re-enactment; and this principle, being first and also most certainly foremost, is manifest throughout the length and breadth of Fichte's philosophy. No previous philosophy ever conceived the freedom of the Ego so boldly and with so uncompromising a radicalism; and the consequences of it – in total support, in grudging partial support, or in opposition, whether apologetic or otherwise – reverberate in much Western philosophy to this day.

But Fichte cannot deny the finitude of the human Ego. And if, for speculative thought, this limitation is *self*-limitation, it cannot be so for the limited – that is, human – self, for which the world forever not only *seems* but also *is* other-than-itself, and just this constitutes its finitude. A split therefore threatens between two realms: the realm of speculative *thought* (for which all is derivative to the pure Ego, an Ego that not merely *has* but *is* freedom, for it is pure self-positing) and the realm of *life* (inhabited by finite selves, limited by 'non-Ego,' that is, a world other-than-self). This split (which would make the thought-realm into an arbitrary construct, without any claim to truth) can be avoided only if there is, as it were, a 'verification' of the thought-realm *in* the life-realm *itself* in which finite selves are *themselves* geared to something *beyond* their finitude, this being manifest in how they both understand themselves and conduct their lives. Otherwise put, Fichte's philosophy requires a *Sitz im Leben*, from which it can be 'assumed' to arise in the beginning and – this is the crux – by which it is 'verified' in the end. As will be seen, the philosophies of Schleiermacher and Schelling, too, require a *Sitz im Leben*, but the *Sitz* is not the same.

Following Kant, Fichte finds his *Sitz im Leben* in the moral sphere: this is not surprising. But whereas for Kant that sphere 'leads to' religion, for Fichte it *is* religion. Here the new ground he breaks comes fully into view. In the sphere of religion – for better or worse – it is Fichte rather than Kant who is the innovator: to move from Kant to Fichte – and then on to Schleiermacher and Schelling – is to enter a new religious world.

Humanity for Kant is rational *but finite*, which is why, on the one hand, humans are free to will but, on the other, unable either to control the consequences of their actions or to be indifferent to them. Kant's religion, therefore, is hope, held by inhabitants of two worlds, the natural and the moral, vested in a God who is Creator of both. In the light of Fichte's religion, however, this hope is a remaining human frailty, in agents who have yet to rise to their full moral stature. To have done so is to have risen above a hope that is now seen as a mere crutch, for it is to have become so totally absorbed in duty for duty's sake as to be indifferent to consequences and, moreover, to these not only when they affect the agent's own fate but also when they affect that of others. From a lower point of view such simon-pure moral high-mindedness may be mere callousness. (It is one thing to be indifferent to how one's actions affect oneself, quite another to how they affect others.) However, the community of which Fichte's moral agent is part is constituted by a shared duty for duty's sake, and by a shared indifference to its consequences.

This breakthrough – it is no less – is possible only because the Fichtean moral agent, while like the Kantian experiencing the object of duty as other, also experiences it, unlike the Kantian, as 'the material of duty, rendered sensuous.' This is a fundamental Fichtean assertion, the importance of which it is impossible to exaggerate. Nature *is meant* to be conquered by moral spirit; it ever tends – so long as there are moral agents – in the direction of *being* conquered; and – if only in the infinite, ideal, never real future – it *is* conquered. As for the community of moral agents, it not only *has* a share in this conquest but *is also aware* of the fact. Negatively, this awareness gives rise to the indifference to consequences, already considered; positively, it is, as will be seen, what religion can be and, at its truest and highest, is.

Inasmuch as Kant and Fichte both link religion with morality, their views on the subject may seem similar if not identical, but in fact the resemblance is dwarfed by the difference. For Kant, morality merely 'leads to' religion, which latter remains a separate sphere. Fichte wipes out this separateness: morality *is* religion. More precisely, it is the 'joy' inherent in the moral agents' experience *itself*, produced by their awareness of having a share in the moral conquest of the world. The conquest is the "moral order of the world," and that order is God. *The joy that is in moral activity is therefore nothing less than a share in God.*[9]

Perhaps not surprisingly, this Fichtean teaching produced a heated – and at the time famous – controversy over atheism. Fichte's own teaching was not directly responsible, but his stubbornness did much to stir it. Against one and all, Fichte insisted on his unrestricted right to teach his philosophy. He also insisted that it was not atheism, and in this he was right. Fichte is no atheist. *His is the historic breakthrough to God internalized, to the God Within.*[10]

The atheism controversy caused the government of Saxony, the controlling authority of Jena University, to prepare an investigation of Fichte's philosophy. On learning of this, Fichte sent off what amounted to an ultimatum. Unless he were summarily exonerated, he threatened, he would resign from his university post. Thereupon the government did something else summarily: it dismissed him. Fichte's rise to academic recognition had been sudden, even meteoric. Now there was a sudden plunge, and the years that followed were restless and insecure, with Fichte not recovering a solid academic post for more than a decade after the atheism controversy, and the crisis it had produced in his life.

This happened in 1799. In the same year the thirty-one-year-old Daniel Friedrich Schleiermacher (1768–1834) wrote – or put the finishing touches on – his *Addresses on Religion.*[11] It was as if he recognized the historic moment for him to come on the scene with this, his pioneer effort.

On Religion became famous subsequently, as the beginning of a career which made its author the first, and perhaps to this day greatest, liberal Protestant theologian. In 1799, however, the *Addresses* are Schleiermacher's intervention in 'the controversy,' but also much more than a share in what, in retrospect, is a petty, long-forgotten squabble. The subtitle of his work is *To the Cultured among Its Despisers*; and since of these Fichte is taken most seriously, the work is a crucial document in the emergence of the God Within. For Fichte, this God is within the joy of moral activity. For the Schelling of 1800 He will be within art. For the Schleiermacher of 1799 He is within religion itself. No wonder the author of *On Religion* subsequently became a theologian and went his own way.

But what is religion? For Schleiermacher it is not beliefs, theologies, sacred Scriptures and their authority: all these are derivative. Primary is an experience. This iconoclastic Protestant clergyman writes that not those are the best Christians who accept a holy Scripture but those whose experience is deep enough to enable them to write one themselves. Holy Scriptures may be part of the religious life, but they can also be a mausoleum of it.[12]

But what experience is religious? The following is Schleiermacher's most famous assertion: the experience looked for is feeling, and feeling is religious when it is radical humility, that is, 'the feeling of absolute dependence.'[13]

Much quoted, this assertion is also much misunderstood. Schleiermacher is not a psychologist of religion, or a social worker who recommends prayer because it is good for you: like Fichte before and Schelling after him, he seeks religious truth. And the truth he finds is understood best – at least in our present context – if it is taken as a radical response to Fichte's challenge, which he rightly considers to be itself radical. In making self-activity ultimate, the self-positing Ego of Fichte's idealism has disposed of the brute facticities of realism – the givenness of the world, of the transcendent God, of revealed Scriptures, of the creatureliness of the self itself. Schleiermacher accepts this disposal. He even welcomes it, for the truth it discloses clears the way to a still higher truth: what for Fichte is ultimate becomes, for Schleiermacher, penultimate. Since the human is finite and the Divine infinite, the joy of Fichte's moral activity consists of travelling hopefully but never to arrive: the Divine and the human remain apart. This apartness is overcome by Schleiermacher's pious passivity, for this is to *have* arrived. *Relative* dependence on things *finite* – food, drink, sleep, illness, mortality, even death – is dealt with by the Fichtean Ego's self-activity. The *presence* of *Infinity*, however, reduces the Ego to *feeling*, and the feeling to one of *absolute* dependence. For Schleiermacher, to have reached this feeling is to have gone beyond Fichte's self-activity: it is to have reached the ultimate.

Divinity is present *for* this feeling, but it is not *in* it, let alone reducible *to* it, for the feeling is one of dependence, and this is on an Other. Schleiermacher therefore asserts a new 'realism.' Rather than a lapse into the old, discredited realism, which is beneath Fichte's idealism, this is a realism beyond it. Divinity, to be sure, is present-as-other, but it is thus disclosed to the feeling of absolute dependence, and to it alone, and manifest as present only once Fichtean moral self-activity, which projects Divinity into the infinite future, is transcended. Fichtean idealism therefore paves for Schleiermacher the way for something higher still, a 'higher realism.'[14]

Schleiermacher and Hegel were colleagues at the University of Berlin – colleagues and rivals. So legendary was their mutual antagonism that the word spread like wildfire when once they were seen walking arm in arm across the campus. No wonder. 'If the feeling of absolute dependence made a Christian,' Hegel once remarked, 'a dog would be the best.'[15] It is easy to imagine how Schleiermacher reacted to that remark.

Yet the author of *On Religion* cannot, himself, have left matters with pious passivity alone, for while of this anyone may be capable, not everyone is capable of writing a Scripture worthy of being considered holy: as well as everyone's pious passivity, his religion requires *someone's* creative activity, and thus from Schleiermacher's step into a 'higher realism' arises the demand for a further step into a higher idealism. With this demand the time has become ripe for Schelling's *System of Transcendental Idealism* of 1800, a work teaching a 'real-idealism,' and culminating in a religion in which activity and passivity are united. That religion is art.

3 The System of Transcendental Idealism

In a series of lectures on the history of modern philosophy, probably delivered around 1827, Schelling writes: 'The actual realization [*Ausführung*] of Fichtean idealism is contained in my *System of Transcendental Idealism* of 1800.'[16] Schelling's work takes its departure from Fichte's *Science of Knowledge* of 1794, which he regards as the first major statement of transcendental idealism, but seeks 'actually to realize' the teaching of that work which is regarded by him as only a fragmentary preparation of transcendental idealism. He attempts to accomplish this task through two closely interrelated steps. One is the enlargement of transcendental philosophy so as to make it encompass a philosophy of nature; the other is the alteration of the transcendental map so as to make art the culminating function of consciousness. This transformation of Fichte's ethical into an aesthetic idealism has profound consequences for Schelling's concept of religion. Fichte is led by his philosophy to affirm a 'religion of joyous moral action.' In his *On Religion* Schleiermacher opposes this with a religion of 'pious passivity.' Both are now superseded by Schelling's art as 'revelation,' for in art activity and passivity are both involved and made one.

Such, as restated by him in retrospect, is Schelling's project in 1800, clearly a major one in the history of philosophy, of religion, and of the relation between the two. It is therefore important for us not merely to state the project but also to consider, in what follows, at least the major steps in its execution.

3.1

The year 1800 found German romantic poets in armed rebellion against the mechanistic conception of nature, as implied in contemporary science. Nature, so many a poem said, was not a mere collection of particles moving according to mechanical laws. This was perhaps how science had to view nature, looking (as it did) at it from without, as an alien object. But this was not what nature was. What appeared to the external onlooker as a mere collection of inert particles was in truth the crystallized external products of an inner, living *productivity* that pervaded and animated everything. Truly to understand nature was to enter into this productivity and to see it manifested in its products. Such an entering was not impossible, for the inward power of nature which was to be known was of the same substance as the mind that was to do the knowing, and in poetic intuition and expression they became one. Nature was an unconscious poet, and the poetic mind that comprehended it was nature reflected and transfigured in consciousness.[17]

This, in brief, is the teaching of the German romantic poets about nature. Like Schleiermacher, Schelling was close to their circle and shared their views. But he attempted to give a philosophical justification of a view which the poets – and Schleiermacher – embraced merely as a matter of romantic faith. As early as 1796, when a youth of twenty-one, he had promised to 'give wings to physics.'[18] And in the years that followed he had written several treatises in which nature appeared as a dynamic whole, a system of tensions and oppositions that struggles from the lowest manifestation of matter up toward mind.

As mechanistic science advanced victoriously through the nineteenth century, the romantic protest came to be dismissed, and with it the kind of philosophy of nature of which Schelling was the most characteristic representative. And special scorn was reserved for Schelling and his kind. For whereas romantic poetry could be dismissed as a protest against science and still be cherished as good poetry, romantic philosophy of nature – 'speculative physics,' as Schelling was fond of calling it – was just bad science and nothing else.

Nobody would dream today of making a case for Schelling's philosophy of nature. (For its counterpart in Hegel's mature thought it may be otherwise.) Still in fairness it should be observed in passing that Schelling's bold and often reckless speculations scorned by the science of his time bear some resemblance to ideas familiar in contemporary natural science and philosophy. It appears that physics, after all, does require 'wings,' although they may have to be put to different use than the one Schelling made of them.[19]

But the historic significance of Schelling's philosophy of nature does not, in any case, lie in his argument against mechanistic science but in that against Fichte, and therefore not in his concept of a philosophy of nature, let alone in its details, but in the relation of his philosophy of nature to transcendental philosophy. For Fichte as for Kant before him, nature is phenomenal, or being-for-self. The sole task of philosophy vis-à-vis nature is to explain its status *as* phenomenal, or being-for-self. As for the knowledge of nature itself, this is left to natural science.

Fichte's distribution of labour is therefore quite as clean as Kant's, for whom science knows phenomena, and transcendental philosophy knows that and why phenomena *are* phenomena.

But whatever else Schelling's philosophy of nature is, it is clearly and above all an attempt to know nature, not as phenomenal for a self, but in itself, that is, in its inner essence and quite apart from any relation to a self. This is why, unlike Kant's first *Critique* and Fichte's *Science of Knowledge*, Schelling's philosophy of nature can come into outright conflict with natural science. But it also comes into another, philosophically more important, conflict: with Fichte's (and Kant's) transcendental philosophy.

Of the fact of conflict there is no doubt. But how is it to be viewed? Fichte never wavered in his view that Schelling's philosophy of nature was nothing but a gross lapse into the kind of pre-critical, 'dogmatic' realism that Kant had disposed of and that he himself, following the master, had abandoned. But on his part, Schelling insisted that, far from a lapse from Fichte's version of transcendental philosophy, his philosophy was a step beyond it, that is, one of the two required for its 'actual realization.' Or, to put it into the context of the foregoing, in his view the 'realism' of his philosophy of nature is by no means the old 'dogmatic' realism done away with by the Kantian-Fichtean transcendental criticism, but much rather like Schleiermacher's 'higher' realism that presupposes that criticism; however, whereas Schleiermacher's realism is merely asserted against Fichte's idealism, that of Schelling is developed from within transcendental criticism itself, with the result – so he holds – that he arrives at a 'real-idealism' that leaves both Fichte and Schleiermacher behind. This is the 'actual realization' of Fichte's 1794 *Science of Knowledge*, brought about in the 1800 *System of Transcendental Idealism*.

Schelling's critique of Fichte may be summed up as follows: Fichte has succeeded in destroying the dualism of dogmatic metaphysics, which asserts a self and a world of independently existing objects. He also has disposed of a variety of dualisms that Kant left unresolved. But he himself remains with at least one unresolved dualism, between a nature that is only for-self and hence phenomenal, and the self for which it is. To be sure, he attempts to resolve this remaining dualism, by regarding nature as non-self but with the ultimate status of being the 'material' of the self's 'duty' and, correspondingly, the self as incompletely real until it has realized its duty. But the moral bridge thus established between self and nature-as-non-self is inadequate. No self has ever realized its duty fully in the past. No self does so now. Fichte therefore holds, and has no choice but to hold, that duty fulfilled is an ideal, lying in infinity. The overcoming of the self/non-self dualism remains an ideal, ever to be pursued but never reached.

All these faults, Schelling holds, are due to one fundamental flaw: 'Fichte understands by Ego merely the human Ego, by no means the universal or absolute Ego.'[20] So long as philosophy stays with the merely-human or finite Ego, nature remains other-than-self-for-self, and the Fichtean dualism cannot be transcended. The question is, of course, how Schelling's own philosophy can transcend the Ego's finitude, and thus 'actually realize' the project that, according to him, Fichte has merely begun.

In the work already cited Schelling writes:

> To be sure, the external world is for me only when I am at the same time, and when I am conscious. This much is self-evident. The opposite is true also: as soon as I exist and am conscious ... I find the world already existing. Hence it is out of the question that the already-conscious Ego should produce the world. But there was nothing to prevent me from going behind what is now a self-conscious Ego, back to a stage where it was not yet conscious; to assume a region below the now existing consciousness, and in this an activity of which I am no longer conscious, and which enters into my consciousness only as a result. This activity could be nothing but the labour of coming-to-self, the becoming self-conscious. Here it is only natural and indeed inevitable that the activity should cease once consciousness is attained. Only the result remains. This mere result, as which it remains for consciousness, is the external world; and this is why the Ego is not conscious of it as a world produced by it, but merely as co-existing along with it. ... The 'I am' is nothing but the process of coming-to-self, and ... it presupposes a having-been-outside-and-away-from-itself.[21]

This passage, advisedly quoted at length, shows how far removed the 'realism' of Schelling's philosophy is from pre-critical dogmatism, and that he understands it as an essential part of an 'actually realized' transcendental idealism. Schelling adopts Fichte's notion of nature as an unconscious force, but whereas in Fichte this force is 'non-Ego' – a function of the self dependent on the self – Schelling inverts that relation: that force is independent of the self – real apart from it – and the self is dependent on *it*. The question is, of course, how Schelling arrives at that independent force. If this were by means of inference from objects, this would be but a lapse into pre-Kantian dogmatism; indeed, a merely-inferred force-in-itself would be nothing but the 'thing-in-itself' all over again, an element in Kant that his successors had lost no time in discarding.

But this is wholly to misunderstand Schelling. His *System of Transcendental Idealism,* like Fichte's *Science of Knowledge,* descends into the self, and reconstructs it as a system of self-constituted functions. Both works come in this descent upon always-existing limiting conditions that can never be manifest to the self as being of its own making. But, unlike Fichte, Schelling does not take these conditions as being ultimately *for*-self, and hence *non*-self. He therefore cannot arrive at a reconstruction in which the self is ultimately *confronted by* nature, the self being wholly autonomous in its own realm and nature being other-than-self and non-self. For Schelling the self is, as it were, *immersed in* nature, and it remains so in all but its highest functions. (Of these – art and philosophy – more will be said below.) Hence he cannot take the self as wholly autonomous in its confrontations with nature, for he must take nature as much as *non*-other-than-self as he takes it to be other-than-self. The nature from which the self emerges, to be sure, is not self, but neither is it simply non-self. *Nature is the finite self's pre-self.*

Evidently nature cannot be understood as pre-self by the finite self, which can take nature only as non-self – as a system of frozen products looked at and acted on from without. To understand nature as pre-self is the task of an 'actually realized' transcendental philosophy. And it achieves this end, not by postulating nature as a system of living productivity, this as an object behind objects, but by penetrating within the finite self below the conditions that constitute its selfhood, 'descending into the depths of nature in order to rise from them to the heights of spirit.'[22] And this descent and subsequent ascent is the work not of the finite self but, as Schelling has told us, of the universal or absolute self.

Since – as may be said in passing – the account just given is not the conventional one, it is well for us to restate its chief thesis: the crucial significance of Schelling's philosophy of nature is its role in his 'actually realized' transcendental philosophy, a role which is indispensable. His quarrel with natural science, such as it is, is wholly secondary, his real quarrel being with philosophies, and with these not for taking nature as the wrong kind of object – say, a collection of particles rather than a self-differentiating whole – but for *the taking of nature as an object at all.*[23] No doubt natural science must take nature as an object, abstracting from the fact that as such it is only for a subject. But philosophies which mistake the abstract object for reality are either blind error – precritical, 'dogmatic' realism – or else, like Fichte's *Science of Knowledge*, half-seeing preparations of the truth. The crucial objective, then, in the two-front war fought in Schelling's philosophy of nature, is to undercut the distinction between subject and object, and this, for him, is achieved by philosophical understanding of nature as pre-self.

But for any hope of success in this effort Schelling must come to grips with a question thus far quite untouched. If the finite self cannot penetrate to its own pre-self *as* pre-self; if among the characteristics that constitute its finitude is this, that it cannot but take nature as a system of frozen objects spread before it in apparent otherness, then how can the philosopher do what the finite self cannot do?[24] He is, after all, himself finite, a finite human being before he is a philosopher. Unless Schelling can answer this question, his 'idealism of the universal or absolute self' must be, not the 'actual realization' of Fichte's transcendental philosophy, but an illegitimate soaring above the limits of knowledge so sharply set by Kant's critical philosophy. Kant was fond of calling this sort of flight *Schwärmerei* (irresponsible ecstasy) and might have applied it even to Fichte. As for Fichte, he might have applied it to Schelling's 'actual realization' of his own philosophy.

3.2

As stated above, in his 'actual realization' of Fichte's transcendental philosophy Schelling takes two steps. Having dealt with the first, we must now turn to the second, the addition of art to the transcendental map. A mere addition, however, would not do what is needful. Art must be, and be shown to be, the culminating transcendental function. Fichte's philosophy must be transformed as a whole, from an ethical into an aesthetic idealism.

The *Science of Knowledge* teaches that theory and praxis are two relations, not between the self and an independent world, but between the self and its unconscious product. In cognition, the self is finite, and must passively accept, as being alien, its own unconscious product, and this is infinite. In praxis culminating in morality, the opposite holds true. For here the world is experienced as finite, forever transcended by the striving of the self, which is infinite. To be sure, both relations are internal conflicts within the self which seek resolution. But neither can ever find the resolution it seeks. If in either relation the self ever overcame the conflict with the non-self, theory and praxis would both cease to be.

If in Schelling's *System of Transcendental Idealism* Fichte's unconscious product of the self becomes the self's pre-self, this transformation is possible only because it is linked with another, the affirmation of yet a third function of the self, in which the resolution of the conflict between self and non-self, merely aimed at by the other two, is forever achieved. That third function is art.

Artistic creation is at once conscious and unconscious, finite and infinite, unfree and free. In this it is like theory and moral action. Like these, too, it starts with conflict. But the nature of this activity, and this conflict, differs from the other two and is unique. In both cognition and morality the conscious self believes itself to be in conflict with an alien world, and only the philosopher knows that the world is not alien, that the conflict is internal. In art, the conflict is *experienced* as internal. Hence in the production that results from this conflict conscious and unconscious self not merely both enter: they are *experienced* as both entering, and it is for this reason that artistic production, while beginning with conflict and dissatisfaction, ends with satisfaction and harmony.

Artistic production involves the conscious and the free. The artist has conscious aims, and uses techniques which must be learned: one does not become an artist without hard work. But hard work alone does not make an artist. Over and above what is planned, conscious, and free there is in all genuine art an element that is unconscious and indeed incomprehensible, and analogous only to fate – in short, genius. This extraordinary notion has appeared already in Schleiermacher, although 'religious genius' may well be considered a problematic concept. It is in art, if anywhere, that the notion has its genuine home.

Genius is the unconscious and infinite element in aesthetic creation, as well as in the work of art. Because of it, the artist can always partly, but never wholly, explain either his aesthetic problem or its aesthetic solution, and his work inevitably reflects this condition.

> The basic character of the work of art is ... an unconscious infinity. ... In addition to what he has placed into it on purpose, the artist seems to have represented in it by instinct an infinity that no finite understanding can wholly explicate.[25]

But – as we have stated – the unique characteristic of the aesthetic conflict is that in it unconscious infinity is not only internal rather than external, but is recognized and experienced as such. Hence this conflict, unlike the cognitive and the moral, ends in absolute harmony. Truth and Goodness are eternal ideals; science and morality live by –

indeed, thrive on – eternal dissatisfaction. But aesthetic production, while beginning with strife and dissatisfaction, ends with infinite satisfaction. And Beauty, unlike Truth and Goodness, is no mere ideal: it is actual, the miraculous presence of the Infinite in the finite, of the Ideal in sensuous appearance.

3.3

The central significance of Schelling's philosophy of nature, we have argued above, does not lie in its case against mechanistic science: just so, we shall argue now, the central significance of his concept of art just outlined does not lie in the argument Schelling might mount against other concepts of art. In both cases, to be side-tracked into these directions would be to lose sight of the central objective – the role played by *both* the philosophy of nature *and* the concept of art within Schelling's 'actual realization' of Fichte's idealism. And the crux is that for the attainment of his objective *the inclusion of a philosophy of nature within idealism is necessary, but that only the role played by art renders this inclusion possible.* Schelling's objective is a 'real-idealism.' It can be attained only if his is an aesthetic idealism.

Fichte's idealism of the finite or human self must be *at least* an ethical idealism, if it is to be an idealism at all: the non-self, for all its otherness, must be experienced as the material of the self's duty, a material that in ideal infinity will lose its independence. Yet his idealism can also be *no more than* ethical: if the non-self were to lose its independence, not in ideal infinity but in the here and now – *any* here and now – the self would, at that point, lose its human finitude and become divine.

In contrast, if Schelling's 'actually realized' idealism is to be of the universal or absolute self; if it conceives nature not as non-self but as the finite self's pre-self, a conception in principle beyond the ken of the finite self: then 'the barriers which Fichte permits to fall outside the self ... [must] fall in the *System of Transcendental Idealism* ... into the self itself. The process ... becomes a wholly immanent one, in which the self ... is occupied only with its own contradiction, to be at once subject and object, finite and infinite.'[26]

If, with Fichte's self-positing Ego, we found the breakthrough to the God Within, with this Schellingian move from Fichte's idealism of the 'finite or human' to his own of the 'universal or absolute self' we come upon a further, no less radical breakthrough in the internalized God's self-disclosure. A new threat of a split between the realms of speculative thought and human life has become manifest, beyond that faced and mastered by Fichte. Like Fichte's *Science of Knowledge*, Schelling's *System of Transcendental Idealism* requires a *Sitz im Leben* from which it may be 'assumed' to arise in the beginning and which 'confirms' it in the end. But whereas Fichte's idealism, limited as it is to the finite or human self, requires only a *Sitz* that is itself finite and human – moral activity, filled with and informed by joy – the *Sitz* required by Schelling's idealism of the universal or absolute self, if a split is to be averted, must itself partake of universality or absoluteness and, the realm of life being human, this may well seem to shatter the limits of humanity. The shift from Fichte's ethical to Schelling's aesthetic idealism therefore involves more than a minor alteration of the transcendental map, but responds to the need for what can only be called a qualitative leap.

Fully aware of this, Schelling's transcendental philosophy as a whole, the philosophy of nature included, employs a 'knowing which is at the same time a producing of its object ..., in which the producing and the produced are identical.'[27] This knowing is a reproducing in thought of a nature already existing as pre-self in life: such is the 'assumption' from the start. But what if this is not knowing at all, but a mere indulgence by speculative thought in its own fancies, falsely projected on an alien nature? This can be refuted only if what is 'assumed' in speculative thought from the start is confirmed by life in the end. The goal of Schelling's transcendental philosophy must be 'to accompany spirit to the aim of all its endeavours, self-consciousness ... from representation to representation, from product to product, to the point where it first tears itself loose from all product, grasping itself in its own activity; where it no longer intuits anything but itself in its own absolute activity.'[28]

This aim – art – is not merely aim. It also justifies the whole enterprise. Art not only occupies a unique place on the map of transcendental philosophy. Because what Schelling puts forward is the transcendental idealism of the universal or absolute self, art is the 'organon of all philosophy.[29]

4 Art as Revelation

4.1

The transformation of Kantian into Fichtean idealism was seen to involve nothing less than a revolution in the understanding of religion – the breakthrough to the God Within. Schelling's idealism is a further breakthrough, from Fichte's 'human or finite' to his own 'universal or absolute self,' understood by him, however, as the 'actual realization' of what is implicit in the Fichtean. Hence while, as will be seen, the change in the understanding of religion is hardly less radical than the change from Kant to Fichte, and again from Fichte to Schleiermacher, no philosophical break is involved, analogous to the one from Kant to Fichte, and this difference leaves its traces in the concept of religion given in the *System of Transcendental Idealism.* The work puts forward two such concepts, of which the first points to the second as superseding it. Schelling's first concept is an implicit critique of Fichte's religion of joyous moral action, while the second is an implicit critique of Schleiermacher's religion of pious passivity as well. Both concepts, as well as the criticism implicit in Schelling's account of them, derive from the fact that Schelling's idealism of the universal or absolute self takes itself as superseding both Fichte's idealism of the finite or human self and Schleiermacher's 'higher realism.'

4.2

We begin with a summary of the first conception.[30] Religion is the belief in the moral order of the world. This belief cannot be sheer, passive acceptance, for the order thus accepted would be blind fate, destructive of freedom: for it to be moral, we must have a share in creating it. The God accepted in religious belief cannot be alien, finished, wholly other: 'Every intelligence may be considered to be an integral part of God, or the moral order of the world.' 'The moral order of the world, one may say, exists as soon as we erect it.'[31]

But this gives rise to the question: 'where is the moral order in fact erected?'[32] This cannot be answered in terms of freedom alone, which assures us of what subjectively ought to be and can be, but not of what objectively will be and is: while sheer submission is to an order which is not moral, purely free activity is moral action without assurance of order. The system of necessity is one of amoral order, while that of freedom is a moral 'system of absolute lawlessness.' To put it in religious terms, while passive acceptance of an objective order is the false religion of fatalism, involvement in moral action alone is no religion at all but, if made absolute, is 'irreligion and atheism.'[33]

This latter may spring from a morally inspired attempt to have freedom unlimited, uncontradicted in its claim to absoluteness by an opposing objective order. But the attempt necessarily fails. Moral agents cannot be unconcerned with the consequences of their actions, hence cannot but act as if these consequences were either within their control, or else in necessary harmony with their purposes. But the former belief is patently false, for the reality they act on is independent of them; and the latter belief cannot be derived from freedom-in-action alone. Thus if, in order to be moral, freedom must take itself as absolute, it is yet paralysed in the attempt. This paralysis shows freedom to be a fragment: moral atheism collapses in internal contradiction.

Morality becomes moral *religion* if it recognizes its own fragmentariness; if it nevertheless asserts its own reality; and if it embraces the only belief that makes this assertion possible. The belief in question is inseparable from morality, for it springs from nothing but freedom-in-active-self-contradiction. But morality is just as inseparable from that belief, for only by dint of it can morality assert its own contradiction-free reality. Thus all genuine religion is of necessity moral, and all genuine morality is of necessity religious. The belief in question is in *Providence* – 'religion in the only true sense of the word.'[34]

Providence, in so far as it is order, is independent, and in so far as it is moral, is not independent of our acting: it is, as it were, a play in which 'we are co-poets of the whole.'

> If the poet *were*, independently of the play, we would only be actors in the play He has created. But if, instead of *being*, independently of us, He reveals Himself only successively, through the play of our freedom *itself*, so that without that freedom He would Himself not *be*, then we are co-poets of the whole, inventors of the special role we play. ... God never *is*, for being is what manifests itself in the objective world. If He *were*, *we* would not be. But He reveals Himself constantly.[35]

Providence, then, is an order dependent on the morally willing, but independent of the morally unwilling. An ancient saying has it that *Fata volentem ducent, nolentem trahunt.* Schelling in effect substitutes: *Providentia nolentem trahet, a volente ducitur.*[36]

Providence thus is *history*, not, however, as understood by the theoretical observer of past and present who, possibly, also forecasts the future. It is history as *believed* in by agents who are *morally involved in* history. Their moral action is in the present, but their religion is geared to the future, to a period in which Providence will not only fully reveal itself but will also disclose that it has, secretly, been at work all along.

'When this period will begin we do not know. But whenever this will be, then God also will be.'[37]

4.3

The summary just completed shows Schelling's stand toward Fichte's concept of religion. His critique of fatalism is support in the atheism controversy: sheer submission to an alien, external God, destructive as it is of freedom, is an immoral religion, and a true religion must spring from freedom, understood as autonomy. But from support he quickly turns to criticism: moral freedom does not, immediately, imply belief in a moral order and hence religion, but on the contrary by itself implies absence of order and hence irreligion and atheism. Moreover, far from being unconcerned with the consequences of his actions, the more genuinely moral an agent is, the more seriously he must be concerned with them. And yet they are beyond his control.

This critique of Fichte's concept of religion must be seen as deriving quite precisely from Schelling's 'actual realization' of Fichtean idealism of the human or finite self. This latter takes as its datum the confrontation of the finite moral self with a nature understood as the material of its duty, a confrontation in which the self knows not only what ought to be but also that it will be: thus the moral experience is inherently complete, and the joy that flows from it is religion. But in Schelling's idealism of the universal or absolute self the finite or human self, to be sure, confronts nature with the autonomous freedom without which it could not be moral. But since it not only morally *confronts* nature but is also itself *immersed* in it, nature being an independent force, the self's own absolute – unlimited moral freedom – clashes with another absolute – that nature, taken as a whole, is beyond its control. Hence, whereas for Fichte religion flows from the completeness of the moral life, for Schelling it flows from its inherent fragmentariness – nay, self-contradiction – and is the belief in a Providence that alone can save its reality.

But the *System of Transcendental Idealism* must not only explain religious belief but also justify it. This it does by showing that there are not, after all, two absolutes-in-contradiction – an absurdity – but only an appearance of two absolutes. What in moral experience appears as an autonomous self-opposed-to-a-nature-other-than-it is in reality immersed in a nature from which it has only partly torn itself loose; and what to religious faith appears as external, independent necessity is in reality pre-self that aims at realization in selfhood. The finite moral self believes religiously in the ultimate harmony between its own freedom and a necessity external to it. The idealism of the universal or absolute self justifies that belief, by showing that both the freedom and the necessity are indispensable aspects in the development of one absolute, the universal or absolute self.

This truth the finite or moral-religious self cannot understand. If it did, it would cease to be moral, that is, act in freedom; it would also cease to believe, that is, commit itself to an order at least partly independent of its freedom. It would *know* rather than believe, and its knowing would be identical with its acting, for it would no longer be of an other – all otherness having been overcome – but absolute self-activity. Such a knowing pervades the *System of Transcendental Idealism,* in the realm of speculative thought. It could be found in the sphere of human life only by shattering the limits of its humanity.

4.4

But, as will be recalled, the Schellingian system of speculative thought, like the Fichtean, would be a mere system of arbitrary 'assumptions' if it did not have a *Sitz im Leben*, a 'verification' in the realm of life; and, in the case of Schelling's idealism of the universal or absolute self, that *Sitz* is art. Hence if, as we have seen, religion-as-belief-in-Providence is validated by speculative thought, and this in turn is 'verified' by art in the realm of life, art indirectly validates religion-as-belief-in-Providence also, and, in validating it, ipso facto also supersedes it. It is *itself* a religion – the ultimate religion there is.

How does religion-as-art both validate and supersede religion-as-belief-in-Providence? By preserving its two absolutes, yet denying their absoluteness by integrating them into *one* absolute. The aspect of free moral activity is preserved, in the conscious aspect of artistic creation. Preserved also is providential order and its aspect of otherness, for in artistic creation 'another, as it were, is experienced as acting through us.'[38] However, it now is only 'as it were' other, for its otherness is within, manifest as genius, that is, the unconscious, infinite aspect of artistic creation. This inner otherness may remain other in the aesthetic struggle, so that here an appearance of two absolutes still survives. But this appearance vanishes when the struggle is over – when, in the completed work of art, finitude and infinity, the conscious and the unconscious, freedom and necessity are reconciled, have become one.

For the moral-religious belief in Providence the Deity remains a *becoming* God: 'If He *were, we* would not be.' Correspondingly, the believing self remains a fragment, which is why it stands in need of religious belief at all. This fragmentariness is now overcome.

But is it overcome in art-as-religion *itself*, or in the *philosophy* that recognizes the religion in art? Or, if in both, what is their relation? (If the 'secret' of the 'golden age' in German philosophy lies in the close cooperation between poet and philosopher, the secret is nowhere as open as in this period of Schelling's thought: but does the cooperation degenerate into a rivalry?)

This was to become a large question in subsequent thought, most clearly spelled out by Hegel, and then also in such distant heirs of German idealism – they would not have liked this description – as Nietzsche and Heidegger.

In the *System of Transcendental Idealism*, at any rate, Schelling's stand seems clear. Philosophy may raise thought above fragmentation, but thought alone. In contrast, 'Art carries *the whole man, as he is*, to the knowledge of the Highest, and in this lies the eternal difference and miracle of art.'[39]

As to what 'the Highest' is, we are left in no doubt. In art God *is*, and so are *we*, for here, and here alone, it is as true that His acting is ours, as that ours is His. Hence 'Art is the sole *eternal* revelation there is.'[40] Nowhere has the God Within found a bolder, more forthright celebration than in this, according to many, the greatest work Schelling wrote in his entire career.

5 Toward Absolute Idealism

The *System of Transcendental Idealism* was published in 1800. In a letter written to a friend Schelling confesses that in 1801 he 'saw the light in philosophy.' Its timing makes this a startling confession, all the more so because Schelling means what he says. In later years he thought of the 1800 work as a mere 'preliminary exercise,' and in a collection published in 1809 he did not include it.

Equally startling is the quality of the works he wrote after having seen 'the light.' *My System of Philosophy* of 1801 is, according to his own claim, authoritative, yet it is incomplete, ends with the feeble explanation that 'time and circumstances did not allow a continuation,' and is, in the words of one critic, 'the emptiest and most insignificant' of all his major works. Other writings of the same period, such as the dialogue *Bruno* and the *Lectures on the Method of Academic Study*, both published in 1802, are elegant, but give the impression of a thinker seeking cover in elegance from systematic rigour. But rigour is demanded by the new 'light' – by the double task of exposing transcendental idealism as being, in principle, guilty of subjective one-sidedness, and of achieving a transcendence of just that one-sidedness, in what Schelling calls a 'system of identity,' with thought assuming a 'standpoint of indifference.' Only thus the 'real-idealism' Schelling has aimed at for so long is at last to find its ultimate 'actual realization.' In short, wanted is no longer a transcendental idealism, not even one of the universal or absolute self, but absolute idealism. The 'light' has at last shown the ultimate philosophy, 'beyond' which to 'go' – so it seems to Schelling in 1801 – is neither necessary nor possible.

But his only reasonably complete statement of absolute idealism was written in 1804, the very year in which he first perceived the 'fall' or break or rupture that at length was, for him, to call the whole idealistic project into question, leading him, after only a few – if significant[41] – further works, into the long silence from which he did not re-emerge until his dramatic 1841 Berlin appearance. Perhaps this is why the 1804 work, entitled *System of Philosophy in Its Entirety*, was left unpublished by him, and published only posthumously.[42]

Schelling abandoned absolute Idealism in 1804. Hegel, his one-time friend and subsequent rival, did not publish his first major work in absolute Idealism until 1807. The preface of the *Phenomenology of Spirit* contains several well-known critical remarks about Schelling, and these widened the already-existing breach between the two thinkers. But it also contains at least one tribute. If 'the times are ripe for the elevation of philosophy to science' (*Wissenschaft*), not the least credit belongs to Schelling, who raised the discipline to the absolute standpoint in which all one-sidedness is overcome. On this Hegel never changed his mind. In his lectures on the history of philosophy – a discipline understood by him as the evolution of philosophical truth – Schelling was invariably treated at the end. Hegel was the incarnate opposite of a Proteus in philosophy. But he never failed to recognize greatness in the friend of his youth, a man with so different a philosophical temperament, and so different a philosophical career.

5 Schelling's Philosophy of the Literary Arts

I

In the summer of 1802 Schelling prepared his lectures on the philosophy of art, which he was to give in Jena in the academic year 1802–3. While in the midst of preparations, he asked A.W. Schlegel for the loan of a manuscript of his on art. 'Your manuscript,' he wrote, 'would be of excellent service to me ... and spare me many investigations.'[1]

This letter is typical. Schelling borrowed freely, not only from A.W. Schlegel (who, incidentally, was glad to lend the manuscript), but also from such other masters as Friedrich Schlegel, Goethe, Schiller, and Winckelmann. Indeed, none of Schelling's works is so dependent on the ideas and research of others as his *Philosophy of Art*.[2]

This fact provides a considerable temptation. The interpreter is tempted to take Schelling's ideas one by one, to trace them wherever possible to sources and origins, in order thus to arrive at a judgment upon his contribution to the field.

But we must resist this temptation. The method of piecemeal comparison implies that Schelling was an aesthetic critic more or less indebted to other critics; and this is a fundamental misunderstanding. Schelling did not intend to compete with the critics. And the precise reason why he felt free to borrow from them is that he regarded his own work as something fundamentally different.

In the above-quoted letter to A.W. Schlegel, Schelling distinguishes between a theory of art and a philosophy of art. The former studies the empirical products of art, the latter, something called 'art in itself,' or 'art in the Absolute.'[3] Now, whatever this latter may be, it is not criticism. It is metaphysics. Schelling never imagined that he had made any substantial contribution to aesthetic criticism:[4] but he did regard himself as more or less the founder of the metaphysics of art.[5] His main contribution is therefore to be sought, not in specific aesthetic concepts or analyses, but in the new function these assume in the context of a metaphysical system. But precisely to this new function the piecemeal approach of the ordinary historian of ideas must be blind.

Our approach to the *Philosophy of Art* must therefore be different. We must first consider the problem which gives rise to this metaphysics of art. For it is by no means obvious what philosophical reasons should make such a metaphysics necessary, nor is it obvious how it is possible. We must then proceed to treat Schelling's ideas on art, not piecemeal but as a system: in conception at least, as an organic whole in which each part has its place.

II

In his *System of Transcendental Idealism* of 1800, Schelling made this remarkable statement: 'Art is the only and eternal organon ... of philosophy.'[6] This may be a commonplace idea among romantic poets,[7] but it is unheard of in philosophy. How did Schelling arrive at it?

We may conveniently treat this doctrine as arising from the problems of Schelling's predecessors.[8] Kant, as is well known, had denied that knowledge is passive reception. In knowing the world, the mind recognizes in it what it has itself placed into it. The world we know is at least in part product of the knowing mind. Fichte went further: he identified reality with production of self. He had therefore to understand the self as a system of necessary functions in terms of which all experience can be explained. Now, the self experiences itself *as* self: but it experiences the world as other than self. If this world is nevertheless to be its own product, it can only be a product in which the self does not recognize itself: in other words, an unconscious product. What we experience as self and world are in truth conscious and unconscious products of self.

Self and world are related in two ways. In knowledge, the self accepts the world passively; in moral practice, it transforms the world in terms of its own ideals. In Fichte's system, theory and practice are two relations, not between self and world, but between conscious and unconscious self. In theory, the conscious self is finite; for it must accept as alien its own unconscious product, and this is infinite. In moral practice, the reverse relation holds. For here the world is experienced as finite, forever transcended by the infinite striving of the conscious self.

The self is thus in eternal conflict with itself. For in neither theory nor practice does it recognize itself in its own unconscious product. Both forever strive toward identity. But if they ever reached it, they would both cease to be.

But Fichte's system has the grave inconsistency of denying what at the same time it must assert. It denies that the self can recognize its own unconscious product as itself, but it also presupposes the opposite. For it claims to do the very thing which is impossible for both theory and practice. Fichte, of course, recognized this difficulty. He started out with an intellectual intuition which, being prior to both theoretical and practical consciousness, is the perception of sheer self-identity. But this obliged him to show how the finite self can reach this perception: how the empirical can become a philosophical self. And this Fichte was unable to show.

Schelling perceives that the system can be saved only if there is yet a third function of the self; and if here the self recognizes itself in its unconscious product. In this function, the self must know itself as at once finite and infinite, unfree and free, conscious and unconscious. It must not only produce, but *know* that it produces. And while it may, like theory and practice, begin with total strife, it must achieve in its production total harmony.

Merely to postulate such a function would be futile indeed. But Schelling perceives its actuality. It is genius and its product, the work of art.

Artistic production, like all production, starts out with a conflict. But the nature of this conflict is unique. In knowledge and morality, the conscious self believes itself to be in conflict with an external world. In art, the conflict is experienced as internal; and conscious and unconscious self are not opposed as enemies. Hence in the production which results from this conflict conscious and unconscious self do not merely both enter; they are also experienced as both entering. Thus every artist has conscious aims and purposes, and he uses techniques which he must learn. For one does not become an artist without hard work.[9] But on the other hand, hard work alone does not make an artist either.[10] In addition to what is planned, conscious, free, there is in all genuine art an element which is incomprehensible, unconscious, and analogous only to fate:[11] in other words, genius. The artist can always partly, but never wholly, explain either his problem or his solution. And his work reflects this condition. 'The basic character of the work of art is ... an unconscious infinity ... In addition to what he has placed into it on purpose, the artist seems to have represented in it by instinct an infinity which no finite understanding can wholly explicate.'[12]

In aesthetic creation the self recognizes itself in its unconscious product. Hence, unlike the theoretical and moral, the aesthetic conflict ends in total harmony. Truth and Goodness are eternal ideals. Science and morality live by eternal dissatisfaction. But Beauty is not a mere idea. It is actual, the miraculous presence of the Infinite in the finite product. And aesthetic experience is infinite satisfaction.

Art, then, is the organon of philosophy because 'in genius ... a contradiction is solved which is absolute, and insoluble elsewhere.'[13] The unity of the self which the philosopher perceives only in abstraction is concretely revealed in the product of art. 'Art is an eternal revelation, the only revelation that exists.'[14]

III

In 1800 Schelling makes art the organon of philosophy. Art, not the philosophy of art. Despite considerable wavering,[15] this must be his conclusion. The philosopher may understand why what the genius does is necessary; but he cannot understand how he does it. To the philosopher, as to the man in the street, art remains a 'miracle.'[16] Hence he can assign the place of genius among the functions of the self. But he can do no more.

But the *Philosophy of Art* of 1802–4 does a great deal more. It offers nothing less than the construction of a system in which all forms of art, and even individual works of art, find a necessary place. And this presupposes, as Schelling clearly recognizes,[17] that in some sense the philosopher's comprehension of the artist's work transcends that of the artist himself.

This shift occurs as part of a more fundamental shift from transcendental to absolute idealism. In 1800 Schelling starts out with a universal self whose highest self-realization is art. In 1802 the starting point is the Absolute; and the self has become a mere aspect included in it.[18] The universal self of 1800, in abstraction, is not beautiful; beauty exists only in the empirical products of genius. But the Absolute of 1802 is not an abstraction; on the contrary, it is absolute, all-inclusive reality. Beauty therefore cannot be denied to it. This necessitates a distinction between empirical beauty and beauty in itself, or beauty in the Absolute.[19] And this again implies the crucial distinction between theory and philosophy of art.[20] This distinction is crucial because (as we have already seen) Schelling's concept of a philosophy of art depends on it. For the task of such a philosophy is, not the empirical consideration of art and beauty, but the discovery of their place in the Absolute. Schelling's transcendental idealism, then, does not make his *Philosophy of Art* intelligible. To understand the latter, we must first understand Schelling's shift to absolute idealism.

Unlike Fichte, Schelling had never regarded nature as the product of the self. In his writings of 1797–9, nature was presented as an independent force which struggled upward from matter to mind. And in his transcendental system of 1800 only the science of nature was the product of the self; nature itself was not. The Fichtean system of consciousness is only one of two systems; the other is the system of nature itself.

But this position is untenable unless the two systems are themselves part of a higher system. For otherwise it remains a riddle how nature can ever be known by science. Consciousness and nature, ideality and reality, cannot be two separate realities; they can only be aspects of a reality which itself is neither. This is the Absolute.

This Absolute must be simple Identity. For difference can be real only from the standpoint of the two subordinate systems. From the absolute standpoint, there is no difference. But, on the other hand, the Absolute cannot be empty identity, and difference cannot fall outside it. For if it did it would be a separate reality. The Absolute must be the bond which unites real and ideal; but what it unites must fall *within* it. It must contain all difference but in a form which denies difference. How is this possible?

According to Schelling, this is possible in only one way. Difference in the Absolute must be quantitative, not qualitative. Whatever exists in the Absolute must have both reality and ideality; and difference is difference of emphasis. All of these emphases (which Schelling calls potencies) must be part of a perfect system. For every emphasis of reality there must be a corresponding emphasis of ideality. And thus the Whole, while containing all difference, will itself be total indifference.

From this it follows that the Absolute may be approached in two ways. Either we may approach it *as* Absolute, in which case it appears as an Identity which absolutely denies difference. Or we may approach it from the standpoint of any one of its potencies. And in that case we perceive it, not in the tranquillity of sheer identity, but as a dynamic system of tensions, in which reality and ideality can return to identity only after having fallen apart.[21]

The method of the former approach may be intuition, but that of the latter cannot. Intuition can perceive the finite as absorbed in the Infinite; but it cannot perceive any particular finite thing. In a philosophical edifice supposedly built on intellectual intuition alone, we do well to suspect an empirical intruder hidden in the basement.

To perceive something as a potency of the Absolute is to perceive it as in perfect balance with all other potencies. From this it follows that the appropriate method must be the construction of a philosophical system. We demand on a priori grounds that all possible proportions of reality and ideality must be actual, and we base our method on this demand. The principle of this method is that the Absolute, like nature, 'abhors a vacuum.'[22]

IV

Philosophy of art is philosophy because it constructs the Absolute. It is philosophy of art because it constructs it in the potency of art. The first task of the *Philosophy of Art* is to understand art as a potency of the Absolute; and this can be done only by defining its place in the total system of identity.

The Absolute has a real side: this has been studied in the philosophy of nature. It has an ideal side: this has been considered in the transcendental philosophy. The philosophy of identity must prove that each side is a potency of the Absolute, and that therefore the potencies within each side are in strict correspondence.

Nature is real or finite; for it is limited, concrete, static fact. Mind is ideal or infinite; for it is unlimited and abstract; and it is not fact but activity. But nature has also ideal emphases, and mind, real. For there is neither absolute reality nor absolute ideality in the Absolute.

Thus nature, or the real, begins with a real emphasis. This is sheer finitude or externality which, taken by itself, lacks all nisus toward universality. It is matter or weight. But this is next countered by an ideal emphasis, a universalizing, dissolving tendency. This is light. Nature culminates in a synthesis of both tendencies. Difference and multiplicity are preserved, but their externality is overcome; for they are united in a whole. This is organism. Organism is the highest potency of nature, and nature is a single organism.

The development of mind is complementary to that of nature. Mind, or the ideal, begins with an ideal emphasis. This is mind in abstract universality, whose expression is science. Science is abstractly universal because it forever seeks, but forever fails, to absorb the particular. Hence the next emphasis must be real, or particular. This mind achieves by turning practical. For while theory is universality striving to absorb the particular, moral practice is particularity striving to realize the universal. But this emphasis too is one-sided. In making itself particular, mind has lost the presence of the universal. The Infinite has become infinite aim; and this aim moral mind can never reach. Thus mind too must achieve a synthesis of reality and ideality. This is art. Genius is universal mind wholly manifest in a particular person. The work of art is the Infinite in a form which is both present and concrete.

We must here note the pattern into which these potencies fall, for this pattern will play a significant role in Schelling's system of the arts. A potency is either abstractly ideal, i.e., an infinite which strives, but fails, to incorporate the finite. This Schelling terms schematic. Or it is abstractly real, i.e., a finite which points to an infinite, but fails to reach it. This is termed allegoric. But the system, as well as each sub-system, must complete itself in a synthesis in which finite and infinite, real and ideal, become identical. This form of existence is called symbolic.

We need not dwell on the place of art among the functions of mind. For we have already considered this point in the system of 1800, and the present doctrine is practically unchanged. But what was then product of the self is now one side in the equation of the Absolute. And this change has new and far-reaching implications.

The equation of the Absolute requires not only that nature should strive toward mind, but also that mind must somehow turn to nature. Science seeks to know it; morality, to transform it; art, to represent it. But this is not to say that there is a complete reciprocity in the relation of nature and mind. At the risk of destroying his equation, Schelling must assert that mind is a higher potency than nature. For while nature strives to dissolve into mind, mind certainly does not seek to disappear in nature.

Nature may strive toward ideality but it cannot reach it. It is therefore a mere allegory of the Absolute. But mind, in striving toward reality, never loses its native ideality. Thus science is not empirical reception, but the bringing of facts under laws. Morality is not obedience to empirical inclination, but the realization of the Ideal. Art finally is not the imitation of nature, but the representation of an infinite Idea in a finite product. The artist does not imitate nature: he transfigures it. Nature is the finite with a nisus toward infinity; art is the synthesis of finiteness and infinity. Nature is a mere allegory of the Absolute; art, its symbolic representation.

From this construction follows the momentous conclusion that art is not only a potency of the Absolute but its highest potency. Nature, and even science and morality, are all one-sided expressions of the Divine. Art is its complete representation in finite form.[23]

This raises the question: how is art, as the highest potency of the Absolute, related to the Absolute itself? We may perhaps say that art is explicitly what the Absolute is implicitly. The Absolute is that pristine identity in which the ideal and the real are blotted out: art is their synthesis after separation. The Absolute is neither real nor ideal: art is the unity of both.

But the terms implicit and explicit are ambiguous. For the explicit may be more, or less, real than the implicit. Thus the Neoplatonic One is more real, but less explicit, than its emanations; but the transcendental Ego of the Kantians is both less real and less explicit than its expressions. Schelling's Absolute may be regarded as a synthesis of the Neoplatonic One and the transcendental Ego. Like the former, it possesses all reality and is thus simple identity; but like the latter, it requires process and contradiction in order to be real.[24]

From this it follows that here the implicit and the explicit are equally real, and that philosophy and art are equally absolute.[25] The philosopher constructs a system whose ultimate aim and effect is the absolute denial of difference.[26] The artist holds on to the finite but builds the infinite into it. What the philosopher achieves by means of ideas the artist achieves by means of the products of aesthetic imagination.

V

Schelling has now defined the place of art in the Absolute. As a result of this definition, he is confronted with a gigantic task: the construction of all forms of art as a world, a system.[27] For if it is true that art represents by means of the aesthetic imagination exactly what philosophy represents by means of ideas, then art must reflect, in a form appropriate to it, the whole system of potencies. It too must have a real side, an ideal side, and the dialectical movement toward synthesis in both. It is little wonder that Schelling is not altogether successful in the construction of such a system. What is surprising is that he succeeds as well as he does.

Nature is the Absolute in finite form. To this must correspond a form of art which, while expressing the Infinite or Ideal, is compelled to represent it in a finite, alien form. This is the world of the figurative arts. We cannot here discuss these in detail, for limitations of space compel us to confine ourselves to the literary arts. Suffice it to say that the figurative arts ascend from music through painting to sculpture. Each represents the Ideal in a real medium and shows, because of the medium, certain analogies to nature. But none of them imitates nature. For they differ from nature in placing the Ideal into the medium. Niobe is cold, mute stone. But there is life in the death of this stone, and Niobe's cry of anguish, though frozen and mute, still resounds.[28]

Mind is the Absolute in the form of ideality or universality. To this must correspond a form of art which expresses the Ideal in ideal form. This is the art of the word. Language is an artistic medium superior to matter in that it is not purely particular. But neither is it, like thought, purely universal; and if it were it could not be an aesthetic medium at all. Language is at once particular act of speaking and universal content.[29] It is real in that, in particular sound, inflection, accent, it expresses particular, present feeling. But it also expresses a meaning which transcends particularity. Language is by its very nature symbolic. It is for that reason the most perfect aesthetic medium, placed at the disposal of the artist, as it were, by the divine Artist himself.

Still, language is only a medium of art, not art itself. For it may, as in prose, be used for non-aesthetic purposes. The art of the word must express an absolute meaning, and it must express this meaning symbolically, i.e., make it live in the particular act of speaking itself. The art of the word is poetry.

In poetry, then, as in all art, there is a necessary connection between form and content. And the system of poetic arts will be at once a system of poetic ideas, and of forms of poetry.

The first form of poetry is the lyric.[30] This may be defined as the real form of poetry, for it represents the finite, particular subject. Not, to be sure, the simply-finite, empirical person: for his self-expression is not poetry at all. Rather, the lyric takes the particular person as absolute; as the particular who seeks, and finds, universality in himself. The lyrical poem is a rhythmic movement, back and forth, between particularity and universality. And the whole process is presented as taking place in the person of the poet himself; he moves with his subject because he *is* his subject. The subject-matter of the lyric is the moods, feelings, passions of the poet himself.[31]

The principle of the lyric is therefore absolute subjectivity or freedom. But this is not freedom as opposed to necessity. Since freedom is here taken as absolute it recognizes no external necessity: it carries its own necessity, as it were, in itself. This freedom is therefore not moral freedom but passion or licence. And the beauty of the lyric is the beauty of absolute licence.

Accordingly, the lyric will recognize no law for either its content or its form. It will dwell, now on the profound, now on the trite; and then again not dwell at all but quickly shift from place to place. It will also shift from rhythm to rhythm, from metre to metre; and it finds the most even metre the least appropriate.

The lyric may thus appear to be sheer chaos. But it is chaos, as it were, with a pattern. Its beauty lies in a licentious playfulness, which scorns an external law only because it carries within itself its own law, latent and inarticulate but nevertheless real.

The radical antithesis of the lyric is the epic. This may be defined as the ideal form of poetry, for it tells a universal story, of which the deeds and fortunes of individuals are merely a part. Nor is it merely an arbitrary story, one story among others. It is a story with an inner necessity; indeed, it is *the* story which the poet hears, as it were, in the Absolute itself.[32] The epic is the universal story because it represents a pristine identity from which particularity has not yet broken loose.

The epic reflects this universality in both content and form. Its content cannot be arbitrary, and it cannot be the random creation of the individual poet. It must be a story of heroes, demi-gods, and gods; and this story must be the product of the entire age. In other words, the material of the epic is mythology. As regards form, the epic must begin and end abruptly, arbitrarily. It must indicate in its form that it tells a story whose true beginning and end lie in infinity; and that therefore any finite beginning and end are arbitrary. The metre of the epic must be the most even. For the epic tells a story which is one, a story equally containing the great and the petty, the profound and the trivial. The very identity of all parts of the story is its essence, and it must never raise its voice.

The principle of the epic is thus objectivity or necessity. But this is not yet a necessity opposed by freedom, and therefore it does not yet appear as fate. In the Homeric epic – the ideal, if not the only epic – there is no instance of rebellion against fate.[33] Men and gods may weep at the dispensations of necessity, but they do not rise up against it. This would be possible only if freedom had an absolute of its own: if it were moral consciousness. But the epic hero is not a moral hero, and mythological gods are not moral gods. Thus in the epic freedom is as yet implicit within necessity. This form of poetry 'represents action in the identity of freedom and necessity,'[34] i.e., in the identity of innocence.

All poetry, being speech, must move. But the lyrical poem makes the particular absolute; it therefore moves absolutely. What is in movement are moods and feelings, and these are the poet's own. But the epic makes universality absolute. It must therefore, though moving in time, symbolize indifference to time.[35] This is possible only if the movement falls, not into the poet himself, but into external actions which he narrates. These move, but the poet himself does not. For he cannot appear in the epic. 'Achilles weeps ... for his friend Patroclus; but the poet appears neither moved nor unmoved, for he does not appear at all.'[36] The beauty of the epic lies in this divine indifference: to symbolize history from the standpoint of God, the poet must, as it were, become God.[37]

But neither the lyric nor the epic is poetry in its highest form. For the epic represents only an identity in which difference lies dormant, and the lyric, a difference which does not recognize identity. In the highest form of poetry *both* must make an explicit appearance. Necessity must become fate, and freedom, moral freedom. They must appear together, and yet both appear as absolute. They must, therefore, become involved in absolute conflict. This happens in tragedy.

Fate and freedom, to be what they are, must both be invincible. For if either of them is not, there is no tragic conflict. But they must also both suffer defeat. For if they cannot touch each other there is no conflict at all. This is the essence of the tragic situation.

Accordingly, it is not enough for the tragic hero merely to suffer, or even to suffer unjustly. For in either case his suffering need not affect his freedom. He might triumph over his suffering with a contempt born of the knowledge of his justice. Fate must attack freedom at its very source and yet, in the very act of destroying it, recognize it. This it can do only by making the hero innocently guilty. The tragic condition in its purity is innocent guilt, and the truly tragic hero is Oedipus.

But this situation is poetically intolerable. The tragic contradiction, though absolute, must be resolved. How is this possible?

Freedom must administer to fate precisely the defeat which it suffers: it must recognize it, yet in the very act of recognition destroy it. This it can do only by ceasing to fight the foe. For just as freedom, to be moral freedom, requires a fate which to oppose, so fate remains fate only so long as freedom opposes it. Oedipus freely atones for the crime of which he is innocently guilty. And this act of atonement ends the tragic conflict. Fate and freedom have both won and lost: they are transfigured into a higher identity.

The tragic theme cannot be told in the form of narrative. For unlike the epic hero, the tragic hero has broken loose from the objective power; and the poet must identify himself with him, in terror and pity. But on the other hand, the poet cannot wholly identify himself with the hero, breaking out into lyrical verse. For he must also detach himself from the hero, and observe his conflict with fate. Thus the poet must, and yet cannot, identify himself with the hero; he must be moved, and yet look on. This is possible only if the tragic hero is presented objectively, as in the epic, yet in a form which enables him to make his case against the objective power: in other words, if instead of being merely narrated, the tragic conflict is enacted. The tragic theme requires the form of drama.

In art, Schelling has told us, 'a contradiction is resolved which is absolute, and insoluble elsewhere.'[38] Both the contradiction and the resolution reach their highest form in the tragic drama. Its beauty is the most inexhaustible. For it symbolizes in the most perfect form the identity of the deepest tranquillity and the most bacchantic frenzy[39] which is the essence of the Absolute.

VI

It is hardly necessary to point out that in the foregoing Schelling has given a system, not of poetry, but merely of Greek poetry. And if it were offered as an account of all poetry it could not be taken seriously. Schelling, however, does treat modern poetry; but he is able to treat it only in terms of a theory of history. This, as we shall see, creates a philosophical problem of the first magnitude. Schelling must relate his concept of art to a concept of history: but the one threatens to destroy the other.

In the *Philosophy of Art* and other writings of the same period,[40] Schelling puts forward an interpretation of history more or less common to the romantics of his age. In this interpretation, history is divided into two sharply opposed periods: the ancient or pagan, and the modern or Christian. In the ancient world, the Infinite lives as embodied in the finite universe. Man finds the presence of God in Nature, and there is no need to seek a God beyond it. Man experiences Nature as a divine, organic unity, and himself as an harmonious part of it. This experience is expressed in mythology. Ancient mythology represents the Divine, as manifold, finite, and present. The last characteristic is perhaps the most important. God is experienced not as Beyond, but as Presence. And the mythology which springs from this experience is therefore not the artificial product of individuals; it reflects the experience of the race.

The spirit of the modern or Christian world is the diametrical opposite. Here the bond once uniting finiteness and infinity is broken. The world has become a godless world, and God, an infinite Beyond. He is no longer present, but has become the object of infinite longing. Man can thus no longer feel at home in the finite world.

From this it follows that while the ancient world was one world, the modern world is broken up into a thousand fragments. For a God who is present is present in one form; but a God who must be sought may be sought in an infinity of ways. Thus while the spirit of the ancient world lived in the social organism, spirit in the modern world lives in the isolated individual.

God, though sought, is never found in the modern world. Hence mythology in the ancient sense is impossible here. Modern mythology, such as it is, cannot be natural but only historical.[41] Its symbols are experienced as forever inadequate, and vanish into the past.

The implications of this view of history for poetry are neatly summarized by A.W. Schlegel: 'The poetry of the ancients expressed possession, whereas ours is the poetry of longing.'[42] In Schelling's view, ancient poetry is the creation of the race; modern poetry, of individuals. Ancient poetry is a complete system; in modern poetry, poetic forms interpenetrate; and if there is a system, it is incomplete. The poetry of the Greeks finds symbolic forms wholly adequate; the symbols of the moderns are experienced as forever inadequate. In Schelling's language, ancient poetry is symbolic, whereas modern poetry is allegorical.

But is then modern poetry not a contradiction in term? Morality may merely seek the Absolute; art must possess it. Art must be symbolic; but the modern age is merely allegorical. How then is art possible in the modern world? Schelling replies: 'Art demands the finite and complete; but the ... modern age destroys ... boundaries and strives toward the unlimited. In this conflict, the individual artist must appear on the scene. He must make his demands in absolute freedom. He must seek to create lasting shapes out of the fickle formlessness of the age.'[43] The modern poet lives, not in a whole, but in a mere fragment. His poetic duty consists in transforming this fragment into a whole of his own. Ancient poetry grew out of a universal mythology. The great modern poets – Dante, Cervantes, Shakespeare, Goethe – had each to create his own mythology.

As modern, then, the modern poet can only seek but not find the Divine. But as poet he must represent a Presence, not a Beyond. Schelling in effect concludes that since God is beyond, the poet must deify the search for God. Romantic subjectivism could find no more eloquent expression.

Of all poetic forms, the lyric is least affected by the great historic change. For it expresses that subjective, particular emphasis which is the universal modern condition. Even so, there are differences. The ancient lyric tends to exalt robust pleasure and manly virtues, while the modern tends to dissolve into romantic longing. The ancient lyric grows out of an organic unity with society; the modern, out of inwardness, and a sense of alienation. It is no accident that ancient lyrical poetry appeared at the time of greatest social harmony, while the modern made its appearance in the fourteenth century, a time of social unrest.

But while the lyric survives in the modern world, relatively unchanged, the epic has of necessity disappeared.[44] For the epic expresses, in pristine form, the identity of finiteness and infinity which the modern world has lost. But there is a modern equivalent of the epic. This is the novel.

The novel, like the epic, tells a story. But unlike the epic, this is not a story which the poet finds ready-made. It is a story of his own invention. The epic poet hears history in the Absolute; the novelist has mere fragments at his disposal which he must transform into an absolute. Hence the epic is *the* story: the novel, one story among others. The epic is a narrative in which the poet himself does not appear. The novel too is a narrative which leaves the poet outside. But here he remains only relatively outside. For the novel as a whole reflects his standpoint. And this standpoint is not, like that of the epic, the standpoint of God; it is only relatively objective, one of many standpoints possible. Thus while the epic is absolutely universal, the novel is only relatively so; and while the epic has neither beginning nor end, the novel has both.

The lyric survives in the modern world while the epic does not. The tragic drama is the synthesis of the lyrical and the epical. Hence it survives, but in surviving is radically transformed.

Ancient tragedy represents the finite or subjective as in clash with the infinite or objective. But in the modern world the infinite is eternal Beyond, and such a clash is therefore impossible. Christianity cannot permit a fate which destroys freedom. It can at best permit a devil. But the devil can only tempt freedom; he cannot destroy it. There is no room in Christianity for the notion of innocent guilt, and the tragic conflict between human freedom and divine fate is here impossible.

From this it follows that tragedy can survive in the modern world in only one way: fate must fall, not into the Deity, but into the subject himself. The hero of Shakespearean tragedy is in conflict, not with a cosmic necessity, but with the necessity of his own character.

But while the fate of the Greeks is one, the number of possible characters is infinite. Hence while the ancient drama represents the tragedy of man, the modern drama can represent only the tragedy of types of men. And the nature of each type has an element of absolute irrationality. This too must find dramatic expression. In Greek tragedy, there can be no extraneous elements. The modern tragedy must on purpose mix the accidental with the necessary, and the comic must irrationally alternate with the tragic.

Goethe's *Faust* comes as close to absolute universality as tragedy can in the modern world. But even this work does not wholly reach it. Faust comes into conflict, not with an objective force without, but with the force of his restless search within. This is his inner fate. But it is the fate, not of man, but of modern man.

VII

From the foregoing it may seem to follow that Schelling must regard modern poetry, if as art at all, at least as an inferior form of art. Art must be the presence in the finite of the Infinite. But modern poetry merely points to the Infinite, and possesses as present merely the search for it. The advent of Christianity, it may seem, was a catastrophe. Genuine art was possible in the ancient world: in the modern world, it is not.

But Schelling seeks at all costs to avoid this conclusion. He firmly maintains that ancient and modern art are equals; that they each possess what the other lacks. Modern art may merely seek what ancient art possesses; but it seeks it in a higher and more comprehensive form. It was necessary that the finite and Infinite should have been separated, in order that the Infinite could be sought in this higher form. And the advent of Christianity, far from being a catastrophe, was on the contrary a meaningful dialectical development. In short, Schelling attempts to save modern art by historicizing *all* art.[45]

But this attempt threatens to destroy Schelling's very concept of art. As we have seen, the central doctrine which gives rise to his metaphysics of art is that art is unhistorical. Science and morality forever seek; art forever possesses. Theory and practice are historical; aesthetic production is not. Now it seems that art too is historical; for both ancient and modern art are incomplete. And with this conclusion Schelling's aesthetic idealism may seem to be destroyed in its foundations.

Schelling can save his metaphysics of art in only one way. This is by becoming prophet. If past art has failed to attain the perfect presence of the Divine, and if art must nevertheless attain this presence, then future art must succeed where the past has failed. And the past must be understood as the dialectical preparation of the final synthesis.

The art of the future will seek the Infinite sought by the moderns; but it will find it in the manner of the ancients. It will preserve the complexity of the modern world, but it will transcend its chaos and disharmony, and be one world. The mythology of the future will incorporate all modern mythologies; but, like the mythology of the ancients, it will be one. The poetry of the future will preserve the infinity of modern poetic ideas and forms; but it will, like the poetry of the ancients, culminate in a supreme synthesis of ideas and forms. The supreme synthesis of the ancient world was the tragic drama of Greece. The synthesis of the future poetry will be drama in a new and higher form; a drama in which all modern ideas and forms of expression can achieve a divine unity.[46]

The philosopher can prophesy this blessed future, though the artist himself cannot. For, at present at least, the philosopher alone stands above history.[47] But he cannot make it come to pass. For he can merely understand abstractly and implicitly what only art itself can make real and explicit. In its search for the new God, art had to turn away from the presence of the old, and set out on a long pilgrimage. Only art itself can lead us to the goal, and establish the new Jerusalem.

VIII

Schelling's *Philosophy of Art* is an uneven work. The profound in it is mixed with the absurd, the mature with the ill-considered. It abounds in obscurities owing to shifts in terminology, or even in doctrine. Schelling appears to have written different parts of the work at different times, without ever welding the parts into a genuine whole. He was himself aware of these weaknesses. For he regarded only a few parts of this work as worthy of publication,[48] and it was never published in his lifetime. The state of the *Philosophy of Art* is such that every interpreter, to give an interpretation at all, has had to omit much that would not fit into it. We wish to make it clear that the present study is no exception.

A number of explanations may be given for these shortcomings. Thus we may attribute them to Schelling's comparative lack of first-hand acquaintance with the arts. For this compelled him to rely to a large extent on the work of others; and it is difficult to organize the finished work of others into a genuine unity. Or we may trace the trouble to his comparative lack of systematic power; for he was notoriously inferior in this respect to Fichte and Hegel. Finally, we may find fault with the whole concept of a speculative system of the arts.[49] Whatever the merit of such explanations, the basic explanation is much simpler. Schelling lectured on the philosophy of art in the years 1802–4. But in 1804 he was already beginning to abandon the system of which that philosophy is an application. And his next major work – the *On Freedom* of 1809 – shows a complete break with it. Like all great philosophers, Schelling never wasted time on working out a philosophy which he had abandoned.

The thesis of 1800 is: art is the only true revelation. In 1802–4 this becomes: the identity of finite and Infinite, striven for everywhere, becomes actual in art. But from 1809 on the finite appears as divorced from the Infinite by a catastrophic gulf. Art becomes the mere creation of finite spirit; and no such creation can achieve the presence of God. If man is to find God, this is now possible only if God reveals Himself. With this conclusion, Schelling loses interest in art and the philosophy of art.[50] For the system of aesthetic idealism must be replaced by a philosophy of revelation.[51]

6 Schelling's Philosophy of Religion

> 'To see clearly is of no value to philosophy, if the discourse does not unite depth of meaning with clarity.' Schelling

I

In 1841 the philosophical world of Berlin witnessed a remarkable event. The sixty-six-year-old Schelling emerged from decades of semi-retirement, in order to destroy the philosophy which he himself had founded no less than forty years earlier. He came to overthrow the Hegelian philosophy of religion, which had grown from his own system of identity.

For years extraordinary rumours had been current about the views Schelling supposedly held. Friends and foes alike had urged him to state them in print. But he had failed to do so. One work he had actually withdrawn from the hands of the publisher. Now that he had at last come into the open, the philosophical world prepared itself for a major event. The press took note of it, and everybody flocked to hear the lectures on the Philosophy of Revelation. The audience included the celebrated and the known; it also included some who were as yet unknown, but were to become very well known indeed in subsequent decades – among them Engels, Bakunin, Burckhardt, and, above all, Kierkegaard.

But if the Philosophy of Revelation was a major contribution to religious thought, Schelling's contemporaries were not aware of it. To their vast disappointment, they seemed to be treated to a confused mixture of an idealist system and orthodox Christianity. And they agreed in condemning the mixture. Kierkegaard rejected it in the interests of Protestant theology, while the Hegelians rejected it in the name of systematic philosophy. The latter were particularly outspoken. 'A shameful apostasy,' cried Michelet, 'such as has never been committed in the history of philosophy.'[1] And Rosenkranz observed: 'It appears that some attach the adjective "Christian" to a thought, like a fig-leaf, as if they had to be ashamed of it in its nakedness.'[2] Nearly everybody was dissatisfied.

Historians of philosophy have agreed with the judgment of Schelling's contemporaries. Indeed, they have created a myth, of that nice and convenient sort found only in histories of philosophy. Schelling, as everybody knows, was a romantic genius. Whoever heard of a romantic genius past the age of thirty? If one is to believe the histories of philosophy, Schelling had exhausted his talents when he was thirty; he spent the remainder of his seventy-nine years mourning his lost genius and envying Hegel.[3] Since nearly everybody does believe the histories, few have bothered to read the *Philosophy of Revelation*. Until today hardly anyone has suspected that it is one of the profoundest works in modern religious thought, equal in importance to the work of Kant, Schleiermacher, and Hegel.

It is indeed a strange fact that the man who published eleven major works before he was thirty should have spent the next thirty years of his life in almost complete literary silence. But this fact is no longer strange if note is taken of the development of Schelling's thought. The young Schelling revels in the new freedom of reason, brought about by Kant and Fichte. The shackles of dogmatism are broken. Reason is no longer tied to mere data outside herself. She can understand the world by the creative development of her own resources. Reason builds up the system of reason. Ten years later Schelling begins to discover facts which the system of reason cannot assimilate. Thus in the very years in which Hegel completes the system, Schelling sees the whole enterprise cast into a crisis. While Hegel rises to fame Schelling withdraws into solitude and silence. In lonely years he wholly rebuilds the foundations of his philosophy. The product of these years is the Philosophy of Revelation, the only significant anti-idealistic philosophy of religion which has grown from the crisis of idealism itself.

II

Among the branches of traditional metaphysics is found a discipline entitled 'natural theology.' This discipline has the task of proving the existence of God and of understanding whatever reason may be able to understand of His nature. Kant, as is well known, restricts the power of reason to experience. He thereby eliminates natural theology; the goals which it has set itself are unattainable. But while limiting reason to experience, Kant makes its autonomy absolute within this sphere. Nothing within experience escapes its grasp. He thereby establishes a new discipline in place of the discarded natural theology: philosophy of religion. Reason cannot answer the question: Does God exist? It can and must answer the questions: What is religious experience? Is there an a priori in religious experience?

The new discipline has the tendency to replace not only natural theology but supernatural theology as well. This latter is based on a divine revelation and the document which records it. No modern thinker quite knows what to do about revelation, for all modern thought is based on the unqualified autonomy of reason. Pre-Kantian philosophers are able to leave the Christian revelation alone, expressing polite if distant esteem. No such cavalier procedure is possible for Kant and his followers. The philosopher now seeks to understand in systematic unity all experience without exception. Among the data of experience is religious experience, which includes the experience of revelation. The philosopher must interpret, not the experience in terms of the revelation, but the revelation in terms of the experience. Thus the authority of revelation gives way to the authority of religious experience, and of reason which is its interpreter. Kant can write: 'Each man must make his god according to moral notions ... there can be no genuine religion on the basis of mere revelation. Without the standard of the ideal of reason, all worship is but idolatry.'[4] Fichte is even more explicit: 'A complete philosophy embraces the whole system of knowledge. ... It contains the content of all possible revelation in organic completeness.'[5]

Kant has denied the accessibility of a God outside experience. This means to the post-Kantian absolute idealist, not that God is inaccessible, but that He is not outside experience. This development is made possible by a momentous step taken by the young Schelling: the assertion of an absolute identity of experience and reality, of the subject and object of experience. Experience itself is reality, and the absolute experience or consciousness is identical with the absolute reality.

This thesis of identity involves a complete reinterpretation of the meaning of religion. Religion is no longer understood as the attempt of man to relate himself to a God outside himself. It is a self-transformation of finite into infinite spirit; and in the true religious experience this self-transformation becomes total identification. The true religious experience and the true God are identical. Idealistic philosophy of religion exhibits this identity in systematic form.

On the basis of the thesis of identity, Schleiermacher and Hegel achieve grandiose syntheses of philosophy and theology. Philosophy asserts the autonomy of human reason and experience; theology asserts the autonomy of God and his Word. These two seemingly conflicting claims are now marvellously synthesized. Man himself is the Absolute; but what is absolute in him is not he but the Absolute. God is complete only in man's religious experience; but this experience is only a manifestation of God. The Christian revelation may be reduced to human experience, but only because all human experience is a divine revelation. There is no more magnificent synthesis of philosophy with Christianity than Hegel's *Philosophy of Religion.* But perhaps Kierkegaard was right: perhaps it is for that precise reason the most dangerous attack on Christianity ever made.

It is easy to regard the idealistic philosophy of religion as a gigantic self-delusion and, indeed, as presumption in its supreme form. How can anyone assert that man, even in his most exalted experience, becomes one with God? But instead of dismissing idealistic religious thought, we must understand the reasons which drive it to this conclusion. If Kant is right, then the assumption of a God outside experience, on whatever grounds, is sheer dogmatism. Indeed, it may well be said to be wishful thinking. If God is to become accessible at all, this can be only if religious experience internally proves its own truth and authenticity. But such a proof is not to be achieved by the sort of romantic confession fashionable in Hegel's day; nor is it to be achieved by endorsements of reputable psychologists which are the fashion in our day. Religious experience can prove its own truth only if it reveals itself as the absolute experience. And this means, however it may be put, that there is some point at which man ceases to be finite spirit and becomes identical with absolute spirit. Philosophy simply organizes all experience in such a way as to unite and synthesize it in this absolute point.

Thus the philosophy of religious experience cannot seek refuge from consistency in an arbitrary external standard of truth. If it is to achieve religious truth, it must seek to expand experience from within into an absolute system. But this does of course not mean that it will succeed. It may be that this momentous aim is unattainable, and that the attempt to attain it falls into self-contradiction. And it would then follow that religious truth becomes visible, not in the achievement of the identity sought by idealism, but in the discovery of necessary failure. The philosophy of religion of Schelling's last period arises from precisely that discovery.

III

In 1809 Schelling writes: 'Regarding the problem of freedom, ... idealism leaves us completely bewildered.'[6] He had always been uneasy about the implications of the absolute system for human personality. In the absolute system, freedom can mean only obedience to a higher necessity. And this implication Schelling had always been reluctant to accept. As early as 1795 he had written: 'The moment a thinker believed he had completed his system he would become intolerable to himself.'[7] Fifteen years later he is convinced that the freedom of decision is real, no matter what the consequences for the system. He writes: 'The genuine and vital conception of freedom is that it is a possibility of good and evil.'[8] But only gradually does Schelling realize that freedom and system are incompatible. Either the absolute identity alone is real, and all separate reality mere appearance; but then freedom too is merely apparent. Or else freedom is real; but then the absolute identity cannot be real, for every free act falls outside it. As to which alternative is the truth Schelling no longer has any doubt. He writes that all freedom is 'absolute beginning ... decision and act.'[9]

The problem of freedom gives rise to the problem of evil. In the system of identity, evil as such is appearance. But if freedom is real, and if it is the possibility of choosing between good and evil, then evil is real also. Every free choice of evil shatters the absolute identity, not only because it is free but also because it is evil.[10]

Thus evil, as such, is a threat to the system of identity. This threat is still further aggravated by its actual manifestations. Schelling comes more and more to feel that idealism has taken evil altogether too lightly. In the system of reason, evil is in the end a mere negation. It is either physical only; or else, if spiritual as well, it is a mere means necessary to the attainment of a higher good. Neither of these explanations, Schelling now feels, does justice to the facts. Evil is in its very essence spiritual. It lurks, not in the limitations of the physical, but in the ambiguous and unlimited possibilities of spiritual freedom. 'Of all creatures only the most perfect is capable of evil. ... The devil is not the most limited but the most unlimited of all creatures.'[11] Nor is evil a mere means to a higher good. Mephistopheles is not as harmless as he pretends when he describes himself to Faust as

> Part of that Power not understood
> Which always wills the Bad,
> And always does the Good.[12]

Evil is a positive force. It manifests itself most clearly, not in small and mean spirits, but in the greatest and most dynamic. In these spirits evil does not flow from cowardice and trepidation, but from a terrible strength, and a genuine enthusiasm. Schelling says: 'Just as there is ardor for the good, there is also an enthusiasm for evil.'[13] In other words, Schelling has discovered not merely evil in its petty forms, the evil of thieves and knaves. He has discovered the demonic. The terrible reality of the demonic shatters the identity of the Absolute.

It might seem that there is an obvious escape from these metaphysical difficulties. Why not turn to radical dualism or pluralism, as philosophers have done so often before, and under similar circumstances? To Schelling such an escape is utterly inadmissible. For since Kant philosophy has learned that every system joins together whatever it puts asunder. No system therefore can assert more than one Absolute without contradicting itself. Radical dualism and pluralism are systems in which reason contradicts itself; they are mere admissions of philosophic failure. Schelling writes: 'Dualism ... is merely a system in which reason mutilates itself and reveals its despair.'[14]

But if this is so, then Schelling is driven into a well-nigh desperate situation. There can only be one Absolute, yet every act of freedom is a new absolute. The Absolute is total harmony, yet evil has a terrible reality. The problem is desperate indeed: but here, as so often in philosophy, the profoundest insights arise from the gravest difficulties.

It must be noted that the problem of freedom appears here in a strange and novel setting. To Kant, freedom means freedom from natural causation. Now it suddenly means freedom from the Absolute. And this involves the most startling reversal. For Kant and idealism, freedom works toward the ideal, toward the divine purpose. Man in his moral freedom is co-worker with God. Now freedom, in its primary meaning, means freedom *against* God. We say: in its primary meaning. If free choice, as such, contradicts the absolute identity, then not only the choice of evil, but *all* choice is in some sense anti-divine. For prior to any particular choice is the choice to choose at all. The primary anti-divine act is not the choice of evil, but the choice of self. 'If spirit is divine, and yet not God, then it is divine and anti-divine at the same time.'[15]

Thus all of a sudden the smooth transition from finite to infinite spirit has disappeared. In idealism, man is the more in harmony with the divine the more autonomously he follows his moral reason. There is no tragic conflict here between God and the moral self. Now such a tragic conflict has made its appearance. Rather than being a harmonious co-worker with God, man is now Prometheus, that infinitely tragic figure who is right and wrong, divine and anti-divine at the same time. He necessarily obeys his moral conscience, yet in so doing necessarily sins against the gods. To be truly moral he must be autonomous, yet this very autonomy implicates him in guilt against the divine. 'Since he is driven by moral necessity, Prometheus is right. Nevertheless he is punished for his deed by infinite tortures. ... For Zeus is right as well; the freedom from God is bought at no less a price. Here lies a contradiction which we cannot resolve but only recognize. ...'[16]

Schelling solves his problem by the doctrine of a cosmic fall. Since absolute identity and human freedom cannot exist together, and yet since both are real, the only possible solution is that an original cosmic identity has been shattered by an original act of finite freedom. In this primeval act, original man, who was like God, sought to make himself God. This cosmic fall is the source of evil.

But by itself, the doctrine of the fall by no means solves the problem of evil. If the fall from absolute identity is the source of evil, how was such a fall possible? Schelling has no other choice but to locate the source of evil in the Deity himself, yet in such a way that this source is not evil in the Deity; it becomes evil only when torn out of the divine identity.

Deeply inspired by the seventeenth-century mystic Jacob Boehme, Schelling develops a concept of divine personality. All personality is a unity, but it is not a simple unity. Personality is the perpetual actualization of selfhood; it is the conscious and purposive control of irrational underlying potentialities. All personality therefore involves two factors: a dark ground, which is the source of uncontrolled vitality, and a self which unites, controls, and directs this ground. God is the absolute personality; He is the absolute Self, holding in command and control His own dark ground. The function of the divine ground is to slumber in the still night of potentiality, as the negative source of the divine vitality. Its function is not to be, but to be potential. This dark ground may be called the demonic in God since, in itself, it is dynamic power without order or control. Schelling can therefore say the daring words: 'The Deity reigns over a world of horrors.'[17]

In God this ground rests in harmonious slumber, fulfilling its vital function. But woe unto the world when Prometheus appears on the scene! Seeking to make himself absolute, he seeks to control the divine ground. But he succeeds only in tearing it out of the divine harmony, and giving it demonic actuality. The world, and he with it, falls under its destructive power. Prometheus-Faust has done his sacrilegious deed. Well may the cosmic chorus of spirits wail, as Goethe makes it wail:

> Alas, alas!
> Thou hast it destroyed,
> The beautiful world

With powerful fist:
In ruin 'tis hurled,
By the blow of a demigod shattered.[18]

IV

This is the point which Schelling reaches in his *Of Human Freedom* of 1809 and his *Ages of the World* of 1811. It appears to him at that time that the doctrine of a cosmic fall has resolved the difficulties besetting the system. But the time for the Philosophy of Revelation has not yet arrived. Thirty years are yet to pass before Schelling presents his final thoughts to his Berlin audience.

For the truth is that Schelling has by no means mastered the crisis of absolute idealism. On the contrary, he has merely exposed it in its full measure. Thus far, he has merely replaced the idealist system by a better system. Yet the very doctrine which has served to correct idealism will inevitably raise the question whether a system – any system – is possible at all.

It must not be forgotten for a moment that the thesis of identity is sole foundation of the idealistic conception of a philosophy of religion. A system of the Absolute is possible only if finite spirit can raise itself to identification with Absolute Spirit. But the precise significance of the doctrine of the fall is to deny the possibility of such an identification. Does this not mean that the whole enterprise of an absolute system has become in principle indefensible? Will not any such system be a mere organization of the human imagination?

Schelling now becomes profoundly attentive to this problem. His Philosophy of Mythology is a study in the religion of fallen man. Man's divine descent makes him a god-seeking being. But because of his fall, his god-seeking is, inevitably, a mere god-positing, though he himself remains unconscious of this fact. But posited gods are not true gods, and mythological religion is idolatry. The fate of idolatry hangs over fallen man, like a heavy cloud. It leads us to ask: is not all religious experience mythological? Is not all god-seeking and god-finding a mere unconscious god-positing? If this is so, then the philosophy of religious experience systematizes mere products of the human imagination. And the attempt to find God in these products is merely the supreme expression of man's inveterate Prometheanism.

Only now is the crisis of idealism fully apparent; and it exhibits the desperate circumstances in which the philosophic concern with the divine seems to find itself. Since Kant, the philosopher can no longer find God outside experience; and now it seems that he cannot find Him within experience either. For the first time since Parmenides, God has become radically inaccessible to the speculative philosopher. It might seem that if God is to be accessible at all, He must break into experience by virtue of the absurd, by virtue of an act whose possibility and actuality are equally unintelligible. In other words, it appears that in relation to the divine, philosophy has suffered total bankruptcy.

And yet the situation is not so simple as that. Schelling does not for a moment consider becoming a Barthian. If reason cannot reach God, this in itself is an insight which can be reached by reason itself. If man has fallen, he can at least know his fallen condition; and in knowing it he in part transcends it. Philosophy of religion requires a point of departure which reason cannot provide. But reason itself can understand that it cannot provide it. In the failure of reason to reach what it yet must seek to reach, the new philosophy of religion will discover its point of departure.

Schelling's first task therefore is to expose the failure of reason to reach God. This task consists simply in a critical re-examination of the idealistic enterprise. Idealism now becomes, instead of a metaphysics, a mere experiment in autonomous reason, carried out by reason in order that it can discover the limits of its autonomy.

What then does the experiment in autonomous reasoning reveal? Surveying the facts of experience, reason finds them to be universally interrelated. One and all, they require an explanation. In seeking an adequate explanation, reason is driven to ever-higher syntheses. And it can stop in this search for consistency nowhere short of the Absolute.

There is nothing wrong with the logic of this movement. The question is only what ontological interpretation it is to be given. Idealism identifies the necessary movement of thought with a necessary movement of reality, and thus identifies its idea of the Absolute with the Absolute itself. But this is an error. For while apprehending real characteristics of the world, reason at the same time ignores others equally real. The system of reason grasps unity and necessity, but must ignore discord, freedom, and chance. Above all, it must ignore existence itself. The system of reason is therefore not a system of reality at all, but an ideal construction.

And yet it is not an arbitrary construction. It arises in response to the needs of the facts. Reason must necessarily seek to explain them; but because its system is merely an ideal construction, it equally necessarily fails to explain them. The system must issue, not in a harmonious solution, but in a paradox.

The last idea of reason is God. As the ultimate synthesis of all existence, God is defined as the necessarily existent. Here the idealist believes he has found the Alpha and Omega: the system is complete. But he is mistaken. For since reason abstracts from existence, it reaches in the end, not the necessarily existent, but merely the idea of the necessarily existent. And this is a self-contradictory idea. Its content is necessary existence, but qua idea, it is non-existent. The form and content of this idea are in inevitable contradiction. This idea expresses the radical crisis of reason: at its culminating point, reason is necessarily driven to seek what it necessarily fails to find. If there is a God, He is incommensurable with reason.

Nor can God be found in feeling. If Hegel is wrong, so is Schleiermacher. The philosopher 'might argue that the God who is mere idea in reason becomes real in feeling. ... But what if one were to show that this so-called real God is a mere creature of our feeling, that every idea has merely psychological significance?'[19] Schelling does not reject reason in favour of feeling. He rejects the thesis of identity. God, if He exists, is external to feeling as well as reason. God must be discovered if reality is to be explained; but reason cannot discover Him. The experiment in autonomous reason ends in despair.

In this despair the new philosophy of religion is to find its point of departure. But how can it find such a point? If there is a radical gap between reason and the Absolute, only a radical leap can bridge it. But can such a leap be anything but arbitrary? Does the despair of reason show that we must leap, and where to leap?

Schelling writes: 'The last idea of reason has this peculiarity that the philosophizing person cannot be indifferent to its existence or non-existence, as he is in the case of every other idea. Here the watchword is: *Tua res agitur.*'[20] Schelling at this point takes a sharp turn. The idea of God is not only the crowning piece of the system, but also the highest aspiration of the system-builder. The system is merely the abstract expression of the spiritual attitude of its builder. The philosopher seeks to absorb in an Absolute not just existence in general but his own personal existence. In philosophic contemplation Prometheus seeks to repent of his Prometheanism, by surrendering himself to an ideal deity. The attempt to reach identity is an attempt to obliterate the self in God.

But it is the tragedy of Prometheus that he cannot undo his deed. The theoretical despair of his thought merely reflects an existential despair which he lives and suffers. For he seeks to, but cannot, absorb his person in his system. He is torn between the self-assertion by which he lives, and the contemplative self-surrender by which he seeks to, but cannot live.

'The self might be satisfied with the purely ideal god, if he could remain in this state of contemplation. But this is impossible. The surrender of action cannot be carried out. Action is inevitable. ... The former despair returns. For the discord is not overcome.'[21]

Thus the problem has suddenly shifted from a contradiction in ideas to a contradiction in the existence of the philosophizing person. And just as the crisis of thought reveals the limits of an autonomous reason, so the crisis in existence reveals the limits of an autonomous life. But whereas thought can be left in suspense, life cannot. The crisis must be ended by a leap.

This leap is a humiliation of reason. For by it there is acceptance, not of the idea of the absolute Existent, but of the absolute Existent Himself. And this reality is not only unknowable but even unthinkable. To this unthinkable reality reason has indeed pointed, but it cannot reach it.

But this acceptance as such resolves neither the intellectual nor the existential despair. How can the philosopher *or* the man solve his problem by accepting a reality wholly outside his reach? The answer is simply that his problem can be solved only if God Himself has solved it. If God is radically outside human reason, feeling, and will, then He can become accessible only if He reveals Himself. No human step can achieve what only revelation can achieve. The leap merely enables the philosopher to recognize and understand a revelation if it has in fact taken place. Schelling writes: 'Him he wants, the God who acts ... who as an existing God can oppose the fact of the fall, the God who is the Lord of being. ... The self cannot arrogate unto himself the task of finding Him. God Himself must meet him with his aid and succour. But the self may will Him, and hope to gain blessedness by His aid.'[22] In other words, Schelling has unmasked the unmoving God of the philosophers as a mere ideal construction. If there is a God, He is the God of Abraham, Isaac, and Jacob. The philosopher cannot ascend to God. But he can find Him if He has descended. The philosophy of religious experience has suffered collapse. Its place is now taken by the Philosophy of Revelation.

V

It might well appear baffling how Schelling, having taken a leap into faith, can ever find his way back to reason. Philosophy may achieve a meaningful concept of revelation, but surely it can go no further. How can it hope to identify an actual revelation? What objective criterion can there be for distinguishing what is revelation from what is not? It might seem that a revelation can be asserted only on the basis of faith, and that Schelling therefore must choose between philosophy and revelation: a Philosophy of Revelation is impossible.

But Schelling denies this fateful alternative. Indeed, the entire Philosophy of Revelation is meant to be its explicit refutation. Schelling does indeed return to orthodox Christianity; but in so doing he does not betray or surrender philosophy.

The Philosophy of Revelation has a clear task and a clear method. Its task is to explain the world, in all its aspects. Its method is to follow rational construction wherever this is possible; for while limited, reason is not impotent. But the emphasis lies, not on what reason includes, but on what it is forced to omit. All those factors which escape rational necessity are explained in terms of cosmic acts of will. The Philosophy of Revelation is therefore a metaphysical system; but it is a system whose unity is, at crucial points, shattered by acts of freedom. These acts are not an a priori necessity, but an a posteriori fact.

The first of these facts is existence itself. Having accepted on faith an Absolute Existent, we ask: why does anything exist apart from Him? From a God beyond all reason nothing can be deduced, and all emanationist theories are in principle mistaken. The world can only be the result of a primordial act of will. Creation must be accepted as a fact for which no further explanation can be given.

But while the fact of creation can only be accepted, its nature can be rationally understood. In creation God manifests Himself as free will, and free will can be rationally analysed. Free will is the freedom to will or not to will. This involves a distinction of potential and actual will; and, since neither potential nor actual will is free both to will and not to will, it further involves the synthesis of potential and actual will, which alone is free to will or not to will. The creation is an organic unity of cosmic matter, cosmic form, and cosmic spirit or freedom.

This doctrine has a superficial resemblance to Spinoza's pantheism. But there are two decisive differences. Unlike Spinoza's *natura naturans*, Schelling's God creates freely; His creation is not an a priori necessity but an a posteriori fact. And unlike Spinoza's *natura naturata*, Schelling's creation is not wholly governed by necessity. Cosmic matter and cosmic form are so governed; but cosmic spirit is free.

Yet the creation is very different from the actual world. The creation is an organic unity; the actual world is externalized, chaotic, and full of evil. The creation has been destroyed, and only a further cosmic act of will can explain this destruction. Schelling here uses the doctrine of the fall developed in earlier years. An act of rebellion on the part of original man has caused universal externality and evil. The original world has become the actual world which is ours.

The question now arises whether all the facts of experience can be explained without further cosmic acts of will. The creation accounts for the element of rationality and order in the world, while the fall accounts for the irrational and chaotic elements. But there is one fact which is explained by neither. This is the fact of human history. From this point on, the Philosophy of Revelation becomes philosophy of history.

History occurs only where there is realization of new meaning. There can therefore be no history either in the original creation or in a merely fallen world. None is possible in the former because no new meaning remains to be realized; none in the latter because no new meaning can be realized. The fall has indeed made history a meaningful problem. It has made what is fall short of what ought to be. It thus raises the problem of which history might be the solution. But in a merely fallen world this solution cannot be accomplished. A merely fallen world exists in time; but mere time does not solve the problem, it perpetually repeats it. Nature exists in mere time; but nature, says Schelling, forever repeats itself in 'melancholy monotony.' If there is a history, it is as yet not understood.

Historical novelty clearly cannot consist in accidental variations of the same fundamental condition. Such variations belong to the realm of mere nature. Historical novelty can consist only in a change of that fundamental condition itself. Hence we can inquire into the nature of human history only after first defining the fundamental condition of man.

Man's existence after the fall is determined by his contradictory relation to God. His divine descent makes him an incomplete and therefore a god-seeking being. But by reason of the fall he cannot find God. This contradictory existence is mythological existence. Man has fallen under the domination of the cosmic powers which are not God but which he, as a god-seeking being, perforce deifies. This mythological existence is the universal fate of fallen man. If it remains unrelieved and unaltered, then man has no more a history than the rest of fallen creation.

Man may, of course, strive to escape his mythological bondage. He may seek to transcend its contradictions, and to reach a higher truth. But if the world is simply fallen he cannot succeed. Indeed, his efforts can only serve to intensify the anguish of his condition. His fate, like that of nature, will be the eternal repetition of the same contradiction, in melancholy monotony.

But Schelling discovers that there is in fact a history of mythology. Mythological deities replace each other, and as they do, they reveal a tendency to transcend the whole mythological condition. This development culminates in the Greek mysteries which reflect a crisis of the mythological consciousness, and therefore an escape from its externality into a higher and more inward truth.

The question is how this history is to be explained. After what has already been said, it is clear that Schelling rejects the categories used by the ordinary historian of mythology. Mythology is neither an invention of the poets, nor is it philosophy in a popular garb. Nor again is it a mere superstition which rational enlightenment might have removed at any time. Schelling regards these views as based on the shallow prejudice of the Enlightenment, and as unable to explain the facts. Mythological man lives and suffers his mythology; he sacrifices himself to the mythological deities, and his final escape into the mysteries is a genuine liberation. No mere accidental human invention or prejudice could have such profound effects. Mythological existence can be explained only in terms of a real domination by real cosmic powers.

But if the mythological condition is no mere human creation, then neither is its development. As we have seen, the unaided efforts of mythological man would only sharpen the tensions implicit in his condition; but they would not alter or remove them. Thus Schelling is driven to the conclusion that mythological history is not a human, but a human-divine history. It can be explained only in terms of a real intervention of God, which relieves and modifies the pressure of the cosmic powers upon the human consciousness.

The question now arises whether all historical facts can be understood in terms of the mythological process. In his youth, Schelling had interpreted Christianity in mythological terms. But now he holds that the facts preclude such an interpretation. The content of mythology illustrates, in varying degrees, man's fallen condition. The content of Christianity is the redemption from that condition. The philosopher understands mythology in terms of standards of truth different from those of mythology itself. Thus mythology proves to be a real relation to the divine, yet at the same time a false relation. But applying his standards of truth to Christianity, the philosopher finds them to coincide with those of Christianity itself. Christianity claims to be an actual incursion of God into history, an incarnation whose purpose is the redemption of man from his fallen condition. The philosopher has already discovered man's fallen condition, and the need for precisely such an incursion, if he is to be redeemed from it. Thus if Christianity is a real relation to God, it will also be a true relation, a relation to God as He truly is.

Is Christianity a real relation to God? If even mythology must involve such a relation, then *a fortiori* Christianity must. Schelling sharply repudiates those who would reduce Christianity to the ideas of the man Jesus. Its essence does not consist in moral ideas, nor even in the idea of redemption and a Christ. Such ideas would merely aggravate to its extreme point the anguish of man's fallen state. But Christianity is not the exposure of man's fallen condition; it is the redemption from it. It is therefore not the teaching of Christ, or the idea of Christ, but Christ himself. Schelling sums up: 'The true content of Christianity is a history into which the divine enters. ... The historical element is not accidental to the doctrine, but the doctrine itself.'[23]

Here the Philosophy of Revelation culminates. Its essential content is revelation: for if God is wholly other than human reason, then He can be accessible only if He has revealed Himself. But it is nevertheless philosophy: for because of its dialectical relation to the divine, reason can by itself understand the need for revelation, and its meaning if and when it takes place.

VI

More than one hundred years have passed since the *Philosophy of Revelation* was written. The critical student of today has little difficulty in bringing its whole bold structure to collapse. Indeed, in retrospect it becomes clear that it retains many of the speculative doctrines which it sought to repudiate.

But it would be rash to dismiss the *Philosophy of Revelation* because of its factual or logical errors. For its essential problem is still the essential problem of religious thought. This problem has divided contemporary thinkers into two sharply opposed camps. But the solutions put forward by each camp are not impressive.

The thinker of the one camp makes religious experience the object of his philosophy. He thus carries on the idealistic tradition. But he has repudiated his idealistic ancestor, and has responded to the crisis of the absolute system by surrendering all aspirations to such a system. Instead, he makes religious experience a mere empirical fact which, he is proud to say, he studies by means of the scientific method. If he remembers his idealistic ancestor at all, he thinks of him with condescension, as dogmatic, pretentious, and, worst accusation of all, unscientific. But he would do well to remember him more frequently, and with less condescension. For the ancestor knew a few things which the descendant seems to have forgotten. He knew, for example, that the philosophy of religious experience requires a criterion of religious truth, and that the merely empirical study of religious experience is unable, not only to find such a criterion, but even to justify the concept of religious truth itself. But in the absence of such a justification, the philosophy of religious experience degenerates into mere psychology.

The thinker of this camp does, of course, dimly realize the need for a criterion of religious truth, but he fails to realize that his standpoint makes a criterion inaccessible. Thus he looks for criteria which he can find, criteria which are empirically verifiable. He finds the useful and the emotionally satisfying, and tries to persuade himself that these are adequate. He may persuade himself; but he persuades no one else, least of all the genuine religious believer. In brief, the thinker of this camp has responded to the crisis of absolute idealism by adopting a half-hearted idealism: but a half-hearted idealism refutes itself.

The other camp has repudiated in principle the philosophy of religious experience. It has responded to the crisis of idealism by turning away from religious experience to God Himself. This can only be a God who has supernaturally revealed Himself. In relation to this God, reason is regarded as wholly impotent. The thinker of this camp tends to combine theological orthodoxy with a radical philosophical scepticism.

But is such a combination really possible? If this scepticism is really radical, it would seem to destroy theology along with philosophy. For if by theology we mean the explication of a divine revelation, then theology requires categories of explication. It requires, for example, the category of revelation. And this category must be rationally intelligible, even if the revelation itself is not. If there are no such categories, then the theologian cannot add a single word of interpretation to the revealed document itself. The theologian may be correct in lifting revelation above the reach of philosophy; but if he wholly repudiates the philosophic concern with the divine, then he refutes himself.

Thus the philosophic concern with the divine is in sore straits in our time. For in one of the two dominant camps the divine has vanished, and in the other, philosophy. But it is of course possible that this whole concern rests on a fundamental mistake, and that the great tradition from the Greeks to the nineteenth century is merely a divine comedy. Many contemporary thinkers are of this opinion; indeed, there are schools of thought which have declared the philosophic concern with the divine to be dead and buried. But one wonders whether the profoundest part of philosophic tradition can be eliminated by a few trifling distinctions or empirical observations. Perhaps this burial has been a little too hasty. Perhaps it proves, not the demise of the interred, but an indecent haste on the part of the undertakers.

If man's concern with the divine is perennial, and if it is at least in part rational, then what is needed in our time is renewal and rejuvenation. Those concerned with such a renewal would do well to take note of Schelling, who first struggled with a crisis which still casts its shadow over us.

7 Schelling's Conception of Positive Philosophy

I

When Schelling died a hundred years ago (20 August 1854), his contemporaries' opinion of him might be summarized as follows. A precocious thinker, Schelling made a great contribution to philosophy around the year 1800, when he was still in his twenties. But he lacked system and thoroughness, and his contribution was soon assimilated and superseded by the system of Hegel. Moreover, he lacked stability. While Hegel spent his whole life working out his system, Schelling changed his standpoint so often as to drive his interpreters to despair. Finally, at least from 1804 on (when Schelling was not yet thirty) these changes were for the worse, for he moved more and more toward mysticism and obscurantism.

This appraisal became conventional opinion, and has remained conventional opinion until this day. In practically any history of philosophy which bothers with Schelling at all one can find this threefold condemnation of his work: that it consists of a number of more or less disconnected systems; that none of these is properly worked out; and that from 1804 on, they get worse and worse. As a result of this opinion, few historians have been interested in Schelling. When in 1944 air raids destroyed the Munich University Library, among the treasures destroyed were thousands of Schelling manuscript pages, mostly written in his later years. It seems that in nearly one hundred years nobody was sufficiently interested in these manuscripts to do anything with them.

But during the last few decades interest in Schelling has revived, at least in Germany and France. This new interest reflects the beginnings of a revision of judgment; indeed, a drastic revision. This is illustrated by the fact that this new interest centres on Schelling's last phase, the phase hitherto most neglected. It is a pity that this revival came too late to make possible the publication of more than a fraction of the manuscripts, before their destruction.[1]

As a result of the new investigations, it has already become clear that the conventional opinion of Schelling is grossly unjust. That opinion is based on the judgment of contemporaries or near-contemporaries. And these were subject to prejudices which made an adequate understanding of Schelling difficult, if not impossible. Schelling's critics were theologians, positivists, and Hegelians. If they were theologians, they looked to Schelling for an apologetic which they did not get, nor were meant to get. If they were positivists, they had even less sympathy with Schelling than they had with Hegel. And if they were Hegelians (as most of them were), they saw the most important criterion of judgment in systematic completeness, the very point in which Schelling was weakest; further, they were bound to regard his development after 1804 as an aberration or an outright betrayal.

To be sure, the conventional opinion is not entirely mistaken. Schelling does lack system and thoroughness; and his consequent tendency to mix the ill-considered, or even the absurd, with the profound confounds the present student as it did the past. But Hegelian prejudices have led to an exaggeration of this vice. Schelling may be weak in execution, but he is strong indeed in programmatic statement. Moreover, the latter strength accounts at least in part for the former weakness. Schelling was able to penetrate with extraordinary swiftness to first principles and ultimate implications. No sooner had he conceived a system than he perceived implications which made it problematic. While others would plod along, working out the details of a system Schelling had outlined, he himself already found it necessary to go beyond it. Thus time and again he faced philosophical crises. If Schelling never worked out any of his systems, this is in part because his systematic tendency was forever at war with his aporematic. But theologians, positivists and Hegelians had this in common: if they were prepared to admit philosophical crises at all, they regarded them as resolved, once and for all.

Because of their blindness to the aporematic element in Schelling's thought, the critics arrived at the opinion that his various systems were more or less disconnected. But this is in fact far from the case. The new system tends to spring from the problems created by the old. Indeed, it is doubtful whether there is any discontinuity in Schelling's development at all.[2] The modern student who fails to perceive a connection does well to suspect that the fault lies, not with Schelling, but with himself.

Because of their prejudices, the critics have been particularly unjust to the philosophy of Schelling's old age. Schelling here made the most radical shift of his entire career. He repudiated absolute idealism, and turned to what can only be called a post-idealistic metaphysics. Absolute idealism now became a mere 'negative philosophy,' i.e., a mere preface (though a necessary preface) to metaphysics proper, or a 'positive philosophy,' which did not as yet exist. But Schelling's critics were either hostile to all metaphysics, or else hostile to all but Hegelian metaphysics. Hence they were unable or unwilling to take the program of the positive philosophy seriously. As a result of their prejudices, Schelling's four-volume *Philosophy of Mythology and Revelation* is still little known, and less understood.[3]

But the climate of philosophical opinion has changed, and in such a way as to explain the new interest in the philosophy of Schelling's old age. At least one school of contemporary thought can approach that philosophy with sympathy, if not enthusiasm. This is existentialism. Existentialist thought, whatever else it is, is post-idealist, not simply non-idealist or anti-idealist. One might almost say that existentialism is misunderstood to the degree to which this fact is ignored. It is no accident that existentialists tend to see the decisive event for modern metaphysics in the collapse of Hegelianism in the middle of the nineteenth century;[4] and it is a most suggestive fact that practically every existentialist seems to have to struggle with Hegel.[5] This would appear to indicate an agreement that one can neither return to a pre-idealist metaphysics, nor remain with idealism. But this is precisely the conviction which gives rise to Schelling's positive philosophy.

This serves to explain, not only why contemporary philosophers do, but also why they should, take Schelling seriously. Schelling is not only the first in a long line of post-idealistic metaphysicians, but he also possesses unique qualifications. For having himself been the founder of absolute idealism, he is the critic who can be trusted most to have understood what he is criticizing. This fact alone should make us suspect that the *Philosophy of Mythology and Revelation* is of first-rate importance not only for historical scholarship but also for contemporary philosophy; or at least for such consciously post-idealistic philosophies as existentialism. On the centenary of Schelling's death, it is fitting to draw attention to this work, which has been ignored for so long, but does not deserve to be forgotten.

II

In 1841 the aged Schelling emerged from decades of semi-retirement and literary silence. He came to Berlin, the stronghold of Hegelianism, in order to present his 'positive' philosophy.[6] Everybody knew beforehand that this was a theistic metaphysics of freedom and existence, and thus not only an attack on Hegel but also a repudiation of Schelling's own former system, the system of identity. In his first lecture, however, Schelling defined the sense in which he repudiated idealistic dialectic: it was an indispensable part of philosophy, but only a part. The basic error of absolute idealism consisted in making the dialectic absolute.[7]

Schelling's lectures were not a success. The reaction of the Hegelians was epitomized by Eduard Gans, who remarked that the Hegelian system could be refuted only by a better system.[8] Perhaps the system had left something unabsorbed; but to recognize the unabsorbed as such was to begin to absorb it. The Hegelians failed to appreciate that Schelling's criticism of the system was radical. He pointed to freedom and existence as facts which no possible dialectical system could absorb; the step from rational system to existence was a *μετάβασις εἰς ἄλλο γένος*.

No less significant is the reaction of that great enemy of the Hegelian system, Kierkegaard. He had come to Berlin especially in order to hear Schelling. At first he showed enthusiastic approval.[9] But his enthusiasm soon waned. 'Schelling drivels quite intolerably,' he wrote. 'His whole doctrine of potency betrays the greatest impotence.'[10]

These two reactions illustrate the problem discussed in this paper. Hegel confronted his age with a choice: an all-inclusive dialectical system, or the salvation of the particular brought about by the surrender of all system. The system was everything or nothing. Schelling's positive philosophy is an attempt to escape this dilemma. It by no means surrenders the notion of dialectical system, but seeks to combine a dialectic of essence and necessity with an undialectical doctrine of existence and freedom. Because of the latter, it displeased the Hegelians; because of the former, it displeased such opponents of the system as Kierkegaard. In their displeasure, neither party subjected Schelling's conception to the impartial examination which it deserved.

III

Dialectic breaks through the apparent externality of things and reaches an inner bond which unites them. Its progression is an 'immanent necessity,'[11] its discovery, an 'inner organism of successive potencies.'[12] By means of this method, the young Schelling had arrived at his metaphysics of absolute identity. In 1801 he had written: 'The absolute identity is not the cause of the universe, but the universe itself.'[13]

The positive philosophy rejects the system of identity but not the method of dialectic. Yet the meaning of dialectic is fundamentally altered. Dialectic does indeed move in an 'immanent necessity'; but it does so on the basis of a prior abstraction from what is outside this necessity. For the structures of thought and reality are not identical. Dialectic constructs a priori a system of essence, but it can do so only by abstracting from existence. Thus it moves necessarily toward God; but this is a non-existent God, a mere idea. God exists necessarily *if* He exists. *Whether* He exists is a question outside the reach of dialectic.[14]

With this fundamental limitation, the first question arises for the new philosophy. In almost literal anticipation of Heidegger,[15] Schelling asks: 'why does anything exist at all? why is there not rather nothing?'[16] The dialectic constructs a priori what can be; it knows nothing of existence.

Schelling does not ask: *does* anything exist? The existence of the world is an empirical fact, and the dialectic is object-related from the start: it understands characteristics of the real world. The problem is that dialectic cannot understand the *meaning* of existence; and this means for Schelling that dialectic cannot absorb existence into a system. Dialectic is fragmentary knowledge[17] and must turn to experience for the knowledge of fact.

It might appear, then, that the dialectic constructs a priori the nature of the actual world. If so, the positive philosophy would have to answer only a single question: why does this world – which is the only possible world – exist? But this would be to misunderstand Schelling's conception and to reduce it to nonsense. If existence resists dialectical absorption, so does individuality. Reality is not in fact the internal unity which it is in ideal construction. The facts not only appear to, but really do, fall outside each other; and their irrational infinity is as inaccessible to dialectic as the fact of existence itself. Experience encounters, as a brute fact, externality; and along with externality meaninglessness and evil. Thus the second question arises for the new philosophy: why is what exists in discrepancy with what it ideally ought to be? Why is the world 'questionable'?[18]

The questions posed by the positive philosophy may well appear nonsensical. How can one ask for the meaning of the meaningless? The meaningless is either ultimately not meaningless, or else it is a brute fact. Schelling emphatically rejects the former alternative: is he, then, not driven toward a simple acceptance of the facts, surrendering the quest for their meaning as itself meaningless? But this would be to ignore the negative achievement of the dialectic. All empirical fact, while indissoluble into dialectic, is yet subject to all-pervasive dialectical qualifications. Dialectic isolates this character of the facts and thus shows them to be in need of explanation. Because of its abstracting from their factuality, dialectic at the same time reveals itself as incapable of the explanation required. Dialectic is thus 'negative philosophy,' in a double sense. It negates absolute idealism as being a false philosophy, and empiricism[19] as being no philosophy at all.

Internal unity and externality, the a priori meaningful and the a priori meaningless, are both real characters of the real world; their togetherness in the same world is the problem requiring a solution. This is the situation which gives rise to the positive philosophy.

IV

The questions of the positive philosophy are not nonsensical, but can they be answered? Qua dialectically qualified, the facts demand an absolute in terms of which they may be explained; but qua facts, they can be explained by no mere idea. The first principle of the positive philosophy cannot be an absolute Idea, but only an absolute Fact. But such a fact is beyond all possible human knowledge. For wherever knowledge grasps fact, it is fact dialectically qualified; and wherever it grasps an Absolute, it is mere idea.

Here the negative philosophy carries out its third and most important negation. It has negated relative fact, as being relative; it has negated absolute Idea, as being mere idea. It now discovers that it cannot think of the Absolute other than as idea, and that it can negate it as such only by negating itself as well. The negative philosophy therefore brings about a radical 'crisis of reason'[20] and sets the stage for a radical leap.[21]

'The last aim of rational philosophy,' says Schelling, 'is to reach God as separate from all relative being.'[22] This aim it reaches in one sense, but fails to reach in another. Examples are Aristotle's *actus purus*, or the 'necessarily existent' of the scholastics. Rational philosophy here has, in its independence, the principle on which everything depends; but it has it as a mere idea. And this means that the end of rational philosophy, far from being the end of all philosophy, involves a paradox requiring a wholly new point of departure. Rational philosophy is driven to the idea of an absolute Individual who necessarily exists; but this idea, qua idea, is universal and non-existent. The form and the content of this idea are in necessary contradiction. In its highest idea reason necessarily points beyond itself; but, equally necessarily, it fails to achieve this beyond.

Schelling refers to this pointing-beyond when he says that reason, in its crisis, becomes 'ec-static.'[23]

Rational philosophy here reaches an unavoidable impasse. From the start, it necessarily abstracts from existence; but what it must *mean* in its last term is the pure Existent beyond all essence. But it cannot attain what it means.

This deadlock can be broken only if it is remembered that rational philosophy, as a whole, is merely the abstract expression of a concrete spiritual condition; it has an existential setting. The idea of God is not only the last concept of reason; it is also the highest expression of a spiritual attitude, viz., philosophical contemplation. In contemplation the philosophizing person seeks to sublate in an Absolute, not just existence in general, but his own personal existence. Contemplation is an attempt at self-surrender and self-oblivion. But just as a mere idea will not absorb any existence, so it will not absorb my own. The logical paradox here turns into a personal paradox which the philosopher lives and suffers. 'The self might be satisfied with the purely ideal God, if he could remain in this state of contemplation. But this is impossible. The surrender of action cannot be carried out. Action is inevitable ... the former despair returns.'[24]

Thus for objective philosophical reasons, subjective personal interest enters. 'The last idea of reason ... has this peculiarity, that the philosophizing subject cannot be indifferent to its existence or non-existence. Here the watch-word is: *Tua res agitur.*'[25] The pure Existent is inaccessible to rational detachment because it abstracts from the existence of the thinker.

The finite spirit is in search of the existing God.[26] But in his life he asserts himself and thus has only finite existence; and in his contemplation he has God, but merely in idea. Existence and idea cannot be synthesized in thought. But they can be synthesized in *will.* From the lonely despair brought about by the search for God, a search at once rational and existential, arises the will, not to posit Him – for any such God would again be idea only – but to accept Him, as prior to all thought and experience. Decision is the radical leap from the last idea of the negative to the first principle of the positive philosophy.[27]

This leap is indeed radical and outside all reason. But it is not arbitrary. The predicament from which it arises is the human condition itself, in which rationality itself is rooted.[28] Thus the individual philosopher has the choice only between taking this leap and remaining within the sphere of the negative philosophy. 'The positive philosophy is genuinely free philosophy: the person who does not will it may leave it alone.'[29]

V

The principle accepted by the leap is by no means an existing God. This would be sheer dogmatism. The leap achieves only what is strictly beyond thought and experience, and yet necessary in order to explain them. The metaphysical principle is individual beyond all universality, existent beyond all essence, and precisely for that reason beyond all thought. The leap from reason into existence has to abandon also God, the highest idea of reason; we are left with an absolute Existent who (or rather which) is unknowable and unthinkable. Schelling calls this existent *Unvordenkliches Sein*, i.e., that being which is forever prior to thought, and which thought cannot encompass. For purposes of convenience, we shall refer to it by using the English term 'absolute Existent.'

The absolute Existent is the principle by which the real world is to be explained. It must therefore be related to the world. But this cannot be a necessary relation; for in that case dialectic would encompass the absolute Existent. The absolute Existent, as the Individual beyond all universality, must be outside all dialectic. The relationship can therefore be only one of free will. Free will is Schelling's fundamental existential category. Reason may explain essence; only will can explain existence. 'Wherever will enters we deal with actual existence.'[30] Free will, for Schelling, transcends all necessity; it is absolute freedom of choice. All free will is therefore a mystery until it acts.[31] The absolute Will is subject to no pre-existing necessity, whether it be a realm of pre-existing possibilities outside itself or its own essence. Indeed, the absolute Existent has no essence; or rather, if it has an essence, it has itself created it. If the absolute Existent is God, He Himself has made Himself God. The Thomists make much of the mysterious passage in Exodus which they translate: 'I am who I am.'[32] Schelling translates: 'I shall be who I shall be'[33] – a translation which, incidentally, would appear to be more faithful to the Hebrew text.

It might appear that to attribute will to the absolute Existent is inconsistent with its supposed unknowability. This, however, is not the case. We know that the first principle has will because it has actually willed the world. Here lies the core of Schelling's 'metaphysical empiricism.'[34]

But an unpredictable absolute Will, by itself, is wholly insufficient for the purposes of the positive philosophy. That Will, as far as the evidence of the facts shows, reveals itself, now as a God, now as a devil, now simply as an omnipotent jester, explaining no more than that nothing can be explained. The positive philosophy has made existence, rather than reason, primary. If it is to move a single step from its first principle, it must now derive reason and universality from the absolute Existent which is beyond both.[35]

Moreover, unless this can be done, the first principle itself collapses. The negative philosophy has led up to an absolute Existent by dialectically relativizing all empirical existents; the validity of this procedure depended entirely on the assumption that these dialectical relations have an ontological status; but this assumption the negative philosophy itself could not justify. Unless the positive philosophy can ground dialectical necessity in the absolute Existent which is itself beyond it, the entire negative philosophy collapses, and we are left, not with an absolute Existent, but with as many existents as there are empirical facts: we have landed, not in the positive philosophy, but in empiricism. The negative philosophy, it now becomes clear, has founded the positive philosophy only hypothetically; the positive philosophy must now directly found the negative philosophy, and indirectly, itself.

We might summarize the situation as follows: if an absolute Reason can explain only rationality, but not existence, and if therefore existence, not reason, must be metaphysically ultimate, then this absolute Existence must be the ground, not only of other existence, but of rationality as well. Schelling must therefore ask: 'Why is there reason? why not unreason?'[36] This is the crucial problem of the positive philosophy; it is, as we shall see, the problem on which it founders.

Schelling proceeds as follows. The absolute Existent and its free Will are a priori unknowable. But we can consider a priori what free will as such involves. Dialectic may examine the *category* of free will, or rather, the category of the absolutely free will. What does such an examination exhibit? Free will is freedom to will or not to will. This involves a distinction between two elements, potential will and actual will. And since neither potential nor actual will is, by itself, free to will and not to will, still a third element is involved. This is the synthesis of potency and act, and this alone is free to will and not to will. These three potencies Schelling calls 'that which can be' (*das Seinkönnende*), 'that which must be' (*das Seinmüssende*), and 'that which is to be' (*das Seinsollende*). They are the fundamental categories of the entire positive philosophy.

It must be clearly realized that Schelling does not move from the absolute individual will to the dialectical category of will; such a move would clearly be impossible. He moves from the category, which is as such an abstract universal, and then seeks to ground it in the absolute Existent.[37] For purposes of convenience, we shall term the dialectical unity of the three potencies the 'absolute Essence.' Since the universal does not, as such, exist, the absolute Essence can only be adjective to the absolute Existent. Moreover, it cannot be an adjective constitutive of the absolute Existent; for (as we have seen) the latter cannot enter into the dialectic. Thus the absolute Existent must freely assume its essence. The absolute Essence, which is the ground of all rationality, is thus in turn grounded, as a primordial accident, in the absolute Existent which is beyond all rationality. Schelling expresses this as follows: 'Absolute Spirit is free in relation to itself; to-be-Spirit is for it only a mode of being.'[38] 'Reason is not the cause of Spirit, but only because [the perfect Spirit] ... exists is there reason. With this conclusion all philosophical rationalism is destroyed in its foundations.'[39]

The positive philosophy has now laid its foundations. It will explain both essence and existence, necessity and freedom, meaning and meaninglessness. It will be able to do so because, on the one hand, the absolute Essence is the ground of all dialectical necessity, and because, on the other, this essence is itself existentially grounded in an act of Will which is not only free itself, but which also imparts to the Essence it grounds, at crucial junctures, radically indeterminate situations.

We shall illustrate the method of the positive philosophy by considering two of these junctures, the creation and the fall.

Creation is the realization of the absolute Essence. By an act of will, the absolute Existent spreads Itself out into the unity of potencies; or, which is the same thing, It makes Itself absolute Spirit. This doctrine differs from pantheism in one crucial respect. The absolute Existent is linked to the creation, not by necessity, but by an act of free will. It does not require it for its own self-realization. Creation is not an a priori necessity but an a posteriori fact.

The creation strictly corresponds to the ideal construction of the negative philosophy, with this difference. It is the product of a real will, and therefore a unity of existing forces, not of abstract ideas.[40]

With the doctrine of creation, the positive philosophy has answered one of its three questions. 'Why does anything exist? why is there not rather nothing?' This question cannot be answered in terms of relative fact or absolute Idea. Something exists because an absolute Existent has willed it.

The second question is: 'Why is there reason? why not unreason?' No rational philosophy could raise, let alone answer this question, since it presupposes what is in question. The positive philosophy answers: there is reason because the absolute Existent has manifested Itself, in the creation, as absolute Spirit.

But has the positive philosophy really answered this question? The creation is by no means an empirical fact; it is an ideal construction. To validate this construction, the positive philosophy must presuppose precisely that absolute rationalism which the doctrine itself puts in question. As we shall see, on this inescapable contradiction the positive philosophy suffers shipwreck.

Schelling's real meaning here is: the absolute Existent is free *whether* to create but not *what* to create. Hence we cannot know a priori whether anything will be; but we can know a priori what will be if anything is.[41]

Only now is the third question meaningful: 'Why is what exists in discrepancy with what it ideally ought to be?' Or, as we may now put it: how are externality, meaninglessness, and evil possible in a creation which, as such, has none of these? It is this question which had led Schelling, many years earlier, to abandon the system of identity.[42]

We are here faced with a radically new fact. And, as in the case of all new fact, only a new act of will can explain it. Where, in the unity of the three potencies which is the creation, is freedom possible? Of the three potencies, we recall, only the third is free to will or not to will. This third potency is man, the original man, or man-in-God. His primordial freedom consists in the bare choice between willing and not-willing. For any particular decision presupposes the decision to will at all. The primordial choice of man is between total surrender to the absolute Existent and total self-assertion.

Since the decision is free, no dialectic can encompass it. But dialectic can work out the consequences attendant upon either choice. The decision not to will would leave the creation wholly unchanged. The decision to will would bring about a radical change. In asserting himself, original man would tear himself loose from the absolute Existent; and, since the other two potencies are synthesized only in him, he would cause, by his own fall, the fall of the entire creation. The fall would bring about universal externality, which is the cause of meaninglessness and evil. Has man in fact fallen? Here the positive philosophy stops constructing and points to the facts.

We have indicated enough of the positive philosophy in order to be able to formulate its conception and method. Negative philosophy is not metaphysics, but the search for the metaphysical principle. Its method is purely dialectical; it reveals the facts as in need of explanation, and progressively eliminates what cannot serve as principle of explanation. Its search for the principle is limited in two respects:

(i) because it abstracts from existence it cannot itself issue into the first principle; it merely leads to a point at which a radical but unmistakable leap can be made; (ii) because its strictly necessary movement is not an ontological movement, it has, as a whole, a merely hypothetical status. It requires validation by the positive philosophy.

Positive philosophy is metaphysics proper. Its principle is an absolute Existent which, qua absolute, is beyond experience, and qua existent, beyond thought. It enters into both by an expression of free will. Its first creation is the dialectical unity of the potencies. This creation, on the one hand, validates the negative philosophy, and, on the other, makes construction within the positive philosophy possible. The positive philosophy explains the actual world. Explanation here involves three terms: (i) the absolute Existent, (ii) the dialectical unity of potencies, (iii) the world of empirical fact. All three terms are required. Only the first term can explain why anything exists. Only the first and second in conjunction can explain the rationality found in the world. And only all three terms in conjunction can explain the togetherness of rationality and irrationality which makes up the actual world. The method of the positive philosophy may be termed 'progressive' or 'metaphysical empiricism.'[43] It starts out, a priori, with the absolute Existent; proceeds, still a priori, to consider the alternative possibilities implicit in the dialectical unity of potencies; but discovers only a posteriori which of these alternatives has become fact. The positive philosophy is thus very far from indiscriminately collecting empirical evidence. It selects for consideration only those facts which, according to its a priori principles, can be explained only by a novel cosmic act of will.

VI

It would appear that Schelling was gravely concerned about the problem which in fact is fatal to the entire positive philosophy. For in one of his last lectures he singles it out for treatment. But here, as elsewhere, he failed to solve it.

The problem is indicated by the title of the lecture: 'On the Source of the External Verities.'[44] Rational truths must have an inherent necessity; but what metaphysics will justify this necessity? After dismissing pre-idealistic metaphysics as inadequate on dialectical grounds, the lecture comes to grips with the crucial alternative: the system of absolute reason, and the positive philosophy. An absolute Reason justifies rationality, but it explains nothing else; it cannot explain (i) the existence and irrationality of the actual world, (ii) its own existential ground. For 'the universal essence exists only if there is an absolute Individual.'[45] The first principle, therefore, cannot be a universal Reason; it must be an individual Existent. But if this is so, how are we to justify the necessity indispensable to rationality? Reason cannot flow necessarily from the essence of the absolute Existent, for the latter has no essence. Nor can it be the product of an arbitrary will, for this would make rationality itself an accident, and destroy the a priori. Schelling ends up by asserting that reason is a 'necessary accident' of the absolute Existent.[46]

But this is surely a mere admission of failure. For if the absolute Essence is in any sense necessary to the absolute Existent, this necessity encompasses the absolute Existent and we have returned to the system of reason; but if the absolute Existent is really beyond reason, the absolute Essence is not a necessary accident, but accident pure and simple. In the terms used earlier in this paper: the transition from the individual Will which is the Absolute to the universal category of free will cannot be made. Schelling himself appears to admit this when he remarks: 'Here is the last limit which cannot be transcended.'[47]

But this admission is fatal to the whole conception of the positive philosophy. For with it vanishes the right to all a priori metaphysical construction. The Absolute might express its will in an indefinite number of ways, rationality being but one of them. Moreover, the absolute Existent itself, as a principle of a cosmic system, becomes indefensible. For the negative philosophy is deprived of its ontological foundation. Dialectic becomes either a mere play of the human mind, justifying no sort of leap, and landing us in empiricism; or else it is merely the dialectic, not of reason-in-reality, but of man-in-his-environment. From such a situation a leap may indeed have to be made; it may even have a certain metaphysical significance; but it will be an entirely different significance, and what is achieved by it cannot be the principle of a cosmic system. To illustrate what may be achieved by it we may point to contemporary existentialism, and perhaps even to certain types of pragmatism.

Schelling's positive philosophy illustrates this profound problem: if the dialectical principle is true that there can be only one Absolute, but if at the same time this Absolute cannot be reason itself, how is reason to be grounded? Rationality must be justified in some way; without such a justification speculative metaphysics, at least, is impossible. Schelling's positive philosophy clearly understands this problem. It fails to solve it.

8 Metaphysics and Historicity[1]

1 Modern Man and the Predicament of History

History is a predicament for man who must live in it. In order to act in history he must seek to rise above it. He needs perspectives in terms of which to understand his situation, and timeless truths and values in terms of which to act in it. Yet the perspectives which he finds often merely reflect his age; and what he accepts as timelessly true and valid is apt to be merely the opinion which is in fashion. Thus while man must always try to rise above his historical situation he succeeds at best only precariously.

This predicament, always part of the human condition, is felt by contemporary Western man more keenly than by man in any previous age. This is in part because of the breath-taking swiftness of contemporary events. Never have men had so much cause to seek a transcending wisdom in terms of which to understand and influence the course of events, and yet to fear that such a wisdom is beyond their reach. For never has yesterday's wisdom become stale so quickly, and hence has present counsel been regarded with so much doubt.

This effect of contemporary events is reinforced by an intellectual development which, in the West, began in the nineteenth century. For a century and a half, Western man has developed an ever-increasing historical self-consciousness. And this has not been without grave spiritual effects. In earlier ages, most men could simply accept religious beliefs or moral principles, as unquestionably true. In this historically self-conscious age, few men can ever forget that what seems unquestionably true to one age or civilization differs from what seems unquestionably true to others. And from historical self-consciousness there is but one step – albeit a long and fateful one – to a wholesale historical scepticism: to the despairing view that history discloses a variety of conflicting *Weltanschauungen*, with no criterion for choice between them anywhere in sight. But when events move as they do today this step is easily taken.[2]

Just how commonly it is in fact taken may be illustrated by a review of three typically contemporary attitudes. The first is what may be called *sceptical paralysis*. Here historical self-consciousness has led to two results: to the insight that wherever there has been a great purpose there has been a great faith; and to the loss of capacity for commitment to such a faith. Hence there is paralysis which recognizes itself as paralysis and preaches doom.[3]

Then there is what may be called *pragmatic make-believe*. Here man, caught in scepticism, seeks escape from its paralysing consequences. Unable to believe and yet seeking a purpose, he falls to pretending to believe, hoping that a pretended might do the work of an actual faith. But it cannot. For a pretended faith is no faith at all. Pragmatic make-believe collapses in self-contradiction.[4]

When men truly suffer from this contradiction they may seek escape in the most ominous form of modern spiritual life: *ideological fanaticism*. Unlike pragmatic make-believe and like faith, ideology asserts itself absolutely. But unlike faith and like pragmatic make-believe, it is shot through with historical scepticism. For it knows itself to be not truth, but merely one specific product of history.

Hence unlike faith, ideology must by its very nature become fanatical. When challenged by a conflicting faith, faith may withdraw on its certainty of *being* true. Because it knows itself to be but one product of history, ideology can achieve certainty only by *making* itself true; and this it can do absolutely only by re-creating all history in its own image. When challenged, therefore, ideology cannot withdraw on itself; it must seek to destroy the challenger. That is, in order to resolve its internal conflict between absolute assertion and historical scepticism, it must engage in a total war from which it hopes to emerge as the only ideology left on earth.[5]

2 History and Metaphysical Truth

Such, then, are the disastrous effects of historical scepticism on the present age. One asks: is the long and fateful step from historical self-consciousness to historical scepticism an inevitable step? Or is it, on the contrary, a mis-step to be avoided at all costs – the mere result of confusion and failure of nerve?

Asking this question, one cannot avoid turning to that most ancient of all philosophical enterprises, metaphysics. For in its long and eventful career, metaphysics has made one claim without hesitation and with the utmost consistency: that the predicament of history, however grave, is not wholly beyond human remedy; that at least when engaged in metaphysical discourse, man can rise above history to a grasp of timeless truth. Such a metaphysician as St Thomas Aquinas may have disagreed with Plato or Avicenna. But he agreed with them that metaphysical truth was timeless. Were the angelic doctor alive today, he would no doubt argue against Descartes, Kant, and Hegel. But such an argument across the ages would itself presuppose the common conviction that metaphysical truth is independent of any age.[6]

But it is a most disturbing fact that what has never been questioned by metaphysicians before has been questioned by metaphysicians since the middle of the nineteenth century. For the first time, the view has come to be entertained that metaphysical truth, far from transcending history, is on the contrary essentially tied to it. And this suggests the possibility of a revolution in metaphysics, more radical than any other ever attempted. When a past metaphysician denied the existence of God he still clung to the idea of timeless metaphysical truth. This idea was itself denied when Nietzsche asserted that God is dead.[7] R.G. Collingwood said nothing new when he affirmed that metaphysical presuppositions are unprovable. But that the validity of these presuppositions depends on their historical setting was a revolutionary assertion on his part.[8] Nor are Nietzsche and Collingwood isolated examples. Among others who would historicize metaphysical truth are metaphysicians as diverse as Dilthey and Croce, Dewey and Heidegger.[9] What is it that metaphysicians of such divergent viewpoints have in common?

If metaphysical truth is timeless, then man, the animal capable of recognizing this truth, must have a capacity which is itself timeless. This is an implication which traditional metaphysicians could easily accept; for they believed in a human nature which, though subject to accidental historical changes, was essentially permanent. But what if there is no such thing as a permanent human nature? What if the distinction between permanent nature and historical change is a false distinction: if man's very being is historical? All the metaphysicians just referred to, and many more, have rejected the doctrine of human nature, and have replaced it with what may be called a doctrine of historicity. And as a result they have been forced to ask whether perhaps just as human being changes throughout history so must metaphysical truth. If man's very being is inseparable from his history, must the same not be true of his grasp of metaphysical truth? And must not then what is metaphysically true in one period of history differ from what is metaphysically true in another? Clearly, the doctrine of historicity is a weighty doctrine, not only in itself but also because of the questions it raises for metaphysics as a whole.

But it is a doctrine difficult to cope with. It cannot, for example, be regarded as obviously true because proved by empirical history. History may show that man is subject to historical change; it does not prove that his very being is involved in this change. The doctrine of historicity is not an empirical generalization but a metaphysical thesis.[10]

Nor can this metaphysical thesis be regarded as obviously false. One cannot, for example, fall straightway to refuting it, in terms of such traditional concepts as substance and nature. For the doctrine of historicity is unintelligible in these terms and indeed implies their falsehood. Before the metaphysician asks whether or not the doctrine of historicity is true he must be sure to have understood it in the terms it requires. But such an understanding is a subtle and complex task.[11]

For this reason, we wish in this chapter to inquire into the meaning of the doctrine of historicity only, and to suspend judgment as to its truth or falsehood. Our inquiry into its meaning will proceed in two stages. We shall first seek to elicit the metaphysical assumptions without which the doctrine of historicity cannot arise, and then seek to state the principal metaphysical categories without which it cannot be maintained. The first effort is to ensure that we understand the doctrine in terms proper to it; the second, to give an understanding of the doctrine itself. But the question which concerns us most of all will be dealt with in the context of the second effort: whether the doctrine of historicity necessitates the surrender of the age-old idea of timeless metaphysical truth.

3 The Presuppositions of the Doctrine of Historicity

Our inquiry into metaphysical presuppositions, like any such inquiry, is apt to arrive at unfamiliar or even abstruse terms. It is therefore prudent to set out with terms which are familiar, and close to common sense.

One such set of terms is furnished by a well-known distinction made by R.G. Collingwood. History consists of actions performed by man, not of natural events which happen to him; and the latter are historical only by virtue of their relation – potential or actual – to the former. Caesar's decision at the Rubicon, or Napoleon's fate at Waterloo, is historical primarily. An eruption of Mount Vesuvius or an earthquake in San Francisco are part of history only secondarily, because they are a challenge to human action. And if they occurred on a star on which no men live they would not be part of history at all.

Collingwood's distinction, though complex, may for the present purpose be expounded with the utmost brevity. A natural event has an 'outside' only. An historical action has an 'inside' as well as an outside. The outside consists of physical bodies and their movement. The inside consists of human thoughts – aims, plans, and decisions. Once the historian has described both the outside and the inside of an action he need no longer inquire why what happened did happen. He has already explained why Caesar crossed the Rubicon if he has correctly described Caesar's ambitions, his appraisal of the political situation, and his eventual decision.[12]

This distinction between natural event and historical action is an assumption, although one which most men would be willing to make – in practice if not in theory. But the assumption is not that there are conscious human beings who believe themselves to be planning, deciding, and performing actions. This is a plain and indisputable fact. The assumption is that on at least some occasions the belief of these agents is a correct belief; that is, that there are occasions when the categories in which the planning, deciding, and performing agents understand their behaviour are the categories in which it must be understood. Men are not invariably subject to compulsive urges when they believe themselves to be making free decisions. Not all imagined acting for reasons is in fact irrational behaviour productive of rationalizations. In short, there is free action, not merely the appearance of free action. This, very briefly and very broadly, is the first assumption.[13]

No doubt it gives rise to baffling questions. Can individuals alone act, or groups as well as individuals? Is all acting rational, or is there irrational as well as rational acting? Does historical action include its consequences, and if so, unintended as well as intended ones? Finally, is the division between natural event and human action an exhaustive division? Or can there be occurrences which are neither? This last question would have been vital to any Jew standing at the foot of Mount Sinai, and to any Christian standing at the foot of the Cross. But such is the secularism of the present age that it is often forgotten.[14]

But there is no need here to raise such baffling questions. It suffices to stress that if the doctrine of historicity is to be maintained, a qualitative distinction between nature and history must somehow and somewhere be drawn. For if it is not drawn, history reduces itself to a mere species of natural process, different from other kinds only in that it happens in or to man. To draw this distinction adequately, the terms 'natural event' and 'human action' may not suffice. But they are certainly both obvious and indispensable.[15]

But by itself, an ontological distinction between natural event and historical action does not justify the doctrine of historicity. As we have said, this is an assumption which most men would be willing to make. But few of these would accept the doctrine of historicity. For it is one thing to admit that men are capable of free action, and hence of a history. It is another thing altogether to assert that man – the being capable of a history – is himself the product of history. Indeed, conceivably those making the first assertion might reject the second as incompatible with it. Is it not the case that man, if capable of free action and hence of a history, must have a nature unalterably endowed with this capacity: a nature, that is, which is radically non-historical?

If this is indeed the case, then the doctrine of historicity must be false, and history as a whole can be of no interest for ontology. For ontology is concerned with being qua being, and hence with human being qua being and qua human. But this concern includes only the capacity for free action, and hence for history, not the actual and accidental uses made of it. If the doctrine of historicity is false, then these latter must be the exclusive concern of the historian. But history, Aristotle says, is less philosophical even than poetry.[16]

The doctrine of historicity, then, requires a second assumption; and this, like the first, may be stated in familiar if not altogether commonsense terms. There are no permanent natures, distinct from the processes in which they are involved; or at any rate, there is no permanent human nature. This assumption, made familiar by modern 'process-philosophers,' was well summarized by Samuel Alexander.[17] Process is productive, not merely of new examples in accordance with patterns, but of new patterns as well as of new examples. There is not only change in accordance with laws. There is also a change of laws themselves. Reality as a whole is an historical process. Only if this assumption is made can man's very being be considered historical. Only then can the ontological inquiry into what man is reduce itself to an historical inquiry into what he has become.

But while necessary, this assumption, by itself and divorced from the first assumption, is not sufficient for the doctrine of historicity. It implies, to be sure, that the processes which constitute human beings are historical as well as natural. But it also implies that the historical is not qualitatively distinct from the natural. If all reality is an historical process, and is so for the same reason, then the processes which make man what he is are in the end all natural.

In the essay already referred to, Alexander speaks of the historicity of *all* things. There is history, he holds, wherever there is novelty and creativity. But Collingwood rightly protests against the implications of such usage.[18] The term 'historical' ought surely to be reserved for determining acts rather than incompletely determined events; for free decisions made by man rather than processes – even 'creative' ones – which occur in him. Or at any rate, if such a qualitative distinction is not made, then the doctrine of historicity reduces itself to nothing more than the ancient doctrine of a Heraclitean flux, which encompasses man along with all else.

The doctrine of historicity, then, requires the two above assumptions, taken in conjunction. (i) History is qualitatively distinct from nature because there are actions performed by man, as well as events which happen to him or in him; and (ii) the distinction between human being and human acting cannot in the end be maintained. Man is not endowed with a permanent nature capable of acting. His 'nature' is itself the product of his acting, and hence not a proper nature at all. *In acting, man makes or constitutes himself.*

To assert this is not to deny that man is largely the product of natural processes. Nor is it even to deny that he is the product of divine creation, or subject to divine influence after creation. But it is to assert that, apart from history, man's very being, qua being and qua human, is deficient. Man is what he becomes and has become; and the processes of becoming which make him distinctively human are historical. But what makes history distinctively historical is human action.

Human being, then, is a self-making or self-constituting process: this emerges as the crucial assumption without which the doctrine of historicity cannot arise. This assumption alone can explain why the ontologist, inquiring into human being qua being and qua human, should turn historian: whether speculative historian in the fashion of Hegel, or historian pure and simple in the fashion of Croce and Collingwood. For if human being is indeed a self-constituting process, then the ontological study of man cannot be divorced from the study of human history. Divorced from history, it would arrive not at a determinate human nature but at a mere abstract and empty possibility; or, if arriving at a determinate human nature, it would mistake for a permanent nature what is in fact a specific historical product.[19]

4 The Concept of Self-making

We have now accomplished our first task – the identification of the assumptions without which the doctrine of historicity cannot arise. But we may well wonder how to proceed with the second task – the understanding of the doctrine itself. Is a self-making process intelligible? If not, how can we determine the categories required by the kind of self-making process which is historical? To ask these questions, one need not share the fashionable fear of taking leave of ordinary language even in metaphysical discourse. Any metaphysician who soars boldly above ordinary language might well ask them. Was Schopenhauer right, when he asserted that a *causa sui* is no less absurd than the story of Baron von Münchhausen, who claimed that, having fallen into a swamp, he pulled himself out by his hair?[20]

But here we must remember a warning given earlier in this chapter. A metaphysical doctrine may well seem unintelligible, and yet in fact be unintelligible only in terms of a metaphysics which is its rival. One does well to suspect that this is so in the present case. For the concept of self-making occurs not only in a relatively brief period of modern metaphysics. It is basic to a whole metaphysical tradition which rivals the major Western tradition in metaphysics. The major tradition asserts that *operatio sequitur esse*. But there is also a minor tradition which asserts that, at least in the case of God, *esse sequitur operationem*. This tradition harks back possibly as far as to John Scotus Eriugena and, passing through such thinkers as Jacob Boehme and Schelling, finds a contemporary representative in Nicolas Berdyaev. In the major tradition, God is understood as Pure Being, and, in substantial strains of that tradition, as creating the world *ex nihilo*. In the minor tradition, God is understood as Pure Freedom who, in creating *ex nihilo*, Himself passes *ex nihilo in aliquid*. The major tradition is ontological, in the strictest sense. The minor tradition would strictly have to be called meontological.[21]

The God of meontological metaphysics would have to be described as a process which (i) because it is pure *making* proceeds from the indifference of sheer possibility of nothingness (μὴ ὄν) into the differentiation of actuality – *ex nihilo in aliquid*; (ii) because it is *self*-making establishes its own identity throughout this process by returning upon itself; or, otherwise put, proceeds into otherness, yet cancels this otherness and in so doing establishes itself; (iii) because it is *absolute* self-making, actualizes *ex nihilo* the totality of possibilities.

Is such a description illogical or unintelligible? It is unintelligible, to be sure, in terms of a logic which, consisting of a simple forward movement, leaves its terms static and unchanged. But to dismiss the doctrine for this reason alone would be to regard logic – one particular logic – as a wholly autonomous court of appeal in matters metaphysical. But what if every logic and hence this logic is itself metaphysically grounded? In that case, it might well be that meontological metaphysics generates a logic of its own, and it is in terms of this logic that it would then have to be understood. And a final judgment as to truth and falsehood would then have to be made, not in terms of one logic arbitrarily taken as absolute standard, but through a confrontation of the conflicting metaphysics themselves.[22]

The above description of the meontological concept of God, however sketchy, suffices to show that it does indeed generate a logic of its own. Its terms alter as the movement proceeds; and they alter because the movement is backward as well as forward: that is, circular. And the logical movement must be of this kind because the real process it describes is a self-constituting process which, in moving forward, integrates and re-integrates its own past into the forward movement.

We cannot here further describe this kind of logic.[23] But we shall henceforth be compelled to use it. We shall be so compelled, that is, if we wish to understand the doctrine of historicity, rather than pass judgment on it before it is understood.

5 Eternity, Temporality, Historicity

Only a self-constituting process can be in its ontological constitution historical. But not every such process is necessarily historical. This may be shown by a renewed consideration of the meontological concept of God.

This concept signifies a process which is at least quasi-historical, because first its moment of *nihil* must be distinguished from its moment of *aliquid,* and because secondly the moments of *nihil* and *aliquid* constitute themselves into an identity. If there were no distinguishable moments there would be no process at all; and if they did not constitute themselves into an identity the process would be merely temporal.

But while *at least* quasi-historical, this process can also be *no more than* quasi-historical. This is because it must wholly transcend temporality. For while, because it is a self-making, it appropriates the past into presentness, because it is absolute, it appropriates the past absolutely and without remainder. And while, because it is a self-making, it anticipates the future as possibility, because it is absolute, its anticipating of possibility is indistinguishable from its production of actuality. Indeed, it is senseless to speak here of either anticipating or possibility. Absolute or divine self-making, then, is only quasi-historical because it is eternal, or wholly present, a process symbolizable only as circular: for it is an absolute returning upon itself.[24] And yet this eternity *is* quasi-historical. Something really goes on. Its end is, and yet is not, identical with its beginning.[25]

To identify historicity proper, then, it will be necessary to distinguish it from mere temporality. But it will also be necessary to distinguish it from the quasi-historicity of eternity. And it will be seen that the concept of self-making marks historicity off from mere temporality; but that to mark it off from quasi-historical eternity another concept is needed, second in importance for the doctrine of historicity only to that of self-making itself. This is the concept of *situation*. Only a being which is a self-making-in-a-situation can be, in its ontological constitution, historical.

First, historicity differs from mere temporality. The temporal past survives in the present only as the present effect of past events. This is true even if the past is remembered, provided memory is regarded, not as a present act of recollection, but as a mere event to be understood solely in terms of past events. The past is historical only if, and to the extent that, it is capable of present appropriation and re-enactment. And human being is, qua being, historical only if such acts enter into its ontological constitution. If man has a permanent nature, then he may no doubt have an historical past; but his nature is not for that reason historical. But if man is a self-constituting process then the historical past must enter into his present being. For this process can constitute and re-constitute itself only if it appropriates and re-appropriates at least some of the past.

Again, the historical differs from the merely temporal future. The temporal future is present only in this sense, that the present is pregnant with but limited possibilities. This is true even if the future is feared or hoped for, provided fear and hope are understood as mere present effects of past events. The historical future is presently appropriated as anticipation. All free acting involves an anticipating, a projecting-into-future. Hence, if there is such a thing as free acting at all, there is also an historical as distinct from a merely temporal future. But only if human being is a self-making does this future enter into its present ontological constitution.[26]

Thus, finally, the historical differs from the merely temporal present. The temporal present is a vanishing point of passage. The historical present is an act of integration in which anticipated future possibilities are integrated with past actualities into present action. If man has a permanent nature, then such acts add up merely to what he *does*. But if his being is a self-making, then they constitute also what he is.

So much for the distinction between historicity and temporality. We now turn to the distinction between historicity and quasi-historical eternity. Most generally stated, historical being is historical – rather than quasi-historical and eternal – because its presently appropriated is ontologically distinct from its actual past, and because, in anticipating the future as a possibility, it does not *ipso facto* produce it as actuality.

The presently re-enacted past would differ from the actual past even if everything humanly capable of re-enactment could be re-enacted; that is, if historical consciousness could reproduce the whole historical past without omission or distortion. I cannot physically, but only in my imagination, re-fight the battle of Waterloo, if only because they who fought it are dead and gone. I cannot literally cope with the San Francisco earthquake, if only because the earthquake is irretrievably past; and if it occurred again it would be a different earthquake. Nor can I, by re-enacting my state of mind at the age of ten, become now ten years of age.

Again, my presently anticipated future would differ from the actual future even if I could anticipate with total accuracy everything capable of anticipation; that is, if I were endowed with the gift of prophetic omniscience. I cannot, by anticipating the actions of future generations, produce either the generations or their actions. Nor can I, by planning for presently predicted future natural catastrophes, produce now these catastrophes and enact my present plans. Indeed, merely by virtue of being planning, all planning is ontologically distinct from acting, and hence involves the distinction between possibility and actuality. Hence all planning is finite, simply by virtue of being planning; and an omniscient being would not plan at all.

Thus, finally, the historical differs from the quasi-historical or eternal present. It is an act of integration which is in principle incomplete. Its return-upon-itself is never absolute, but fragmented by the loss of a past which it cannot recapture, and by the refractoriness of a future which refuses to be subdued into presentness. It is, in short, a returning-upon-self within the limits of a *situation*.

These limits are many and varied in kind. But those thus far referred to are all of the same kind. Historical acts of self-making all occur on the basis and in the context of events which simply *happen*, independently of all acts of self-making; that is, of *natural events*. All historical acting occurs in a *natural situation*; otherwise it would not be historical at all.[27]

Historical being, then, differs in its ontological structure from temporal and eternal being alike. At its lowest, it may lapse into a dream-like flux barely distinct from a merely temporal passage. At its highest, it may rise to actions which make it seem to fall but little short of eternity. But it is only so long as it transcends temporality to some degree that it attains to humanity and historicity; and it is only so long as it does not transcend temporality absolutely – that is, so long as it remains finite – that it remains historical and human.

6 The Concept of Situation

We must now consider the relation between situation and situated self-making. That relation has a characteristic which is of the greatest importance for the further development of the doctrine of historicity. But it is easily overlooked or explained away.

We have seen that self-making, to be both human and historical, must be finite. But if the situation which situates it were not ontologically other than it, self-making could not be genuinely finite. Its limitations, such as they were, would be subject to possible elimination by acts of self-transcendence. On the other hand, if the situation were *wholly* other than the self-making it situates, then the latter would not be a finite self-making either. It would either be a simple product, and hence not a self-making at all, or else it would be subject only externally to bounds, unaffected by them in its inner structure. In the latter case, it would be finite in one respect, self-making in another. But we have already seen that this is impossible. It is by virtue of its historicity that human self-making is finite; yet only if historicity is permeated in its inner structure by temporality can it be historicity at all.

The relation between situation and situated self-making, then, is a dialectical relation. The situation which situates self-making must be other than it; and it must yet enter into its ontological constitution, thus losing some of its otherness.

This dialectical characteristic is easily ignored or explained away, but with grave consequences. To ignore the aspect of otherness in the situation is to lapse into the kind of idealism which regards all limitation of the self as the self's own self-limitation. And to stress nothing but the aspect of otherness is to lapse into the kind of naturalism for which the self is, in the end, the mere product of its environment.[28] Uneasily between these extremes would rest the attempt to dispose of dialectic by means of a dualistic doctrine, for which the self is, on the one hand, subject to external bounds, and on the other, unaffected by these bounds in its internal self-constitution.

Such a doctrine might identify the aspects of otherness in the situation with the *actual* limitations which it imposes on self-making, and the aspect of non-otherness with the self's *awareness* of these limitations. And it could point out that the self is subject to natural limitations quite regardless of its awareness of them; but that, once the self *is* aware of them, they have become part of its inner constitution.

But there can be no dualism between self and self-awareness – the former described as a simply passive, the latter as a simply active aspect of self-making. If the self qua subject to natural limitations were simply passive it would not – or not yet – be a self at all, since the self is *ex hypothesi* a process of self-making. And if awareness were wholly active, then the self would, in becoming aware of limitations, *ipso facto* transcend them; indeed, there would be no difference between self-awareness and self-images created at random. But the self, qua subject to limitations, is already a self and hence not simply passive; and self-awareness *is* self-awareness precisely because it does not, simply by virtue of being awareness, transcend the limitations which it is aware of: hence it is not simply active.

The conclusion then, is clear. If human being is a situated self-making, then the relation between it and the situation which situates it must be dialectical. Finite self-making must be understood as limited by a situation which is other than it, and which still enters into its internal constitution; and nevertheless finite self-making must *be* a self-making, not the mere product of external events. But how this dialectical relation manifests itself depends on the type of situation by which self-making is situated. Yet the only type thus far referred to is the natural situation.

7 The Concept of Historical Situation

But the concepts of self-making and natural situation are not yet sufficient to describe the structure of a being which is qua being historical. At least one further concept is needed – that of *historical situation.*

No one can doubt that there are historical situations. The sphere of possible human acting is circumscribed not only by natural events but also by other human actions. To deny this would be to deny the obvious.

The question is not, however, whether there are historical situations but whether they affect man's very being. If man has a permanent nature, then historical situations affect only its accidental manifestations. But if human being is a self-making, then, in affecting the possibilities of human acting, historical situations must affect also the possibilities of human being. The concept of historical situation must be, in that case, an ontological as well as an historical concept.[29]

If human being is a self-making, then there is need for two concepts of historical situation which are *prima facie* wholly distinct. First, an individual's present possibilities of acting are affected by his own past acting. On the one hand, he can do higher mathematics now because he has done lower mathematics in the past. On the other hand, because he has faced up to grief and sorrow he has lost his childlike innocence. No doubt an individual's past acts of self-making affect his present acts in varying degrees, from the lowest form of subconscious influence to the highest form of conscious recollection. But if human being is a self-making, they must all affect them to some degree. For personal identity is, in that case, nothing but the process which integrates past acts of self-making into present acts; and personality is a history which begins at birth and ends with death.

But there is need also for a second concept of historical situation, and of the two this indeed is the more obvious. The acting of men is affected by that of other men, as well as by their own. Mozart has created possibilities of experience which but for his work would not exist. And citizenship in a Greek city-state is a possibility lost for men of this century. If man has a permanent nature, then our specific twentieth-century situation is irrelevant to that nature and its essential possibilities; and the twentieth-century situation concerns only the historian, not the ontologist. But if human being is a self-making, then our twentieth-century situation is not irrelevant to the concerns of ontology. In circumscribing what contemporary man can experience and do, that situation, in that case, circumscribes also what contemporary man can be and is.[30]

What is the relation between historical situation and historically situated self-making, in the two senses just described? We have already dealt in general with the dialectical relation between situation and what it situates. What remains to be shown is how this applies to the historical situation.

Here, as everywhere, the situating must remain other than the situated, if the latter is to be situated at all. Still, historical otherness must differ from natural otherness. The natural situation simply limits; and the situated is free toward this limitation only in that it can accept it.[31] But the historically situating cannot simply limit the historically situated; for here the situating and the situated are both human action. Despite this fact, the historically situating must do *some* limiting, if what it situates is to be situated at all. But because of this fact, the historically situating augments as well as limits. For the freedom of the situated toward the situating cannot be confined to the acceptance of alien limitations. Because the situating and the situated are both human action, the freedom of the situated extends to the appropriating of aspects of the situating, that is, to the integrating of these into its own process of self-constitution. Natural facts such as lost childhood and present middle age are limitations which I can only accept. Historical facts such as the work of Mozart can become part of myself to the extent to which I can appropriate them. But in so far as I in fact do so, the historical other at once loses its otherness and augments my selfhood.

Unlike the natural situation, then, the historical situation both limits and augments what it situates; and it is the togetherness of both which alone can constitute a situation as historical. If the historically situated could ever appropriate the totality of what situates it historically, it would rise above history.[32] And if the historically situated were ever wholly incapable of appropriating any part of what situates it historically, it would fall below history. In both cases, history would be lost. Every historical situation, then, *qua* historical, is a conjunction of limitation and opportunity; as it were, of fate and freedom.

This conclusion gives rise to another which is no less important. Natural situations fall into types; and if and when they bring forth qualitative novelty it is, so to speak, by accident. But in the case of historical situations, the possibility of novelty is part and parcel of their essential structure. For any free and novel act enlarges the scope of subsequent acting, so long as it remains capable of being appropriated. But if human being is a self-making, this implies that the scope of human being differs from one historical situation to another; that, to the extent to which it is historically situated, man's very humanity differs from age to age.

8 Historicism

These conclusions give rise to the question with which we began this lecture. The question then was: does the doctrine of historicity imply the surrender of the idea of timeless metaphysical truth? We can now give a more precise formulation: if human being is an historically situated self-making, must all its activities be historically situated – metaphysics included?

Prima facie, the case against the metaphysical claim to timeless truth is overwhelming. First, if human being is a self-making, then metaphysics too must be a form of self-making. In rising to metaphysical knowledge, self-making may or may not be creating the truths to the knowledge of which it rises. But the knowledge itself must, at any rate, be part of the self-making process. And if metaphysical truth is transhistorical, then metaphysical knowledge must be a transhistorical form of self-making.

But secondly, a transhistorical form of self-making seems *prima facie* impossible. If man has a permanent nature, then it may be possible to distinguish between finite capacities and capacities such as that for metaphysical knowledge which transcend finitude. But if human being is a self-making, then such a distinction between aspects which leave each other unaffected is surely untenable. For the self-making process is one in which all aspects are integrated into a single whole; and it is only by virtue of this integration that the self attains to selfhood at all.

Thus the above-made distinctions are subject to qualification. No doubt one must distinguish, as we have distinguished, between the history which is the life of an individual, and the history which is the life of a civilization. But if human being is a self-making this distinction cannot be absolute. For individual self-making integrates into a present unity not only its own past actions but also the effect on it of the acts of others. Thus merely by virtue of living in the twentieth century, an individual is, qua individual, different from what he would have been had he lived in another century.

Further, we did undoubtedly well to distinguish between natural and historical situation. But if human being is a self-making, one cannot distinguish absolutely even between these. Who can doubt that at least man's attitude toward his natural limitations differs from one civilization to another? Moreover, bearing in mind the facts of modern technology, who can believe that even man's actual natural limitations are wholly unaffected by history?[33] The conclusion seems inescapable that, if human being is a self-making, it is *radically* historically situated; that there are no aspects of a man's being which are wholly unaffected by the historical situation in which he exists.

If this is the case, then how can metaphysics be an exception? The metaphysician may claim to be rising above history, to timeless truth. And the metaphysician who regards human being as a self-making may try to save this claim by interpreting metaphysics as a transhistorical form of self-making. But if human being is a self-making, must not the transhistorical integrate itself with the historical, and thus itself become infected with historicity? It may seem, then, that the distinction between the historical and the transhistorical, if admissible at all, is only a relative distinction; a distinction, that is, which appears absolute only to a standpoint which is itself historically situated.

This conclusion, if accepted, revolutionizes the very concept of metaphysics. Metaphysics, once regarded as aiming at timeless truth, is now reduced to an activity aiming at what *seems* timeless truth, from the standpoint and within the limits of an historical situation. All metaphysics, that is, is reduced to a sequence of historically relative *Weltanschauungen*.

The consequence of this is that metaphysics is in principle superseded by history. For, on the one hand, the metaphysician – the person who lives by a particular *Weltanschauung* – cannot recognize its historical relativity; for if he did he could no longer live by it. On the other hand, *somebody* must recognize the relativity of all *Weltanschauungen*, and in so doing he passes beyond all metaphysics. This somebody is the historian.

The historian's history of *Weltanschauungen* is, to be sure, forever incomplete in one sense; but it is forever complete in another. It is forever incomplete because, itself written from an historical standpoint, it must be rewritten in every age. But it is forever complete in that it leaves no room, beyond the history of metaphysics, for an independent inquiry into metaphysical truth.[34]

The position thus arrived at is known as historicism. This term has been given many meanings. But only one of these deserves to be called classical. Historicism, in the classical sense, is the position which asserts that all philosophical are superseded by historical questions. It is 'the assertion that the fundamental distinction between philosophical and historical questions cannot in the last analysis be maintained.'[35]

9 The Refutation of Historicism

But historicism is radically and unqualifiedly untenable; and if the doctrine of historicity necessarily led to historicism it would, for that reason alone, be untenable as well. History may stand in need of being rewritten in every age. The philosophy which recognizes this truth cannot itself stand in need of being so rewritten. All other acts of human self-making may be historically situated. The one exception must be the act by which self-making recognizes itself as self-making, and as historically situated. But if this exception is impossible, then the whole doctrine collapses in internal contradiction.

Historicism is faced with a dilemma from which there is no escape. Either it renounces all philosophical assumptions (but then it can make no philosophical assertions; it is, in fact, not historicism at all but simply history),[36] or else it insists that philosophical are superseded by historical questions (but then it is committed to philosophical assumptions which are ruled out by the thesis itself). In this chapter, we have endeavoured to outline the ontology which historicism, as a metaphysical position, would seem to require. But this ontology implies that historicism must be false.[37]

Thus one of the two questions which we ask in this lecture is answered in what would seem a thoroughly conclusive manner. The doctrine of historicity, far from implying the surrender of the ancient claim to timeless metaphysical truth, is on the contrary compelled to re-assert this claim, if it is not, like historicism, to collapse in internal inconsistency. And thus the most dangerous metaphysical assault ever made on the idea of timeless metaphysical truth has failed. And this failure emboldens us to predict that no similar assault will ever succeed. It would be hazardous indeed to predict the metaphysics of the future, or even that there will be a metaphysics in the future. But it would seem wholly safe to predict that, so long as there is metaphysics at all, it cannot abandon the notion of timeless metaphysical truth.

This crucial conclusion has weighty implications for the doctrine of historicity. It implies that that doctrine, in order to be tenable, must after all find room for transhistorical possibilities of self-making. Moreover, such possibilities, once granted in principle, can hardly be confined to philosophy. Can one dismiss Kierkegaard's claim that Christianity, if a possibility at all, must be substantially the same possibility in the nineteenth century that it was in the first? Can one dismiss the possibility of a radical religious conversion?[38] And can one deny that Mozart, were he alive and at work today, would only *per accidens* be a different Mozart? It would be rash indeed to exempt the arts wholly from historicity; and the example of modern art is enough to give even the rashest pause. At the same time, any single work of genius is a living witness testifying that the total historization of the arts is absurd.

10 Hegel

But what is true of many false but profound metaphysical doctrines is true of historicism. Refutation is easiest. More difficult is sympathetic understanding. Most difficult of all is what combines both: a genuine response to the challenge.[39]

Such a response was given before historicism ever appeared on the scene, in the philosophy of Hegel. Hegel perceived with the utmost clarity a truth wholly beyond the comprehension of historicism. If human being is a self-making, then it must be composed of both finite or situated and infinite or non-situated aspects. It must have finite or situated aspects, for otherwise it would not be human. And it must have infinite or non-situated aspects, for otherwise it would be incapable of philosophical self-recognition. Hegel further perceived that, if human being is a self-making, its finite and its infinite aspects must, and yet cannot, integrate themselves into a unity. They must do so because self-identity consists of precisely that integration. They cannot do so because neither aspect can reduce itself to the other. If the infinite reduced itself to the finite aspect, the result would be a relapse into historicism. And if the finite reduced itself to the infinite aspect, man would cease to be human. Hegel expressed all this in a single statement, remarkable enough to be considered a key statement in modern metaphysics: 'I raise myself in thought to the Absolute ... thus being infinite consciousness; yet at the same time I am finite consciousness. ... Both aspects seek each other and flee each other. ... I am the struggle between them.'[40]

And yet it is a fact that Hegel in the end let go of this struggle. No subsequent existential thinker exceeds Hegel in emphasis on man's human limitations. Nevertheless he ended up asserting the sublation of man's finite in his infinite aspect. To be sure, this assertion, like all of Hegel's assertions, was made for excellent reasons. For if man remains an unresolved struggle must not his finite infect his infinite aspect, thus rendering philosophy impossible?[41] Still, while few definitive judgments have as yet been made on Hegel, one such judgment has long been made, less by subsequent philosophers than by subsequent historical developments. Hegel's own transhistorical synthesis of the historical and the transhistorical was destroyed by the recalcitrance of subsequent history. And the same fate would befall any attempt to bring Hegelianism up to date. Indeed, it is only because of this failure on Hegel's part that historicism could appear on the scene even after Hegel himself had refuted it.[42]

11 The Concept of Human Situation

We are thus left with this inescapable conclusion: if the doctrine of historicity is to be maintained, human being must be understood, after all, as the Hegelian struggle between aspects which seek each other and flee each other; and that struggle must remain in principle unresolvable. The aspects must seek each other because human self-identity must be achieved, if not in integration, so at least in the search for integration. And the aspects must flee each other because if they found each other the result would be either a self-refuting historicism or else a Hegelian elevation of man above humanity. If human being is a self-making, then man is not merely accidentally involved in this unresolvable struggle. This struggle then constitutes what man *is*.

This conclusion, we say, is inevitable. But it gives rise to one crucial question: can human being be this struggle and yet be capable of rising to philosophic self-understanding?

This question has received an answer of the utmost profundity, from the existential philosophers of our own time. According to their teaching, human being manifests, in a thousand forms, the unresolvable struggle which is its essence. But one or some of these forms are qualitatively distinct from all the others, because in these human being *recog-*

nizes itself as a struggle which is in principle unresolvable. This recognition must itself be a form of the struggle, for if it rose above it the struggle would not be unresolvable. At the same time, it is a qualitatively unique form because it understands the struggle, in principle and as a whole.

This doctrine implies a revolutionary concept of metaphysical cognition. In other forms of cognition, the knower may assume the standpoint of a detached subject viewing an object or a world of objects. The self-as-struggle which knows itself as struggle cannot adopt such a standpoint. For to do so would be to break up the reality of unresolvable struggle into two pseudo-realities: a subject which, being a detached spectator, is not involved in the struggle; and an object which, being a mere object-*for*-understanding but qua object incapable of *self*-understanding, is not involved in the decisive struggle, either. If human being is unresolvable struggle, then it cannot achieve philosophical self-understanding through the kind of cognition achieved by a spectator – a definition given *ab extra*. The definition required must be a *self*-definition; and this can spring only from existential attempts at radical self-transcendence, in which human being, seeking to rise above the unresolvable struggle which is its essence, recognizes its radical limitations by foundering in the attempt.[43]

These attempts must be radically individual, made by each person for himself. But the knowledge attained through them is radically universal. For this is not a person's mere knowledge of his personal situation. It is his knowledge that he is both in principle situated and yet able to recognize his situatedness. This knowledge is universal; and the person who has acquired it has risen to philosophical self-understanding.

It follows, then, that existential philosophy must introduce yet another crucial concept into the ontology of human self-making; and this concept, once introduced, surpasses the concepts of natural and historical situation in significance. The new concept is that of *human situation*.[44]

This concept is additional to those of natural and historical situation. But the human situation is not a source of additional limitations. Rather, it is the ontological ground of both the natural and the historical situation, and is in turn individuated only in these. Correspondingly, the recognition of the human situation cannot be divorced from that of the natural and the historical situation; it is achieved when the natural and the historical situation are understood radically, as specific manifestations of a universal condition. It is the radicalization of the natural and of the historical situation which discloses the human situation.

This radicalization, however, achieves a qualitatively new insight. A person discovers his natural situation when he comes upon such individual limits as his lost childhood, a disease which afflicts him, or the frailties of old age. He discovers his human situation when he sees, in the foundering attempt at radical self-transcendence, that temporality and mortality are universally part of the human lot. Again, a person discovers his historical situation when he faces up, say, to the unique historical limitations and opportunities of the nuclear age. He comes upon his human situation when he recognizes that all history is a conjunction of compulsion and freedom, and that to be subject to the one and to be challenged to realize the other is universally part of the human condition.[45]

Thus the human situation manifests itself only in the natural and the historical situation, and is yet irreducible to them. And the recognition of the human situation occurs only in and through that of the natural and the historical situation; yet it achieves a universality which marks it off from these latter forms of knowledge. It is the very acceptance of a particular and indeed unique limitation, whether natural or historical, which achieves philosophical universality in the moment of radical anxiety in which a man, recognizing his ultimate finiteness and yet bound to it even in the moment of recognition, is brought face-to-face with Nothingness.[46] And it is the very grasp of a unique historical opportunity, different from all others, which nevertheless becomes a paradigm of what all human freedom is, in the awe-inspiring moment in which there is acceptance of responsibility for humanity as a whole.[47]

So much for the existential concept of human situation. We must now consider two of its implications, which are of the utmost importance for our present purpose. The first of these is startling indeed. It is the need for a radical revision of the whole doctrine of human self-making.

So long as one grants only the natural situation, one admits, to be sure, an other-than-man, as a condition of human self-making. But this other does not constitute, in any way, human being in so far as it is distinctively human. And so long as one grants only, in addition, the historical situation, one does indeed admit something other than self-making which contributes to the constitution of its very humanity; for self-making integrates part of the historical other into its own self, and without this other it could not constitute itself at all. But the historical other is not, after all, other-than-human but merely other than the particular self-making which it situates. In short, so long as only natural and historical situation are granted, as necessary conditions of human self-making, the conditions admitted do not threaten the autonomy of self-making itself. Human being, qua being and qua human, can be understood as at least collectively a wholly autonomous human product.

But this is no longer possible once the concept of human situation is accepted. For on the one hand, the humanly situating, like the naturally situating, is not human. On the other hand, it contributes, like the historically situating, to the constitution of man in so far as he is distinctively human. This does not mean that the human situation reduces human being to a mere product; for like every situation, the human situation must stop short of this. But it does mean that the humanly situated must be something less than, and qualitatively different from, an autonomous self-making. For like every situation, the human situation is other than what it situates and yet enters into its internal constitution. But the other in this case is radically other than human being, and yet helps constitute it *qua* human.

This, then, is the radical revision required by the concept of human situation of the doctrine of human self-making: *human being must be understood as something more than a mere product, and yet as something less than a self-making. Instead of a self-constituting, it must rather be the accepting or choosing of something already constituted, and yet also not constituted, because the accepting or choosing is part of its essence.* Thus once more we have come upon a dialectical relation between the situating and the situated. But in the present case – that of the humanly situating and the humanly situated – this dialectic focuses on the relation between the self qua accepted and the self qua accepting, or between the self that is chosen and the self that does the choosing.

This dialectic is of the greatest subtlety. The self that is chosen must already be a self, for otherwise the self that chooses would not choose but make itself. And yet the chosen self cannot be a self, ready-made apart from the choice, for then there would be no essential choice; and the self as a whole would be a mere product. Correspondingly, the self that chooses must originate in its act of choice, for otherwise it could not choose itself but only this or that. And yet if it wholly originated in its act of self-choice it would be self-production. What emerges from this dialectic is the distinction – fundamental in every form of existential thought – between self and *authentic* self. The self is self whether or not it chooses itself. But only through self-choice does it become authentic self.[48]

However the dialectic of self and authentic self may further be developed, it is clear that the replacement of the doctrine of self-making with a doctrine of self-choosing has in turn a most weighty consequence concerning metaphysics as a whole. So long as human being is understood as a self-making, metaphysics as a human enterprise must clearly be regarded as part of the self-making process. And this in turn compels one at least to entertain the possibility that the truths known by metaphysics too are affected by human self-making, that man has at least a share in creating the realm to the knowledge of which his metaphysics rises.[49]

But once human being is understood as a humanly situated self-choosing, this possibility is at once wholly excluded. For what situates man humanly is not produced by man but on the contrary the condition of all human producing. And in rising to metaphysics man recognizes this fact; but in recognizing it he recognizes the otherness of the Other that situates him. This Other is the Other *par excellence.*

In this recognition the Other must, and yet cannot, remain wholly unknown. It must remain unknown, for if human being were to know It it would cease to be situated by It. Hence all supposed knowledge of this Other is but pseudo-knowledge, due to pseudo-detachment from, or pseudo-transcendence of, the human situation. And yet this Other cannot remain wholly unknown. For to know its otherness is to have passed beyond simple ignorance. We have seen that existential metaphysics originates in the recognition of man's human situation, as a dialectical mystery. We now see that this metaphysics culminates in pointing, as to a vastly greater mystery, to the ultimate Other which situates man humanly. And this pointing-to is itself dialectical. It expresses an ignorance which knows the grounds of this ignorance, or a knowledge which knows that it is ignorant, and why. The Other that is pointed to thus remains undefined, and is yet given names. But the names express Mystery. They do not disclose It.[50]

12 Conclusion

In this chapter, we have endeavoured to show that the doctrine of historicity requires the assumption that human being is a self-constituting process; and what doctrinal provisions must be made once that initial assumption is granted. But why should that initial assumption be made at all? Why should human being be regarded as a self-constituting process? This is a question which we have thus far failed to raise. Hence our whole discourse, thus far, is a mere fragment; as it were, an incomplete metaphysical hypothesis.

It must, we fear, remain such an hypothesis. For it is much too late to deal properly with a question which requires solid treatment in its own right. And our concluding remarks can do no more than stress the need for such a treatment.

The doctrine of human being as a self-making was first put forward, under the influence of Kant, in opposition to three competing doctrines; and against two of these it won a resounding victory. The first was the kind of substantialism which, regarding the human self as no less ready-made than matter, offered a mere caricature of selfhood. The second was the Humean kind of mental process which, being a simple rather than a self-constituting process, does not deserve to be called mental at all. To be sure, the war on these two doctrines has had to be re-fought again and again. For empiricism has the habit of raising its head, no matter how often and how decisively it is refuted; and the same is true of attempts to reduce the self to the non-self which, however disguised as naturalism, evolutionism, or behaviourism, are never very far from crude materialism. The war has always had to be re-fought; but it has always been re-won: by Heidegger, Jaspers, and Collingwood in our own age no less decisively than by Fichte, Schelling, and Hegel in theirs.[51]

But the doctrine of human self-making was originally asserted also against a third doctrine: the classical doctrine of a permanent human nature. And the history of this conflict, unlike the other two, has been complex and ambiguous.

Kant's immediate followers did not object primarily, or even at all, to the notion of human permanence. What they did object to was the notion of a human nature, that is, to the notion of a reality ready-made prior to the self's own acting, and yet fully human. Thus Fichte held that the self had to be wholly self-produced in order to be a self at all; and that to regard it as in any sense constituted by another – even if that Other were God – was both metaphysically and morally intolerable.[52]

But subsequent history shows a steady retreat from the extreme Fichtean position. Already Schelling and Hegel insist that the self requires a background other than itself for its self-constitution, although they are idealistic enough to believe that in the highest form of the self's self-constitution no aspect of otherness remains.[53] A far more radical retreat is carried out by Kierkegaard. Kierkegaard lays no less stress than his predecessors on the self as a process of self-activity. Possibly he even exceeds them in emphasis. For that being-a-self is a responsibility rather than a given fact is a thesis which is stated in his writings with unmatched pathos. At the same time, he radically breaks with the idealism of his predecessors. And the essence of the break lies in his insistence on existential limitations which, being universally human, define man's very humanity. Hence idealistic self-making reduces itself to existential self-choosing: to the appropriating acceptance of a gift which is, and yet is not, fully real before the gift is accepted.

Viewing the history of this retreat, one may well wonder whether the whole doctrine of human self-making must not be abandoned altogether, in favour of the classical doctrine of a human nature. After all, even Aristotle did not deny that a specifically human characteristic such as rationality is not actual until man himself actualizes it; yet this did not prevent him from regarding it as a potentiality grounded in human nature. What if speculative thought can contemplate the human situation, as described by existential philosophers, and identify a human nature as its ontological ground?

But at least one crucial objection would be made to such a project by thinkers such as Kierkegaard, Jaspers, and Buber. They would object that the self cannot qua self become an object of speculative thought; and that to treat it as such is incompatible with the demands to be made in behalf of selfhood. They would insist that the human situation can only be existentially encountered, not made an object of detached thought, and that hence any attempt to discover a human nature as the ground of the human situation is doomed from the start. And when offered a concept of human nature, no matter what particular concept it might be, they would no doubt dismiss it, as a mere objectifying construction.

Does the classical doctrine of a human nature have the resources to meet this objection? More generally, can it assimilate the insights into selfhood, achieved from Kant and Fichte down to Heidegger and Collingwood, without suffering collapse in this process of assimilation? Can it, perhaps, mount a counter-attack, based on the indispensability of speculative thought? For that existential philosophy cannot wholly dispense with such thought is all too obvious.[54] These are vital questions; and they invite what might well become the most profound metaphysical dialogue in our time.

One fact, above all, augurs well for such a dialogue. In its existential form, the doctrine of human self-making has been driven to the conclusion that a reality other than man has a share in the constitution of human being qua being and qua human: a reality which cannot be either nature which is less than human, or historical action which is only human. But this is a view which the classical doctrine of human nature has held or implied all along.

13 Epilogue

The British Museum Library possesses a Schelling volume with marginal notes by no less a person than Samuel Taylor Coleridge. On page 9 of the volume Schelling writes: 'Ich bin, weil ich bin. Das ergreift jeden plötzlich.' 'I am because I am. This truth seizes hold, all of a sudden, of everyone.' Writing under Fichte's influence, Schelling here asserts that the self is the absolute source of its self-constitution, and that in great moments it becomes intuitively aware of this fact. Coleridge comments, naively and yet with the utmost profundity: 'Jeden?' 'Everyone? I doubt it. Many may say: I am because God made me.'[55]

9 The Historicity and Transcendence of Philosophic Truth

'Whenever we situate the divine within the historical we always fall into the fluctuation and changeability that is proper to everything historical.'
Hegel

Introduction

The paper which follows is meant to be self-contained, and independently intelligible and defensible. But limitations of time forced me to write it very tightly, and to give only bare hints, both of the wider context into which its argument belongs, and of the use made of the history of philosophy. I have therefore thought it wise to add some introductory notes.

(i) The paper is limited to *philosophic* truth; the fact that 'I am writing these words now' will not be true tomorrow does not come under scrutiny. This is enough to rule out any attempt to give a general definition of truth. As for a specific definition of philosophic truth, this emerges in the paper only incompletely because it is held (with Hegel and Heidegger – despite the scarce references to Hegel in the paper, his spirit lurks in it everywhere) that such a definition ought to emerge from the context of discourse. Discourse here is directly focused, not on the nature of philosophic truth, but on its historicity and/or transcendence.

(ii) The core of the paper is an interpretation of, and argument with, the earlier and later Heidegger. But the sections which precede those devoted to that task are by no means inessential. They seek to establish a context quite different from the Heideggerian, and implicitly or explicitly repudiate basic but questionable – or at least not self-evident – Heideggerian assertions.[1]

(a) In the early and certainly in the later Heideggerian view, the eternal verities of the *philosophia perennis* are a mere (albeit historically inevitable) mistake, deriving from an original forgetting-of-Being; and the exposure of the mistake (also historically conditioned, if not inevitable) ends it. The present paper suspends any such judgment, and treats the loss or surrender of eternal verities by modern philosophers as merely a contingent fact. Hence its entire argument is only hypothetical, and the question whether or not modern philosophy can recover eternal verities remains unanswered.

(b) In Heidegger's view, nothing radically new has occurred in the history of Western philosophy from Plato to Nietzsche; and his own quest for Being is a wholly new, albeit historically conditioned, departure. In the view developed in this paper, the radically new occurrence in the history of Western philosophy – at least so far as the historicity and/or transcendence of philosophic truth is concerned – is the Kantian philosophy; the Heideggerian philosophy is only the last (although the most radical, and among contemporary philosophies the most significant) manifestation of a revolution initiated not by Heidegger but by Kant. It is not possible here even to sketch the interpretation of Kant on which this view rests. It must suffice simply to say that this interpretation is much indebted to Heidegger's Kant-interpretation,[2] and yet fundamentally critical of its failure to do justice to, or indeed to take account of, the Kantian primacy of practical reason.[3]

(c) In the later Heideggerian view, the metaphysical *ratio*[4] is not only superseded, but in its claim to transcendence also dissipated, by a higher 'recalling' thinking whose truth is historical; hence all 'rational' argument between philosophies across the ages is impossible. This paper assumes that such an argument *is* possible, and hence that the Heideggerian and earlier philosophies may conceivably be subject to a common standard; and it bolsters this assumption with the argument (1) that the earlier Heideggerian philosophy has a common ground with philosophies since Kant; and (2) that *any* 'recalling' thinking such as is called for by the later Heidegger must make use of the metaphysical *ratio* in the very act of superseding it; hence that it cannot dissipate its claim to transcendence and universality.

(d) Because of its failure wholly to face up to the last-named fact, the Heideggerian philosophy is for all its radicalism in decisive respects a less adequate statement of the issue of the historicity and/or transcendence of philosophic truth than some philosophies which preceded it. If time permitted, the paper would go beyond its present conclusion, and resume an argument, left inconclusive, between the Hegelian and Schelling's 'positive' philosophy. Unlike Heidegger, Hegel confronts the finitude of the human *ratio, and also* the fact that the thinking which confronts it cannot dissipate the *ratio*; and he seeks to resolve this impasse by means of a self-elevation of the finite human *ratio* to divine infinity. Schelling's 'positive' philosophy is a confused, inconclusive, but nevertheless radical and profound exploration of the alternative. The *ratio* both remains finite and recognizes its finitude; hence it is limited to a 'negative' philosophy which points beyond itself. But can the 'Being' which is beyond the *ratio*, and to which the *ratio* points, both *be* beyond the *ratio* and yet establish rather than destroy the pointing *ratio*? The 'positive' philosophy gives no adequate answer to this question; but it states the question with a profundity which (despite valuable insights added by left-wing Hegelians, phenomenologists, and existentialists) is unmatched until this day.[5]

(e) Even those who would doubt or deny that the Hegelian is superior to the Heideggerian philosophy, as regards the 'ontological' concept of historicity, may still be persuaded of the superiority of the Hegelian over the Heideggerian 'ontic' judgments upon history. (In the case of neither thinker are such judgments a matter of philosophic irrelevance.) The later Heidegger seems to suggest that contemporary philosophy speaks German only, just as the ancient was confined to Greek;[6] and he explicitly states that Germany is the centre of Europe, that the quest for Being is connected with the fate of Europe, and that the fate of Europe determines the fate of the earth.[7] Hegel was incapable of such a German, or even European, parochialism – to call it nothing worse. He suggested that the World-Spirit might emigrate to America, even at a time when Europe and Germany were at a cultural peak from which they were soon to tumble. Today, he would without question be open to those stirrings which may well mark the end of the hegemony of Western culture and of white man.

(iii) This paper is a further development of one aspect of my *Metaphysics and Historicity*.[8] That work, however, centres on the theme of selfhood, whereas this paper ignores that theme. This is not because of limitations of time alone. In the thinking of the later Heidegger, selfhood no longer plays an essential role. Despite this fact, and contra Heidegger, philosophic truth and selfhood may well be intrinsically connected. But whether or not this is the case requires an independent examination which cannot here be given.

(iv) The external occasion of this paper was a personal letter to me by Professor Leo Strauss, in which he criticized my disposal of the historicism of the later Heidegger.[9] His criticism convinced me of the inadequacy of my merely formal-dialectical 'refutation,' which was in fact anticipated by Heidegger himself.[10] The present paper is an attempt to come more deeply to grips with Heidegger's historicism. And I am indebted to Professor Strauss for making me more fully aware of its challenge – as well as for his tireless insistence that the eternal verities of the *philosophia perennis* must not be lightly or thoughtlessly dismissed.

I

For the tradition known as *philosophia perennis*, the expression 'historicity of philosophic truth' is a contradiction in terms. The philosopher escapes from the cave of history into a realm of eternity, and not until he has done so has he reached philosophic truth. Historical circumstances may favour or hamper this attainment. They are in either case accidental to the truth attained.

It does not at first sight seem necessary, or indeed possible, to abolish or even qualify this sharp dichotomy between philosophic truth and history when modern philosophers suffer the loss of, or abandon, the eternal realm of the *philosophia perennis*. For philosophic thought seeks radical universality, and the truths to which it lays claim transcend history even if they encompass not eternity but merely all time or all history. And so inescapably is philosophic thought bound up with universality as to remain universal even in its disclaimers to universality. Nothing compels a man to enter into the circle of the philosophic *ratio*. But it *does* seem that, once having entered into it, he can find no philosophic means of escape from it.

Thus it should cause no surprise that to the widespread modern surrender or loss of the eternal realm of the *philosophia perennis* corresponds no equally widespread surrender of claims to universal, and hence transcendent, philosophic truth. Heracliteans may cast all things into time – except their Heracliteanism. Empiricists may reduce all knowledge to the history of sense – except their empiricism which does the reducing. Historicism – this alone a strictly modern phenomenon – seems at first sight no exception to the rule. For those who would bind all truth to specific historical situations cannot so dispose of the truth of historicism itself.

Nor is there *prima facie* force to the objection that philosophic thought does not always, and perhaps does not ever wholly, lay hold of the truths it seeks. For the defects of philosophic thought seem only *per accidens* due to the historical circumstances in which it is formulated, and in essence due to its partial or total failure to meet the standards of rational argument. And it is on this failure, not on their respective historical situations, that philosophers fasten when they engage in argument across the ages. Thus emerges *one* universe of philosophic discourse.

II

But it would be rash to dismiss the claims of history upon philosophic truth too lightly. Indeed, once the eternal realm of the *philosophia perennis* is lost or abandoned, these claims cannot be dismissed at all, and the question then arises whether historicity permeates philosophic truth so thoroughly as to destroy every vestige of transcendence.

The loss of an eternal realm of truth may not necessarily mean the loss of all universal truth. Not unnaturally, modern philosophers are tempted to throw in their lot wholly with the physical sciences, which seek universal truths of fact. But, first, these truths belong to the province of these sciences, and philosophy becomes the mere second-order inquiry into them. And secondly, it is not certain whether these truths are, as philosophic truth aims to be, absolutely universal, or merely relatively so. Does Einsteinian physics grasp universal truths about the universe, or merely truths universal to an historically limited understanding? If the latter, are not the second-order philosophic truths merely historical truths about Einsteinian science, not transcendent truths about science?

History looms still larger when the philosopher throws in his lot with the social rather than the physical sciences. In the case of the latter, it is presumably the knowledge alone which is historical.[11] In that of the former, the reality may well be historical as well.[12] A present social scientist may assert universal truths about man. A future historian may show historical limitations in these truths – if truths they are – as regards both subject and object; i.e., that they represent, not the universal view of the social scientist but, say, the historical view of the mid-twentieth-century American social scientist; and that their object is not man, but, say, mid-twentieth-century American man. But if historicity invades the first-order truths of the social sciences must it not likewise invade the second-order truths of the philosophy of the social sciences?

But so long as one confines philosophical attention to the sciences one may conceivably deny the claim of history upon philosophic truth; one does not, in any case, come upon the source of that claim. The scientist may conceivably step outside history; but he is, abstractly, a spectator of the world, and the world is, abstractly, his object. Existing man cannot step outside history. For he is involved in the world, and his knowledge of it is one of involvement; and the world known and the knowledge are both historical. This is a world marked by certainty mixed with risk, planning mingled with gamble, factual appraisal along with evaluation and the need for decision, fear, guilt, and death as well as joy, faith, and hope. John Dewey called it the world of experience. We shall here use the less ambiguous, well-established German equivalent, *Lebenswelt.*

How can philosophic thought relate itself to the *Lebenswelt?* The *philosophia perennis* was *independent* of it, and yet possessed *standards* by which to *judge* it; for its eternal truths included the Good, the Beautiful, the Holy. A philosophy bereft of an eternal realm, however, has no such standards. It merely confronts, in the *Lebenswelt,* a history of *beliefs* in the Good, the Beautiful, the Holy. And if it seeks to preserve its truths in a transcendent purity free of all historical taint, it cannot enter into history and become a partisan in the history of the conflicting beliefs. It must adopt toward the *Lebenswelt* what may be called a strategy of indiscriminateness. The man who exists in the *Lebenswelt* may discriminate and choose between claims to truth. The philosopher who reflects on these claims judges that they are, equally and indiscriminately, mere opinion, unworthy of a *philosopher's* acceptance; for they cannot be *known* to be true. Or he may even judge that they are, equally and indiscriminately, unworthy of *anyone's* acceptance; for they cannot *be* true. (Thus logical positivism reduces all moral, aesthetic, and religious truths to mere illusory objectifications.) The *philosophia perennis* could *both* possess transcendent truths *and* discriminate, in terms of these truths, between claims to truth made in the *Lebenswelt.* Without an eternal realm, philosophy can keep its truths free of all historical taint only at the cost of loosing this discriminating power. The transcendent truths have become so meagre as to force the philosopher either to wash his hands, indiscriminately, of the claims to truth made in the *Lebenswelt,* or else indiscriminately to destroy them.

But such a philosophic stance gives rise to a war between claims to truth made *in* the *Lebenswelt,* and philosophic truths asserted *about* these claims; a war for which the *philosophia perennis* has no precedent. The philosopher may adopt a strategy of indiscriminateness toward the

Lebenswelt. The man who lives in that world cannot do likewise, but on the contrary *must* discriminate and choose, i.e., accept *some* of the claims to truth made in the *Lebenswelt* as *being* true. And in this very act of discriminating choice he testifies against the philosopher. To his indiscriminate philosophic destruction he opposes a discriminating affirmation – which the philosopher must share, if not qua philosopher, qua man. And to his indiscriminate detachment he opposes a discriminating commitment – which the philosopher can avoid only so long as he remains a spectator. His testimony *in* the *Lebenswelt,* in short, shows either the falsehood, or at least the inadequacy, of the philosophic doctrine *concerning* the *Lebenswelt. This* war between life and philosophy is one which philosophy cannot win.

This points to one conclusion. Having lost the eternal world of the *philosophia perennis,* philosophic thought cannot keep itself unsullied by history but must rather become involved with history, i.e., with the discriminating between claims to truth which occurs in the *Lebenswelt.* Having lost its goal in eternity, it requires roots in history; or, to use another well-established German term, a *Sitz im Leben.* This conclusion, however, gives rise to a fundamental problem, which is in fact the sole concern of this paper. *How can philosophic thought be rooted in history, and emerge from history, and yet reach a truth which is transcendent?* For, as will be seen, philosophic thought can reach nothing less and still be philosophical.

III

The problem just stated is in evidence in much current 'ordinary'-language-philosophy. For here the strategy of indiscriminateness toward the *Lebenswelt,* adopted by logical positivism, is systematically abandoned. 'Ordinary' language *is* the language of the *Lebenswelt;* and ordinary-language-philosophy makes no indiscriminate judgments of its meaningfulness or meaninglessness, but rather discriminating judgments of what meaning it has.

But at least as thus far developed, ordinary-language-philosophy seems to reflect the stated problem rather than to confront it. Must philosophy examine the logic of *any* ordinary language – the moral language of a Himmler as well as a Schweitzer, or the religious language of *Mein Kampf* as well as the Bible? But while in that case it preserves its transcendence of history it remains committed to the strategy of indiscriminateness adopted by its positivistic ancestor. Or is it confined to the logic of the *true* ordinary language? But then it becomes involved in history, in the *Lebenswelt,* in the first-order commitments of ordinary language; and the question is how it can achieve transcendence. For the most part, current ordinary-language-philosophy would appear to evade rather than confront this crucial question – an indication that its emancipation from logical positivism is as yet incomplete.

IV

The question is confronted rather than evaded in a European tradition initiated by the Kantian philosophy. To be sure, Kant himself shows as yet few signs of recognizing that the *Lebenswelt* is an historical world. He does, however, take the *Lebenswelt* seriously, as well as hold that at least some philosophic truth has its *Sitz im Leben* in it. Moreover, three conclusions, arrived at by Kant, who does not yet give history its due, will be seen to re-emerge as inescapable after attempts have been made radically to historize both the *Lebenswelt* and all philosophical truth. (It is to argue the last-named point that Kant's thought is here briefly considered.)

Kant rejects the view that all knowledge is object-knowledge, obtained by a spectator. Some knowledge is obtained by the participant who is forced to act in the *Lebenswelt*. Thus of moral obligation I do not say 'it is certain' but 'I am certain.' Yet the latter certainty is not only no less certain than the former but also, more importantly, no less objective. I do not merely *feel* obligated but *am* obligated: the *certainty* is of a *truth*. Independent of object-knowledge, this certainty is independent also of philosophy. I do not need philosophy in order to know that I am morally obligated; and if I did not have this knowledge, philosophy could not furnish it. Indeed it is the philosophical knowledge which depends on the moral knowledge. I *do* have philosophical knowledge of my moral freedom, but only because it is presupposed by the obligation of which I have moral knowledge. Further, the range of the philosophical does not exceed the range of the moral knowledge. For I can understand only the fact of my freedom, not its nature, and certainly not its nature from the standpoint of God.

But then does not philosophic *reduce itself* to moral knowledge? It does not, for between them obtains a *mutual* dependence. Obligation is the *ratio cognoscendi* of freedom. Freedom is the *ratio essendi* of obligation. I *believe* that I am free because I believe that I am morally obligated. Only if I *am* free can the belief in my being-obligated *be* a *true* belief. Philosophic thought achieves a transcendent grasp of the whole structure of experience, and thus can demonstrate the *possibility* of my freedom. Thus the sophisticated moral consciousness is enabled to do what the naive does anyhow, i.e., assert, along with the actuality of obligation, the *actuality* of freedom.

Three conclusions relative to this paper emerge from the above-sketched doctrines. First, freedom is a transcendent philosophic truth, tested against the whole range of human experience: it *is* a truth, not merely a necessary – albeit, from a scientific standpoint, fictitious – presupposition of morality. Secondly, this philosophic truth, while transcendent, has a *Sitz* in the *Lebenswelt,* not a dwelling place in eternity: it does not extend but only authenticates the knowledge of moral obligation which exists in the *Lebenswelt.* The third conclusion is the most important, for it makes possible the coexistence of the other two: *the moral truth which is the* Sitz im Leben *of the philosophic truth is 'universal and necessary.'* Only on this condition can the philosophic truth which *has* this moral truth for a *Sitz im Leben* itself be universal and necessary, i.e., philosophical. Not without cause does Kant claim that the moral knowledge of obligation and the philosophic knowledge of freedom have a common source: they are both manifestations of 'reason.'

V

But *is* the Kantian moral truth, if a truth at all, universal and necessary? Only by virtue of abstraction from history. (i) I ought to do what anyone else in my place ought to do: but my place may well be historically unique. (ii) My obligation does not extend beyond my freedom: but my freedom is limited by historical conditions. (iii) The *Lebenswelt* includes more than moral claims to truth. What of aesthetic truths of creative insight, existential truths of care, anxiety, guilt, and death, the religious truth of a redemptive Presence? Once adopting a *Sitz im Leben* at all, can philosophic thought long avoid facing *all* claims to truth made in the *Lebenswelt,* and avoid facing them as such totalities as are intended by yet another well-established German term, i.e., *Weltanschauungen?*[13]

To face up to the *concrete Lebenswelt,* however, is to recognize that it is an *historical* world; that the claims to truth made by *Weltanschauungen* conflict and change; and that, the eternal realm of the *philosophia perennis* having vanished, no recourse is possible, for a discriminating choice, to timeless standards of truth which transcend history. And with this insight the spectre of historicism comes on the scene. What if the philosophic claim to transcendent truth is a mere built-in illusion? What if philosophic truth is not a grasp of totality but at most such a grasp from the perspective and within the limits of an historical situation? How can philosophic thought have as a *Sitz* a *Weltanschauung* within the historical world and yet reach a transcendent grasp *of* the historical world?

Two nineteenth-century answers are instructive. Hegel answers: if the philosophic grasp of history occurs at the end of history.[14] History has not ended in Hegel's own time in any manifestly absurd sense: external history goes on. It *has* ended in that the essential human-historical possibilities – i.e., the *Weltanschauungen* – are in idea consummated. Hence whereas prior philosophies reflect historical *Weltanschauungen* Hegel's own philosophy marks their end. It is total comprehension.

But what if our philosophic thought, too, occurs in the midst of history? This is the main burden of Marx's and Nietzsche's anti-Hegelian protests. According to the protests, Hegel's thought does not comprehend the history of the *Lebenswelt.* It is merely the ideology of the *bourgeois*-Christian world, and a monument to its decadence. And a new future *Lebenswelt* will supersede both the *bourgeois*-Christian world and its Hegelian comprehension.

But then why are Marx's and Nietzsche's own philosophies not mere ideologies – the one reflecting the *Lebenswelt* of the alienated proletariat, the other, that of an alienated individual aware of his alienation from the Christian world? If they were, they could not, as they both do, point to the end of history: in the one case, to a post-historical classless society; in the other, to an overman, post-historical because capable of surrender to an eternal recurrence.[15] How then can their philosophic thought – which, unlike Hegel's, occurs in the midst of history – achieve, like Hegel's, a transcendent grasp of history?

Only if the situation in which it occurs is one of *crisis,* and one of *final* and hence *universal* crisis. The proletariat is *absolutely* alienated, hence representing *all* mankind in its crisis. And European-Christian culture is *radically* decadent, hence marking the death of *all* gods. Only on this condition can the future pointed to by Marx and Nietzsche be as surely the end of history as the present comprehended by Hegel.

The Hegelian and the anti-Hegelian philosophies have two things in common. First, while having a *Sitz im Leben* in history they reach a transcendent grasp of history. Secondly, they can do so only because this *Sitz,* while unlike the Kantian historical, is like the Kantian 'universal and necessary.'[16]

VI

But what if philosophic thought occurs neither at the end nor in the final crisis of history, but rather in the midst of a history with a wholly open future? A philosophic thought in need of a *Sitz im Leben* cannot then encompass history but threatens to be encompassed by it, the reflection of a mere *Weltanschauung* to be followed by other, unpredictable *Weltanschauungen*. Are not the *Lebenswelt* and philosophy both reduced to radical historicity? Historicism seems inescapable.

But the reduction to historicity, were it total, could not come to consciousness. There could be historically situated *Weltanschauungen*: not historicism, which is not itself a *Weltanschauung* but rather a *Weltanschauungslehre*, i.e., the doctrine concerning the historicity of *all Weltanschauungen*. And the truth claimed for *this* doctrine is not historical but transcendent. It is this contradiction which was noted at the beginning of this paper.

But after the intervening reflections it is no longer sufficient to dispose of historicism by means of a charge of formal self-contradiction. For it has emerged that, given the loss of eternal truths, philosophical thought requires a *Sitz im Leben*, and that the *Lebenswelt* is historical. Historicism is an impasse arising from these circumstances; and it calls, not for charges of formal self-contradiction only, but also for an inquiry into whether, and if so how, the *Lebenswelt* can provide a *Sitz*, *both* for the historically situated *Weltanschauungen and* the philosophical insight into their historicity. No work has undertaken this task as radically and comprehensively as Martin Heidegger's *Sein und Zeit*.

The relevant doctrines of that work may be stated as follows:

(i) Philosophic thought must turn its back on the eternal truths of the *philosophia perennis*[17] and hence preface its quest for Being with an existential analysis of *Dasein*;[18] this latter is historical, not *per accidens*, but in its essential constitution.[19]

(ii) The existential analysis of *Dasein* is not a contingent *historical* manifestation of *Dasein* but rather the understanding of the *structure* of its *historicity*. Its truth, while not 'eternal,' is not historical but transcendent. For 'the basic factual possibilities'[20] which it discloses *are* basic only because they are *exhaustive*. *The transcendent truth of* Dasein's *historicity both incorporates historicism and transcends and refutes it.*

(iii) But how is this refutation possible? The existential analysis is not by a philosophic thought which has risen *above Dasein*: such a view, and the doctrines which follow from it, are but a hidden remnant of the spurned eternal verities. The existential analysis of *Dasein* must itself be a possibility of *Dasein*.

(iv) But this necessity gives rise to what (for the purpose of this paper) is *the* crucial question of *Sein und Zeit*. Philosophical *analysis* understands the historical *structure* of *Dasein* as such, i.e., its *historicity*: this philosophic understanding is called *existenzial. Dasein itself* has an understanding and a self-understanding which is *historical*: this non-philosophic understanding is called *existenziell*.[21] The one is a transcendent grasp of *existentiality*; the other, an historical manifestation of *Existenz*. *How then can the former have a* Sitz *in the latter?* For 'without *existenziell* understanding every analysis of existentiality is rootless and groundless (*bodenlos*).'[22]

(v) The *existenzial* philosophic analysis can refute historicism only because *Dasein's existenziell* understanding also and already refutes it. This latter refutation occurs when, in the midst of its temporal-historical condition, *Dasein* grasps *the whole* of its condition, in such 'privileged' disclosures as care, anxiety, death, 'openness' (*Erschlossenheit*), and 'decisiveness' (*Entschlossenheit*).[23] These disclosures *are* privileged because in them *Dasein* comes to *know* the limitations within which it *is*. The knowledge, however, is not a rise above these limitations but rather their 'authentic' confrontation. No other 'wholeness' but this authenticity is possible for *Dasein*. *And it is the* existenziell Sitz im Leben *of the* existenzial *philosophic analysis*.

(vi) And yet such an analysis may well seem to be a 'phantastic understanding.'[24]

> Whence is one to derive what constitutes the 'authentic' *Existenz* of *Dasein*? ... Is the provided interpretation of the authenticity and wholeness of *Dasein* based on an ontic grasp of *Existenz* which, while possible, is not binding for everyone? The *existenzial* interpretation will never wish to make arbitrary decisions concerning *existenziell* possibilities and liabilities. And yet, must it not justify itself concerning *those existenziell* possibilities with which it gives the ontological interpretation its ontic ground?[25]

The *existenzial* analysis seems a phantastic undertaking, then, because it is caught in a 'circle':[26] the *existenzial* interpretation rests on an authentic *existenziell* understanding, yet it must itself decide what *existenziell* understanding *is* authentic and what is not. (So precarious a possibility is authentic *existenziell* understanding as to call for a 'counter-thrust' by *existenzial* analysis, against philosophical interpretations resting on *existenziell* unauthenticity.)[27] Does this circle not serve to show that *any* historical claim to *existenziell* authenticity may have its own *existenzial* interpretation, i.e., that, after all, historicism has won out?

(vii) But the 'being of *Dasein*' is itself 'circular,' and a philosophy wholly disavowing eternal verities must 'wholly leap' into this circle, rather than vainly seek escape from it.[28] *Dasein* as originally *cares* about its being-*in-the-world* as it *is* in the world, caring merely about *this and that.* And a philosophy which gives the structure of this original care-about-being-in-the-world itself *manifests* this *existenziell* care *by Dasein* even as it understands the *existenzial* structure *of* it.

So much for the relevant doctrines of *Sein und Zeit.* We derive from these one fundamental conclusion. *The* existenzial *analysis* can *reach a transcendent-universal truth concerning historicity – the structure* Dasein – *only because a transcendent-universal truth is manifest in history – in the* existenziell *understanding of* Dasein. A veritable gulf separates the *Critique of Practical Reason,* which precedes historicism, from *Sein und Zeit,* which follows it. Yet the two works share two formal but crucial characteristics. Heidegger reclaims, after historicism, the transcendence for philosophic truth which Kant had claimed before it. And he can, like Kant, make this claim only because he finds, as *Sitz im Leben* of the transcendent truth of philosophic thought, a transcendent truth manifest in the *Lebenswelt.* To be sure, the respective transcendent truths differ greatly in content. The intervention of historicism has undermined the content of the transcendent, and the 'uncanniness of thrown individuation' is far more radically historical than the categorical imperative.[29] Yet the empty truth which remains – a 'pure that'[30] without what, a 'decisiveness' without decision[31] – retains its transcendence, and does so precisely at the price of emptiness.[32]

VII

But *has 'Sein und Zeit' ultimately* overcome historicism? The gulf between Kant and Heidegger, after all, is most grave. A common, non-historical 'reason' unites Kant's moral knowledge of obligation with his philosophical knowledge of freedom. In contrast, Heidegger's *existenziell* understanding and his *existenzial* interpretation well-nigh fall apart, for the radical historicity of all authentic *existenziell* decisions demands an open *existenzial* category of decisiveness. And yet this latter cannot be *wholly* open – hence wholly empty – lest all differences between authenticity and unauthenticity vanish. Nor is this decisiveness in fact wholly open. Though a 'freedom-toward-death,' it rules out an authentic pagan-Stoic suicide.[33] And though singled out for decision, it leaves no room for call of God.[34] *Sein und Zeit* seems caught between returning to a Kantian-style rejection of the *naked* historicity of the *existenziell* decision, and remaining with an historicism which can give only an historical, not a transcendent, category of decisiveness. Could it be that *Sein und Zeit* gives the structure, not of *Dasein,* but merely of post-Christian

Dasein, i.e., of a *Dasein* marked by the absence of the Christian God, who yet rules out an authentic pagan-Stoic suicide even in His absence?

But we are spared the labour of these questions by the thought of the later Heidegger,[35] for this embraces an historicism far more radical than that which *Sein und Zeit* has overcome.

The *existenzial* analysis of *Sein und Zeit* is merely prefatory to *Dasein*'s quest for Being. This quest now discloses the historicity, not merely of *Dasein*'s quest for Being, but of Being itself. The history of philosophy, from Plato to Nietzsche, is dominated by the metaphysical *ratio*, which is in search of universal truth. But this *ratio* and this truth are themselves historical phenomena, marked by a primordial forgetting-of-Being. This forgetting-of-Being is itself part of the history of Being, which is why the metaphysical *ratio* and its truth are no mere errors. But to recognize this condition is, nevertheless, to go beyond both the *ratio* and its truth, toward a 'recalling' thinking of their forgotten Ground. Such a recalling opens itself up to original Truth. This original Truth is the Presence of Being, not a universal statement about Being. And it changes historically, according to the history of Being itself. These few indications of Heidegger's later position,[36] in no way able or intended to do it justice, nevertheless suffice to show it to be an historicism whose radicalism cannot be exceeded. How could it be more radical when it asserts the historicity, not merely of the human *Lebenswelt*, but of Being itself?

Heidegger does not shrink from the implications of his radical position.

(i) If the philosopher is a 'rational' thinker, then the 'recalling' thinker is no longer a philosopher. He dwells, rather, in the neighbourhood of the poet. Both are beholden to language, the 'house of Being,' which is in turn as historical as the Being it houses.[37]

(ii) The 'recalling' thinker not only goes beyond, but dissipates the metaphysical *ratio*, 'in the vortex of a more original questioning.' He does not, to be sure, 'abolish metaphysics. As long as man remains the *animal rationale*, he also remains the *animal metaphysicum*.' But he *does* destroy the universality and transcendence of the *ratio*. Any recalling of Being – itself forever historical because of the historicity of Being – *transforms* metaphysics.[38]

(iii) 'All refuting is silly in the sphere of essential thinking.' This applies not only to the recalling thinking but also to its interpretation of the history of metaphysics. For it understands past metaphysics, not in the 'rational' terms in which this latter understands itself, but rather as part of the history of Being which it recalls, whereas past metaphysics rests on a forgetting-of-Being.[39]

(iv) Since all thinking-of-Being – recalling as well as metaphysical thinking – is of the essence of *Dasein*, the future of Being and the future recalling-of-Being will help transform not only the metaphysical *ratio* but the essence of man as a whole.[40]

(v) The above are all not rational-metaphysical statements *about* recalling thinking but rather themselves *samples of* such thinking. (Hence they can only 'hint something,' but 'prove nothing.') This recalling thinking, like all recalling thinking, is historical. Present recalling thinking is *between* the past metaphysical forgetting-of-Being and an as yet future thinking-of-Being. For 'we are too late for the gods and too early for Being. Man is the poem of Being, as yet only begun.'[41]

Can Heidegger's recalling thinking maintain itself in this all-consuming historicism? It cannot. We need not here inquire whether Being has a history, and if so whether man is its 'clearing' (*Lichtung*).[42] For even if one grants both these theses one must still deny that the recalling thinking of the history of Being can destroy, or even indefinitely transform, the metaphysical *ratio*. On Heideggerian grounds this *ratio*, to be sure, becomes derivative rather than primary; even so it remains in its own derivative sphere, unassailable. Heidegger makes only the first point, but either does not ponder or else implicitly denies the second, when he asks: 'Has reason constituted itself to be the ruler of history? If so, by what right? If not, whence does it obtain its mission and its role?'[43]

That the *ratio is* unassailable in its own sphere is shown by Heidegger's own recalling thinking. For this can remain distinct from poetry only so long as it preserves the *ratio* in the very act of transcending it. Heidegger writes : 'Language is the house of Being. In this house dwells man. Thinkers and poets are guardians of it.'[44] What thinking is this? It is not, to be sure, rational-metaphysical thinking: it goes beyond it. But neither is it poetry: it is a thinking *interpretive* of poetry. More precisely, it is a thinking which interprets poetry, itself, and the relation between itself and poetry, all with a view to Being. But it can be such an interpreting only so long as it dialectically negates the insufficiencies of the *ratio*; and this it can do only so long as it preserves the *ratio* in the very act of negating it. A recalling thinking which simply destroyed the *ratio* would become incapable of ontological interpretation, collapse into an ontologically uninterpreted poetry, and destroy, not the *ratio*, but itself.[45]

VIII

No assault on the transcendence of philosophic truth can be more formidable than one which derives from the historicity of Being. Martin

Heidegger has made such an assault, and it has failed to destroy transcendent philosophic truth. This result calls for a renewed philosophic quest, if not for the timeless in an eternal world, then for the non-temporal and non-historical in the human *Lebenswelt*. The philosopher may be unable to escape from the cave of history. He does find, however, that a light from beyond the cave shines into the cave itself, and that it lights up both the lives of men who must live in history and the philosophic thought which seeks to understand it.

10 Hegel on the Actuality of the Rational and the Rationality of the Actual

I

In the preface to his *Philosophy of Right* Hegel writes: 'Was vernünftig ist, das ist wirklich; und was wirklich ist, das ist vernünftig' – 'What is rational is actual, and what is actual is rational.'[1] In paragraph 6 of the third edition of his *Encyclopedia of Philosophical Sciences* he repeats this statement verbatim, calling it 'simple.' Few interpreters, however, have ever found it so. Even friendly critics are baffled; hostile ones dismiss it as either scandalous or senseless. Two centuries after Hegel's birth there is thus still room for a modest exposition of the meaning of this famous (or infamous) Hegelian statement, much more so for one of its 'simplicity.' Both tasks, however – and in particular the second, seemingly hopeless one – should be undertaken in full awareness of two conditions which the *Encyclopedia* passage considers evident but which can be taken as such no longer. One is possession of (or at least respect for) 'religion.' The other is the kind of philosophical 'culture' which includes 'knowledge' of 'God.'

II

The charge 'scandalous or senseless' was popularized if not originated by Rudolph Haym's influential *Hegel und seine Zeit.*[2] Little troubled by any possible difficulties concerning the meaning of Hegelian 'rationality' (to which he correctly ascribes moral as well as logical significance), Haym concentrates his critical attention on Hegelian 'actuality.' Does this latter term signify any and all existing fact? But then the Hegelian statement is scandalous and 'the theories of the divine right of kings and of absolute obedience are innocent and harmless compared to the terrifying doctrine which sanctifies the existing as such.' Or does it signify only such existing fact as is in accord with Hegelian notions of logic and morality? But then the statement is indeed harmless but also an 'empty tautology.' Haym is not unaware of Hegel's effort to distinguish between 'existence' and 'actuality.' Yet he asserts that the whole Hegelian 'system, as it stands, results *exclusively* from a continuous, veritably unholy, *confusion* of two concepts of actuality.' (Italics added.) We are thus told that Hegel's statement – indeed, his whole system – suffers shipwreck on a basic dilemma; and the view expressed by Haym has been shared to this day by countless critics, not all of them hostile or superficial. Thus recently Sidney Hook has written: 'One interpretation of the distinction between the actual and the existent gives us a sheer tautology; the other, a scandalous absurdity.'[3]

III

But is it plausible that Hegel's statement (not to speak of his system in its entirety) is destroyed by an, after all, extremely obvious and elementary dilemma when it is formulated with obvious care,. put in a prominent place, and repeated and defended in another, hardly less prominent place? Or could it be that preconceptions on our part preclude an understanding? No less than three such preconceptions are brought to light in a brilliant passage in Franz Rosenzweig's *Hegel und der Staat* – an extraordinary, never fully appreciated work. The passage merely mentions these in passing; we must first of all fully expose them and explicitly set them aside. Rosenzweig writes:

> 'What is rational is actual': immediately from ... [a] discussion of the world-historical significance of the Platonic state leaps forth, as if shot from the pistol, this famous (or infamous) dictum. It has by no means been valid ... from all eternity but only since, through Christianity, the Idea of the divine Kingdom on earth has become a moral demand and thus the standard by which all human institutions are to be judged. Since then, however, it has been *actually* valid. And because for the agent the task of making Reason actual is fixed, cognition has – since then! – the task of examining Actuality – *become* actual since then! – with a view to discovering how Reason has been actual in it. *Only* because the Rational has become actual – principle of action! – is the Actual rational – principle of cognition! The second half of the dictum, which in contradiction to Hegel's own usage has always been adduced as the kernel of the

> thought –'Hegel's assertion of the rationality of the Actual' – is thus in fact merely the consequence of the thought, revolutionary in its core, of the actuality of the Rational – a thought expressed in the first half.[4]

(i) Some critics have considered the order of Hegel's two-part statement insignificant. Others, as Rosenzweig states, have seen its essence in the second part. Still others have actually reversed its order, thereby misquoting Hegel.[5] Each case reflects mistaken, however seemingly natural, preconceptions, serious enough to make an understanding impossible. A reversal of Hegel's own order may seem to compliment him in that it attributes to him a 'modern' critical view for which 'ontological' assertions about history must be justified by prior 'epistemological' assertions about human knowledge. Yet Hegelian 'rationality' is not primordially a standard *in us* (logical, moral, or both), nor is his 'actuality' exclusively 'the world *without* us.' Hegelian 'rationalism' is far closer to Platonic idealism (a closeness hinted at by Rosenzweig) than to modern – Kantian-moral, not to speak of epistemological – subjectivism. And if, like Haym and others, one investigates Hegelian 'actuality' while paying little attention to his 'rationality' one risks projecting upon Hegel non-Hegelian conceptions – and then charging him with either senselessness or scandalousness.

(ii) It may seem proper to suppose that Hegel's statement is valid either 'universally' or not at all. Not so according to Rosenzweig. Hook asks what shamans and medicine-men would assert of their own cannibalistic societies if they were Hegelian philosophers.[6] On Hegel's own view (and Rosenzweig's correct interpretation) such societies could not produce Hegelian philosophers; indeed, even Greek society could produce only Platonic and Aristotelian, but not Hegelian, idealism. For Hegel the actuality of the Rational is a *specific historical condition*; and only if and when that condition exists is the recognition of the Rational in the Actual a philosophical possibility. This assertion, to be sure, leaves Hegel with two questions which may permit no easy answer. One concerns the *origin* of the specific historical condition in question, and the possibility of a philosophical comprehension of that origin. The other is whether –and if so with what philosophical consequences – that altogether crucial historical condition may *pass away*.[7]

(iii) Once having identified the actuality of the Rational as a specific historical achievement, we are predisposed to look for exclusively human achievements – moral, cultural, political, technological. Once again Rosenzweig warns us. At least in its own self-understanding the decisive Christian event is a divine-human event, not a human event only. And since the 'principle of action' precedes the 'principle of cognition' the former must first of all be taken in its own terms before it can be taken in philosophical terms. To be sure, *both* parts of Hegel's statement are philosophical; yet *neither* part would be possible without a *pre*-philosophical form of historical existence which, if not entirely religious, has in any case an indispensable religious dimension. Hegel's statement is a translation and transfiguration of a (partly) religious into a philosophical affirmation. In attempting to fathom the meaning of the second, we are well advised first of all to retranslate it from its philosophical into the appropriate religious terms, with a view to discovering what meaning, if any, is yielded by them.

IV

In Hegel's own view it is 'unnecessary to cite religion' in defence of his statement, and he confines himself to a passing reference to divine Providence (*Encyclopedia*, §6). Today such citing, while no longer unnecessary, may be altogether brief if its sole purpose is to dispose of Haym's dilemma. Consider the following Christian (it is Christianity which Hegel's 'religion' refers to) affirmation: 'God's Providence governs the world, and the world is the place where His Providence may be recognized.' Some Christian theologians may have their doubts about divine 'Providence,' preferring instead 'Grace' or 'Revelation' or 'Redemption.' All will have vast and intricate difficulties with the distinction between worldly events in which God's Providence (or Grace or Revelation or Redemption) is, and is not, manifest. None of this matters to establish one fundamental point: unless on other, here irrelevant, grounds all theological statements are dismissed as senseless, *the statement in question is neither tautologous nor scandalous*. Not the first, for one may affirm a God who remains indifferent to the world or, indeed, a *deus absconditus*; not the second because, with the possible exception of certain 'heretics,' no Christian theologian affirms a divine Providence (or Grace or Revelation or Redemption) which has an *indiscriminate* worldly presence. The vast and intricate difficulties bound up with the distinction between such worldly events as do, and such as do not, manifest a divine Presence, concern the correct conception of the distinction, and even more the correct identification of instances: they do not concern the fact and necessity of a distinction as such. This remains assured if only (except, as has been said, for certain 'heretics') because the world is not identified with or dissipated into God even though God is its Creator and Redeemer.

Thus, at least if retranslated into its pre-philosophical form (or rather into its religious aspect), Hegel's statement, while possibly causing difficulties, causes none of Haym's difficulties. There is no tautology. There is no obviously scandalous absurdity. There is no 'confusion' between 'the actual' ('worldly events manifesting God') and the 'merely existing' ('worldly events not manifesting God'). Indeed, for those 'possessing religion' the statement is 'simple.'

V

But then, the Hegelian statement is not a Christian theological one but rather gives the Christian 'true content' its 'true [i.e., philosophical] form.' This feat is not external to the content, as may be the case when a philosophy attempts to prove an affirmation which in religion is accepted on faith – and the affirmation itself remains unaltered. The philosophical 'form' alters the religious 'content' in that it transfigures the externality which remains between its terms. To express Hegel's purpose in the simplest (i.e., historical) terms, 'the Rational' cannot be *exclusively* a God *external* to man and world if Hegel is any kind of Kantian; and 'the Actual' cannot be *exclusively* a natural and/or human 'world' (or a divine manifestation in that world) if Hegel is any sort of Spinozist. Religious 'representation,' though expressing a form of spiritual life in which all things are inwardly related, is nevertheless forced to resort to a symbolism in which 'God,' 'man,' and 'world' have the 'form' of mere side-by-sideness. The 'form' of Hegel's philosophical thought transfigures this side-by-sideness (and thus religious life itself) into a single, self-explicating, spiritual self-activity. And the question arises as to whether in this process the significant differences which remain between 'God' and 'world' vanish when these religious terms become, respectively, 'the Rational' and 'the Actual' – with the dire consequences asserted from Haym's days to our own.

A brief comment on a single Hegel passage will suffice to answer this question for the modest purposes of this chapter. Hegel writes:

> I am to make myself fit for the indwelling of the Spirit. ... This is my labour, the labour of man; but the same is also the labour of God, regarded from His side. He moves toward man and is in man through the act of raising him. What seems my act is thus God's and, conversely, what seems His is mine. This, to be sure, runs counter to the merely moral standpoint of Kant and Fichte; there the Good always remains something yet to be produced ... , some-

> thing that ought to be, as if it were not already essentially there. A world outside me remains, God-forsaken, waiting for me to bring purpose and goodness into it. But the sphere of moral action is limited. In religion the Good and reconciliation are absolutely complete and existing on their own account.[8]

We comment:

(i) The 'moral standpoint' of Kant and Fichte is valid in its own 'sphere,' and for it 'the highest is infinite process.'[9] In this sphere 'the Rational' is infinite but at the price of being an ideal *in us* only, the world being 'God-forsaken' except in so far as we already *have done* what we ought to do and can do.

(ii) This standpoint is *both* valid in its own 'sphere' *and* limited, i.e., superseded by a religious sphere. Infinite process is not *absolutely* highest, for in 'religion' the highest is *already* accomplished. Yet this must leave – albeit limited – room for the persistent validity of a human action for which 'the highest' is forever *yet to be* accomplished. As for philosophical thought, it must explicate a 'reconciliation' which is already implicit in religion itself.

(iii) Some religions (and their philosophical transfigurations) do not make possible such a reconciliation. Thus the Spinozistic 'divine Substance' (according to Hegel, the philosophical transfiguration of Judaism) dissolves the world (and thus human freedom), being itself 'acosmic.' Christianity (and the Hegelian philosophical 'Subject' which is its transfiguration) possesses the 'indwelling of the Spirit' by virtue of whose activity 'what seems my act ... is God's, and ... what seems His is mine.' A dialectic of divine giving and human receiving, it 'raises' human freedom instead of dissolving it.

(iv) The freedom thus achieved, however, would still dissolve *moral* freedom (and thus be acosmic in a Hegelian if not a Spinozistic sense) unless, rather than self-sufficient as 'religious' (i.e., cultic), it preserved and indeed demanded for its own completion a 'secular' (i.e., moral and political) counterpart, in which what 'religiously' is *already* divinely achieved is 'secularly' forever *yet to be* achieved, by an action which is human. As for the Hegelian philosophical comprehension of this relation between the 'religious' and the 'secular,' it must so internalize it as to preserve rather than dissipate the difference.

VI

The famous (or infamous) Hegelian statement which is the subject of this essay may thus be expounded as follows. Since the rise of Christianity the Rational has become actual; but whereas Christian faith has from the start grasped the religious aspect of this event (that through the indwelling of the Spirit all is accomplished), it has been left to secular reality, often indifferent or even hostile to the Christian faith, to grasp its secular aspect (that through human action much, if not everything, is forever yet to be accomplished). Only the existence of these two aspects make the philosophical (instead of merely the theological) formula true. Andonly the existence of this truth renders possible the Hegelian philosophy – the recognition of the rationality in the Actual.

In the *Encyclopedia* passage in which he repeats his controversial statement first made in the preface to the *Philosophy of Right*, Hegel remarks that philosophical 'culture' is necessary for its comprehension. Of this culture he tells us that it must know 'not only that God is actual, the most actual, indeed, alone truly actual, but also ... that existence in general is partly appearance and only partly actual.' He does not tell us, but rather takes for granted, that the philosophically cultured recognize that appearance is not unreality or illusion but brute, existent fact – that for his philosophical 'thought' the distinction between existence and actuality remains as vital and indispensable as the corresponding distinction in 'religious representation.'

VII

Four major omissions will have been noticed in the above account. All are due to the modesty of the task claimed in the initial paragraph. First, all references to the *Logic* have been avoided: we have sought to show that Hegel *seeks* to distinguish between existence and actuality, not whether or how he succeeds. Second, all references to the *Philosophy of Right* have been avoided, and this despite the fact that the controversial statement which has been under discussion occurs in the preface of that work: we have sought to show that Hegel *can* and *does* distinguish between 'actual' and 'merely existing' states, not that his criteria of distinction are sound or even defensible – much less that soundness or defensibility attaches to his political judgments. Third, we have refrained from inquiring into the *origin* of what Rosenzweig refers to as Hegel's 'principle of action.' (See above, section III.) This is no insignificant question. For Christian faith the divine incursion into history may drop from heaven; Hegel's actuality of the Rational cannot. Moreover, the question does not lose its significance when Hegelianism takes an atheistic, left-wing turn: Marx projects the actuality of the Rational into the post-revolutionary future; unless there are present origins of this future this projection reduces itself to a groundless hope and an empty conceit.

The fourth omission is most serious, and it concerns the question most of all in need of contemporary examination. Can the historical conditions producing the actuality of the Rational (and hence the rationality of the Actual) pass away? (See above, section III.) The religious incursion into the world of God in Christ may or may not leave room for subsequent eruptions of demonic evil in the world which produce genocidal industries with by-products including human skin made into lamp-shades, human hair used for pillows, human bones turned into fertilizer. Hegel's actuality of the Rational leaves room only for world-historically insignificant evils to be disposed of as relapses into tribalism or barbarism. In their post-Enlightenment optimism all but a few modern philosophers have ignored or denied the demonic. Hegel's philosophy – which unites Christian religious with modern secular optimism – is the most radical and hence most serious expression of this modern tendency. This modest essay has inquired only into the meaning of Hegel's philosophy. Any inquiry into its truth must confront its claims with the gas chambers of Auschwitz.

Epilogue
Holocaust and *Weltanschauung*: Philosophical Reflections on Why They Did It

Corruptio optimi pessima est

1 The Unanswered Question

I once asked Raul Hilberg the following question: 'Raul, you have thought as long and hard as anyone about how they did it. Now tell me, why did they do it?' Hilberg heaved a sigh and replied: 'They did it because they wanted to do it.'

I reported this incident at the 1985 meeting of the Eastern Division of the American Philosophical Association.[1] In the ensuing discussion someone substituted, 'They did it because they *decided* to do it.' This emendation, I believe, is acceptable to Hilberg, who is given neither to absolving people of responsibility for their decisions, nor to overlooking the fact that one does not do everything one wants to do.

Both answers, however, give rise to the further question of why they should have wanted – let alone decided! – to perpetrate a crime as unprecedented as it was 'irrational.' That Hilberg is aware of this further question his sigh would suffice to prove. But there is more. He has explained again and again that in his life-long struggle with the Holocaust he has limited himself to 'small' questions, for fear of giving too small an answer to the 'big' question.

Claude Lanzmann's *Shoah* has followed the same course. Not once in his masterful film does he ask either a victim or bystander and least of all a criminal why they did it: had he asked this question, he would surely have got too small an answer. Answers which are too small have invariably been given and received by those who have failed to be supremely wary in getting anywhere close to the 'big' question.[2]

I shall confine my present attention entirely to that question. I must therefore state what I take it to be. It is not why the Nazis practised brutality on a scale hitherto unknown; built a vast system of concentration camps; preached and practised an extreme form of racism; fanned the most radical conceivable antisemitism; put it into practice through laws that disenfranchised Jews, undoing a century of emancipation; staged the worst pogrom in a history not lacking in pogroms; or even why at length they resorted to genocide of the Jewish people. To these (and other) questions historians may find answers, citing historical parallels. For me the 'big' question is why they decided quite literally to '*exterminate*' the Jews, i.e. murder *every available* Jew; why they *acted* on this decision, not letting even the old die in bed; and – this surely most startling but also most revelatory! – why this action *remained sacrosanct* even when at length it became contrary to their most elementary interest, i.e. when their own Reich was in its death-throes. For me, that it was and remained sacrosanct will always remain a searing fact because of Bertchen Bacher. A spinster, my grandmother's best friend, and already old and frail, she was the most inoffensive of persons. Yet they would not let even her die in peace.

Among those who count, only a few such as Himmler – *der treue Heinrich* – gave up, betraying their Führer as well as their own *Treue*. Not most of the others. Eichmann diverted trains from the crumbling Eastern front so as to send more Jews to their death. The SS did not flee when the Russians approached Auschwitz; rather, at risk to themselves, they force-marched their victims westward, making sure that they perished by the thousands from exhaustion or shooting on the way.

As for the Führer himself, this is how he acted in the end. Trapped in his Berlin bunker, he had already expressed satisfaction at what he thought – perhaps hoped! – would be the annihilation of his own German *Volk*: the Russians would win, nay, being the stronger after all, would *deserve* to win, for such were the laws of social-Darwinist justice. Yet now, when it was time for suicide, he composed a 'political testament' that did not view Jews by these same standards. To be sure, they were strong, nay, stronger than the Russians and indeed near-omnipotent. Yet they were not the master-race that deserved to rule mankind, but rather its 'poisoners.' It was they – not the Führer himself – who had caused this most terrible of wars, just as they had caused every previous one. And Hitler's last words to his *Volk* – for this purpose, it seems, it must survive, after all – were an appeal to 'practice merciless resistance to the world-poisoners of all nations, *das internationale Judentum*.'[3]

2 The 'Big' Question and the Nature of Historical Explanation

It is not a philosopher's task to ask questions that baffle historians. His task is, however, to reflect on the nature of historical explanations; and, attending to the 'big' Holocaust question while engaged in this task, I shall here direct the historian's attention to a dimension of the question that has been insufficiently explored, if and when explored at all. Two theories of historical explanation have commanded philosophical assent in recent decades. Let both be tested with Hilberg's 'big' question in mind.

3 The Covering Law Theory and the Holocaust

The first theory may be called positivist since it asserts that explanation in the sciences is all of one kind, and that therefore explanation in history does not differ in principle from, say, explanation in physics.[4] To be sure, physics aims at universal laws, through which the physicist both predicts the future and explains the past, whereas the historian explains nothing more than past particulars and is, moreover, rarely helped by success in this effort in predicting the future. This difference, however, is not one of principle but merely of situation and degree. Of situation: unlike the physicist, the historian cannot make – much less repeat – experiments by which to test his hypothesis. Of degree: human affairs are too complex to yield laws of human behaviour as precise as those of physics. Taken together, these two differences suffice to explain why a professional historian, say, of post-World War I Europe was but little better qualified to predict the course of the Nazi movement than the amateur historian Winston Churchill. (In fact, of course, the qualifications of the whole lot, taken together, were much worse.) They also sufficed to explain why historical explanations rarely take the precise form '*x* caused *y*,' and mostly the vaguer form '*x* led to *y*' or 'sooner or later was bound to lead to *y*.' Yet, consciously or not, in explaining past particulars the historian implies general laws of human behaviour; and if he does not, he explains nothing. He may then still be engaged in separating fact from fiction, and thus also scholarship from journalism, novel-writing, and other unscholarly activities. However, in venturing beyond establishing to explaining the past, his activity is, in that case, to paraphrase Aristotle, less scientific even than poetry.

This so-called 'covering law theory' of historical explanation rests on the dogma of the unity of the sciences. Its plausibility to historians, however, derives far more from examples adduced in support. Hence in testing the theory by the 'big,' baffling question about the Holocaust, we shall shed light not only on that question itself but also on the whole theory – and, as will be seen, its limits.

It is not difficult to find law-like generalizations implied in accounts not only of Nazism but also of the Holocaust. 'Economic distress tends to cause social upheaval'; 'defeat in war may lead to nationalist extremism fuelled by resentment': no account of Nazism seems able to dispense with these generalizations, dubious though they are. (They *are* dubious: like Germany, America suffered the great Depression; yet it produced not Hitler but Roosevelt.) Add to these two 'laws' yet a third, and no account of the Holocaust seems able to dispense with all three, thus conjoined: 'given a centuries-old calumny of one identifiable group, that group is apt to serve as scapegoat in times of economic distress, especially when this latter is compounded by national humiliation and resentment.'

These law-like generalizations explain much about the Holocaust: they come nowhere close, however, to the 'big' question. The Jews-as-scapegoats 'law' may have some plausibility so long as one deals with the early Nazi period, when Jewish-blood-spurting-from-knives was a song bellowed from the house-tops; all plausibility is lost when public incitement was turned into top-secret action. And plausibility becomes sheer absurdity when at length the 'big' question comes into view. Jewish scapegoating by the Nazis was presumably meant as a means, first, to bringing Nazism to power and, then, to preserving and strengthening it. Yet *in extremis* the relation became reversed: such power of the Nazi Reich as remained became a means to the murder of more, and still more, Jews.

When confronting this extremity the positivist theorist may protest that nobody can ever explain everything; that, for example, he himself could not so much as describe, let alone explain, every trivial thing that had occurred in the single classroom hour he has just spent expounding his theory – the itches, scratches, yawns of his students, the little noises from outside, and so forth. In this, however, he ignores that 'why they did it' is not a trivial thing. Of all questions raised by the Holocaust, it is the most important.

Forced, after all, to confront the 'big' question, the positivist may call for the historian's heaping laws upon laws, bringing his general laws ever closer to the Holocaust's particularity, with a view to capturing at length the scandalous 'why' of it. 'Given sufficient time, radical anti-semites sooner or later believe their own propaganda.' 'Given sufficient stress, they continue to believe in Jewish power even when events –

events like the Holocaust – demonstrate Jewish lack of power.' 'Given sufficient time *and* stress, they become so fanatical in their beliefs as to die for them rather than question them.' Grant these or similar 'laws,' and you reach not only the *infima species* 'events *like* the Holocaust' but the Holocaust itself, its 'why' included.

What has in fact been reached, however, is the *reductio ad absurdum* of the theory. By the time the compounding of laws has reached that great, baffling 'why,' the historian, like the old-fashioned metaphysician with his old-fashioned God, is left with a class with but a single member. To make matters worse, the crucial characteristic of that single member is insanity. This, to be sure, is no little matter. Terms such as 'insanity' and 'paranoia' keep creeping into historical accounts of the Holocaust, all-but-unfailingly so as they approach the 'big' question.[5] This fact ought to provoke thought. It does not provoke our thought here, however, for what matters presently is only this, that 'insanity,' 'paranoia,' and similar 'explanations' are all answers too 'small' to the 'big' question.

4 The Covering Law Theory Modified

The covering law theory of historical explanation has now been widely abandoned. Its model, 'given *a*, *b* is probable, if not necessary,' has yielded to the less doctrinaire and more sober 'given *a*, *b* is possible.'[6] With this there is no need to quarrel. Much has been said, and much more needs to be explored, about the circumstances that made the Holocaust possible. The 'big' question, however, is not how it was possible, but why it became actual; not how they could decide to do it, but why they made the decision.

5 The 'Idealist' Theory of R.G. Collingwood

We must therefore attend to the second prevalent theory of historical explanation, 'idealist' in that it stakes all on human decisions and their 'why.' Only nature, asserts R.G. Collingwood, its most distinguished exponent of recent decades, consists of 'events.' History consists of 'actions'; and these, unlike events, have an 'inside' as well as an 'outside,' the latter being the action itself, the former, the 'why' of it in the mind of the agent. Give the reason (or reasons) why an agent did what he did, and you have explained the action. To look for behavioural laws beyond these reasons is a doctrinaire mistake.[7]

Like its positivist rival, this theory depends for its plausibility less on abstract doctrines than on examples cited in support. Collingwood's own favourite example is Caesar crossing the Rubicon. Few actions of great moment have ever been based so clearly, on the one hand, on one man's decision who, on the other, was so obviously rational. Bismarck may have been as rational as Caesar; yet the actions that led to the founding of his German Reich were not his alone, nor his in conjunction with those of other individuals equally rational; they were also – far more – all those countless ones motivated by a yearning for national unity, a yearning explosive ever since Napoleon at Jena dealt the death blow to the Holy Roman Empire of German Nation. However, 'actions' such as these – they are those of a 'movement' – are group-actions rather than individual ones; and while their 'inside' may be ideas, they can hardly be called rational.

Never in all history was a movement so clearly the work of a single individual as was National Socialism. That a decision as crucial as the Holocaust stemmed from a *Führerbefehl* was therefore evident to people both honest and level-headed long before it was demonstrated.[8] Its 'why' may therefore seem to fit well into Collingwood's model, since, after all, individual 'actions' are less problematic for it than collective ones. Yet despite the *Führerbefehl*-institution the 'big' question is not about Hitler alone. Himmler may have complained that his particular Hitler-order was hard; in the end he was even *treulos* enough to disobey it: yet while obey he did, he approved of it.[9] In Jerusalem Eichmann protested that he had been a mere cog in the wheel; he contradicted his own protest when he cited Kant's categorical imperative.[10] And simple common sense is very nearly enough to demonstrate that the death-marches, occurring as they did in the last, chaotic days of the Reich, were ordered not by Hitler but by 'decent'[11] subordinates.

To be sure, among the torturers and murderers were robots who obeyed orders blindly, as well as sadists who enjoyed obeying them. The 'big' Holocaust question, however, involves not such as these, but only the 'idealists' – Himmler until he became *treulos*; Eichmann, the SS murderers, and countless others to the very end – who, to cite an obscure Nazi philosopher's novel version of Kant's categorical imperative, asked themselves while doing what they did whether the Führer, if he knew, would approve; who acted on the presumed Führer's will as though it were their own.[12]

The 'why' of the Holocaust, then, is not a case like Caesar's crossing of the Rubicon, after all. This is true of the 'action' itself, for it was collective rather than individual. It is true also of its 'inside,' for this was not 'rational.'

What was the 'inside' of the 'actions' of these many quasi-Hitlers, as well as of the one and only – and irreplaceable! – real one? More precisely, what did it prove to have been all along in the extremity that showed forth its truth?[13] One asks this, the 'big' question, and arrives once more at insanity. To be sure, they were all responsible decision-makers, not human flotsam carried into catastrophe by waves of 'laws.' The decisions themselves, however, were insane. Yet insanity, as we already know, is too 'small' an answer to the 'big' question.

We thus have reached an impasse once more – or would have reached it were it not for the *nationalsozialistische Weltanschauung.*

6 Hitler's *Weltanschauung*

Back in 1938 Hermann Rauschning, a one-time Hitler supporter but now resolute foe, advanced the thesis that Nazism was a 'revolution of nihilism' that aimed at nothing but naked power. He would not destroy the Jews, Rauschning reports Hitler as saying, for he needed a visible enemy for Germans to focus their hate on; indeed, if Jews did not exist, he would have to invent them.[14] But then came the Holocaust. And since, moreover, there is nothing to suggest that, had Hitler won the war and made the world *judenrein*, he would have 'invented' new Jews to take their place – Slavs, blacks, to say nothing of Englishmen[15] – the Rauschning thesis is destroyed by the facts. Yet it survives.

An explanation emerges, strangely enough, from a work aimed at refuting that thesis. As is well known, there was a *nationalsozialistische Weltanschauung.* Equally well known is, or ought to be, that it was formulated authoritatively by Hitler himself, and solemnly invoked on all proper occasions. Yet, Eberhard Jäckel argues,[16] historians have neglected that *Weltanschauung*, and in a brief but powerful book he sets out to remedy that defect. In so doing he puts forward a thesis of his own but, to his credit, does not hurl it at the reader, proceeding instead to examine the evidence. Hitler, ruthlessly Machiavellian in his means, Jäckel asserts, was by no means Machiavellian in his ends: he aimed, not at power for power's sake, but rather at goals set forth in his *Weltanschauung* – the 'granite-like foundation of ... [his future] actions.'[17]

What were these goals and that *Weltanschauung*? To cite only aspects presently relevant, the German *Volk* needs *Lebensraum*, and armed conquest is a just way of getting it: such are 'nature's' social-Darwinist 'laws.' Armed conquest is practical as well as just, provided the aim is pursued in alliance with others. Natural allies are Italy and Britain, both *Völker* with *Lebensraum*-needs of their own, with the British being fellow-'Aryans' to boot. Italy would expand in Southern Europe and Africa;

Britain overseas; and in return for a free hand in those parts of the world, these two powers would let Germany expand eastward. They would do so gladly, moreover, since, in destroying Russia, Germany would destroy also the world-citadel of Marxism, the common enemy of them all. Only two further aspects of the *Weltanschauung* need to be mentioned here: the *Führerprinzip* and antisemitism. Hitler would not merely happen to be Führer: it was a *Prinzip* that there should *be* a Führer, and that Hitler himself would be he. This one principle emerged together with the other, for in his own mind (if not yet outside it) Hitler became Führer with his Vienna-'conversion' from 'cosmopolitanism' to 'antisemitism.'[18] To be sure, the account of that process in *Mein Kampf* – theatrical, self-inflating as it is with all that talk about 'greatest inner soul struggles' – deserves little credit: in all likelihood Hitler was an antisemite since childhood. The account does deserve credit, however, in so far as it marks the birth of a *Weltanschauung*. Nor may one take lightly the theatrical self-inflation that accompanies the retrospective account – a retrospect that was to last till Hitler's death.

Such, then, was the *Weltanschauung* that was to be the 'foundation' of the Führer's subsequent 'actions.' But what happened when, with actions in full swing, the actors failed to play their pre-assigned roles: when Britain turned enemy rather than ally; when Italy, no heroic victor, became instead a defeated coward; and when Russia, easy prey though it was to be by dint of its 'Jewish Marxism,' refused to expire? What of the *Weltanschauung* remained 'granite-like' then?

Jäckel keeps asking this question. He also keeps looking for the *Geschlossenheit* – comprehensive unity – that, as he rightly insists, a full-blown *Weltanschauung* requires. He does find the necessary *Geschlossenheit*, but only after much labour and in the book's very last few pages. Yet the reader seems to have guessed it – the great mystery – all along, for he has read the book with care, and has been startled by the unique character of its third chapter.[19] Why, *das Judentum* gives the *Weltanschauung* its needed *Geschlossenheit*.[20] It solves the large problem, showing what Hitler is *for* by showing what he is *against* – internationalism, pacifism, and parliamentary democracy, poisonous Jewish inventions all! *Das Judentum* also solves the small problem – why the actors failed to play their pre-assigned roles. Why had Britain turned hostile? Because Churchill was jewified! Why was Russia winning? Because Stalin, no Jewish Marxist after all, deserved to win! The *Weltanschauung*, then, had been right, and remained right even *in extremis*: only in Italy's case does Hitler admit to a mistake, and even that one was due, not to his *Weltanschauung*, but merely to misguided personal kindness.

In the extremity that showed forth its truth, then, the *Weltanschauung* survived, but in part only. Not among the surviving parts was the thousand-year-Reich, its right to ever more *Lebensraum*, or even to *Leben* itself. All these, the Führer himself included, went down in a self-destructive, nihilistic fury that confirmed what had been true all along in the Rauschning thesis, after all.[21] Rauschning had been wrong all along, however, in two respects: the Jews were the poisoners of the world, and – except for acts of mistaken kindness – the Führer was always right. These two parts of the *Weltanschauung* were veritable pillars. They remained standing to the end. And they were 'granite-like' because they confirmed each other: *that the Führer was always right was proved by the Jews being the poisoners of the world; and that the Jews were the poisoners of the world was proved by the Führer being always right.*

Evidently we have, for yet a third time, arrived at insanity; indeed, if the mind's self-enclosure in its own circle, immune to all external evidence, is what *constitutes* insanity, we have reached a classic case of it. We must therefore, at this late point, alter the strategy we have followed thus far. Earlier we simply dismissed 'insanity,' as 'too small' an answer to the 'big' Holocaust-question. Simply to dismiss it is possible no more. Instead, we must think again.

Does history lack in mad, megalomanic dictators? With his 'Heil Hitler,' his 'Hitler youth,' his *Führerprinzip* and all the rest, does Hitler not rank with the maddest of them? Way back in ancient times Nero fiddled while Rome burned, having set the city on fire himself in order for his musical genius to be inspired by the sight.

But the parallel fails. Nero fiddled alone; no quasi-Neros fiddled with him or under him. In contrast, if Hitler was insane, so were Eichmann, the SS, Himmler until he became *treulos*, and indeed – in the extremity that showed forth its truth – the whole Nazi Reich. This however, is the crux: *whereas a mad Nero is an explanation, a whole Reich-as-madhouse is not; whether or not recognized as such, such a purported 'explanation' is but an admission on the historian's part, witting or unwitting, that nothing has been explained.* The 'why' of the Holocaust, then, is a truly great predicament for the historian in the practice of his craft.

He may be helped somewhat by pondering the second difference between Nero's Rome and Hitler's Berlin; indeed, by pondering it ourselves we reach at length the goal of the present inquiry. When Nero's Rome burned, nothing remained sacrosanct, not even the emperor's fiddling. In contrast, two things – but two things only – remained sacrosanct when Hitler's Berlin was aflame: the *Führerprinzip*, and the murder of more, and ever more, Jews. Indeed, if Hitler's 'political testament' is taken seriously – and this it must be – these two things were to remain sacrosanct not only unto death but, in Nibelungen-like *Treue*, even beyond.

This difference exists because Hitler's Berlin, unlike Nero's Rome, had a *Weltanschauung*.

7 What *Weltanschauung* Means in German History

As used in languages other than German, the word *Weltanschauung* has lost its German meaning. On their part, Germans are too close to their own history to reflect on that meaning and its role in their history. Even Jäckel, among the most perceptive, refers to *Weltanschauungen* other than Hitler's, but never stands back to ask – ask in depth – precisely what '*Weltanschauung*' means in German history.

An ideology is confined to history. Hence such crimes as Stalin's murder of the peasants and the Cambodian genocide shatter the imagination, to be sure, but remain within the limits of intelligibility. That it was to be otherwise with Hitler's *Weltanschauung* is evident as early as in his 1924 'dialogue' with Dietrich Eckart which, though still confined to history, is already 'world-historical' enough – as well as world-historically-anti-Jewish enough – to make Moses into a bolshevist and Lenin into a Jew.[22] That the as-yet-not-*geschlossene Weltanschauung* was to transcend history altogether is announced in a much-quoted passage of *Mein Kampf*:

> If, with the help of his Marxist creed, the Jew is victorious over the other peoples of the world, his crown will be the funeral wreath of humanity, and this planet will, as it did thousands of years ago, move through the ether devoid of men.[23]

Much quoted, this passage is little understood, even though Hitler himself, so to speak, lends a hand when, in the second edition, he 'corrects' 'thousands' into 'millions.' *Millions* of years in the past? Perhaps millions *again* in the future? Why did such passages not mark their author as a raving madman? Nothing is explained by the fact that *Mein Kampf* was the world's 'least-read best-seller,' for Hitler said much the same often enough in his speeches. Nor by the fact that antisemitism was rife in Germany: except in Germany, few antisemites, however extreme, ever made Jews into a cosmic principle.

Historians may never succeed in answering this question satisfactorily. They will fail entirely unless they understand – understand in the depth that the subject requires – that whereas an ideology remains with history, the scope of a *Weltanschauung*, in the context of German history, goes beyond things historical and extends to the cosmos. An encyclopedia article, published in Germany in 1931, declares that the 'true problem' of a *Weltanschauung* is to find 'a firm, unified framework for life that transcends the achievement of the senses, of thought, of the sciences – to find it with the help of other powers.'[24] The author, himself a Christian, will not have guessed how – and how soon – the 'problem' would be 'solved.'

Nothing in history quite compares to the role of *Weltanschauungen* in nineteenth- and early-twentieth-century Germany. Like people elsewhere, Germans had opinions, beliefs (religious and/or other), interests, belonged to clubs and political parties. To have a *Weltanschauung* was something special. It deserved respect, even awe, if only it had the three characteristics a *Weltanschauung* requires: cosmic scope, internal coherence or *Geschlossenheit*, and a sincere commitment on the part of its devotees. (Whether it was right or true by external criteria – such as, in Hitler's case, elementary decency or facts about Jews – mattered little or not at all.) Hence when the *nationalsozialistische Weltanschauung* appeared, it was respected simply *because* it was a *Weltanschauung*: not despite the fact that it was cosmic but because of it; not despite the fact that it slandered 'good' as well as 'bad' Jews but – indiscriminate attacks on *das Judentum* being necessary for *Geschlossenheit* – because of it. And the pimp Horst Wessel became a saint, not despite the fact that he died needlessly but, having died because he had refused a Jewish doctor's aid, because of it.

Who had a *Weltanschauung* in Weimar Germany? Even the communists had only an ideology. As for the others on both right and left, they had at best a few principles, i.e. fragments of a *Weltanschauung*. The fragments of the Weimar 'traitors' on the left, of course, were held in contempt, and not by the Nazis alone. But right-wing would-be restorers of the Kaiser's *Reich* did not fare well, either. It was for lack of a *geschlossene Weltanschauung*, Hitler claimed, that the Kaiser had lost his war – and won over many hankering for the Kaiser's return. Once in pre-Nazi days an argument erupted in my high school class. The subject was German war-time policy toward Belgium. The Kaiser's government had violated Belgian neutrality but subsequently apologized. The handful of Weimar democrats in the class attacked the violation and lost. But so did the Kaiser's defenders, and they were the great majority who usually set the tone. It was the handful of Nazis that won the argument: the Kaiser had been right in violating Belgian neutrality – but should have blamed the violation on the Belgians. The Nazis won because they – and they alone – had a *geschlossene Weltanschauung*. They continued to win. And their *Weltanschauung* continued to remain *geschlossen* when Hitler started his newer and better war on Poland; and when his war ended, with Eichmann keeping on sending his trains, with the SS force-marching the Auschwitz survivors westward, and with the Führer himself composing his 'political testament.'

Arguably this end marks the nadir of all history. One must understand it, however, as the nadir of *German* history – and hark back from this to its zenith, for then the German notion of *Weltanschauung* was born. Their best age once earned Germans the title of *Volk* not only of *Dichter* but also of *Denker*. Their worst age came when Hitler was not only their *Führer* but also their *Denker*. *Corruptio optimi pessima est.*

The greatest German age began when Kant – *der Alleszermalmer*[25] – having smashed metaphysics, placed moral duty into the vacated place, thus giving it cosmic significance. Two decades later, in 1807, what for Kant was absolute was described by Hegel[26] as *die moralische Weltanschauung*, i.e. first, a *Weltanschauung*, and second, only one among others. This was no whim on Hegel's part but rendered inevitable by intervening developments. In 1797 Fichte[27] wrote

> What philosophy one chooses depends on what kind of person one is. A philosophical system is not a dead piece of furniture that one can accept or reject at will, but is rather animated by the person that holds it.

This well-known statement is widely taken to mean that philosophy is a cluster of personal idiosyncrasies, something that Fichte would not have dignified by the name of philosophy. The philosopher rather faces up to a serious but new philosophical problem. Since Kant, the philosopher can – and therefore must – choose between two philosophical systems, the one – realism – making objective reality ultimate, the other – idealism – subjective freedom, with each reducing to appearance what to the other was reality. Though coherent, however, neither system sufficed by itself to lay claim to truth. The new problem is that whereas both are coherent neither can refute the other and therefore demonstrate its own truth. Hence – lest the choice be arbitrary – the claim to truth made by either must be backed by the person that affirms it. The word *Weltanschauung* doubtless existed before in the German language. But this is how it became a respected notion in philosophical discourse – and, Germany being Germany, in German discourse as a whole.

What Fichte showed to be a problem quickly turned into a predicament. In 1797 he affirmed two possible *Weltanschauungen*, a 'realist' suffused with a weak freedom overwhelmed by cosmic necessity, and an 'idealist' with a freedom so strong as to maintain itself against the whole universe. In 1799 Schleiermacher followed with yet a third, the religious *Weltanschauung*,[28] and only one year later Schelling with yet a fourth, the aesthetic one.[29] With the exception of the soon-forgotten 'realism' (acknowledged but not held by Fichte), these *Weltanschauungen* all were supported by philosophical argument, as subtle as it was honest, for their *coherence*; they also all culminated in the noblest of human experiences affirming their *truth* – respectively, moral freedom, religious devoutness, and the aesthetic creativity by which truth is wedded to beauty. By dint of their very plurality, however, they also willy-nilly introduced arbitrariness into philosophical discourse. Even so, however, there was yet no reason to fear the spectre of *Weltanschauungen* that would owe their *Geschlossenheit* not to philosophical honesty but to lies and slander, and that would affirm their truth not through noble experiences but mass murder.

Then came Hegel. A philosopher of unequalled modern greatness, he confronted the predicament of the plurality of *Weltanschauungen* with unmatched integrity, but sought to overcome it with an all-comprehensive system of thought in which all *Weltanschauungen* were accorded partial truth, and none more than a partial one. However, as every German *Privatdozent* worth his meagre stipend was to intone for the rest of the nineteenth century and well into the twentieth, the Hegelian synthesis has 'collapsed.' Not many have added that, with this collapse, the great age of German *Denker* came to an end.

No end came, however, to the multiplicity of *Weltanschauungen*, with few Germans deterred from giving them respect by the fact that the level of humane culture and philosophical subtlety was rapidly declining. Count Gobineau was a Frenchman, and Houston Stewart Chamberlain, an Englishman. Yet the coarse trash of both became *Weltanschauungen* only in Germany. Nor was respect paid to the trash only by the coarse. The chief German booster of the Frenchman was Richard Wagner, and the Englishman became his son-in-law. Nothing influenced the young Hitler quite as much as getting drunk on Wagner's music.[30]

A wide gulf still exists between Hitler and Wagner, to say nothing of the vast one between the darkest period in German history and the brightest. Our task is not to explore this gulf, but merely to point to it, for future historians concerned with the 'big' Holocaust question to ponder and explore. In doing both they are given food for thought by the fact that Schelling's call for a future union of beauty and truth – a 'new mythology' in which music and drama, dance, poetry, and philosophic thought were all at one – found a response in Wagner's musical dramas; and on these the young Hitler got drunk.

Pondering the twofold gulf ourselves, we on our part say only this: if *der Nationalsozialismus* was the acting out of a *Weltanschauung*, and if anti-semitism was the 'granite-like' core of it,[31] then neither the Führer nor his 'decent' followers could be satisfied with a *Halbheit* that would have *Geschlossenheit* but stop short of confirming its truth. The 'solution' of the 'problem' posed by the Jewish 'poisoners' of the world, in that case, had to have *Ganzheit*, i.e. be 'final,' and remain so to the end. Not even Bertchen Bacher, in that case, could be allowed to die in bed.

8 Reality and Theatre

Did Hitler believe his own *Weltanschauung*? Some say that nobody dies with a lie.[32] A dubious thesis, in Hitler's case this may be wholly false. An actor, Hitler was a nobody who became a somebody when he found his *Weltanschauung*. In order to die a somebody, he may well have played to the end a role in a tragedy that he himself had had the main share in writing. If so, the Holocaust, unique in any case, is also a unique tragedy. Like other tragedies, it inspires terror and pity – terror because of the criminals, pity because of the victims. But enacted on no mere stage, it offers no way for us, no mere spectators, of purging these emotions.

9 Epilogue

When Hitler died, did German *Denken* come to an end? An understandable reaction, it offers no way out, however, for the spectre of Hitler, his Reich, his Holocaust, all keep on haunting the world and will keep on haunting it.[33] The times therefore call for a new generation of *Denker* – they can only be German – who will not escape into rarefied realms of 'Being' or generalized 'revolts against transcendence,'[34] but rather assume responsibility for their history, pondering the history of German *Denker*, from its bright beginning to its catastrophic end.

Notes

Preface

1 See the comments on page vii of *Encounters between Judaism and Modern Philosophy* (New York, 1973).

Chapter 1 Kant's Philosophy of Religion

1 Preface, *Religion innerhalb der Grenzen der blossen Vernunft*, in *Kants Gesammelte Schriften*, Prussian Academy ed. (Berlin, 1902–55), VI, 6. (Henceforth referred to as *Werke*. Unless otherwise noted, all references are to this edition.)

2 *Critique of Pure Reason* B832–3. (Henceforth cited as *Cr.p.R.*) This division also appears in a letter (*Werke*, XI, 414) and in the introduction to Kant's handbook on *Logic* (*Werke*, XI, 25). In the last two versions the three questions are 'referred to' a fourth, 'What is man?' Just how seriously one should take this fourth question and, if so, what sort of 'anthropology' (*Werke*, IX, 25) it would involve, are issues beyond the scope of this essay.

3 Scriptural passages such as Romans 9:18 ('He hath mercy upon whom He will, and whom He will He hardeneth'), if taken literally, are for Kant the '*salto mortale* of human reason' (*Religion innerhalb* [*Werke*, VI, 121]).

4 Kant asks, and must ask, not 'What *ought* I to hope?' but 'What *may* I hope?'

5 We shall make no attempt to defend Kant's teaching in all its versions, some of which we find frankly indefensible. (See below, note 34.) We do maintain, however, that the texts justify our interpretation. The *locus classicus* is, of course, the Dialectic of the *Critique of Practical Reason*. (Henceforth cited as *Cr.pr.R.*) But of hardly less great importance would appear to be the following texts: *Critique of Judgment* §§84ff (henceforth cited as *Cr.J.*); Preface to the first edition of *Religion innerhalb*; *Cr.p.R.* B823–59; *Reflections*, 6132, 6173, 6454, 6876 (*Werke*, XVIII, 464, 476ff, 724ff; XIX, 188ff); *Über den Gemeinspruch* (*Werke*,

VIII, 279ff). Especially in view of its late date (1797), a relevant passage in 'Von einem neuerdings erhobenen vornehmen Ton in der Philosophie' (*Werke*, VIII, 397) is of special significance.

6 To be sure, much obscurity attaches to Kant's concept of happiness. (See H.J. Paton, 'Kant's Idea of the Good,' *Proceedings of the Aristotelian Society*, n.s. 14 (1944–5), especially IX–X.) However, these obscurities do not concern our present purpose. Whether happiness can be directly aimed at; if so, whether it is definable (*Grundlegung zur Metaphysik der Sitten* [henceforth *Grundlegung*, *Werke*, IV, 417ff], also *Cr.J.* §83); if so, whether it is subject to change (*Religion innerhalb* [*Werke*, VI, 26]): all these are questions outside our scope. What is central to our purpose is solely Kant's certainty – and in this he does not waver – that 'to be happy is necessarily the desire of every rational *but finite* being' (*Cr.pr.R.* [*Werke*, V, 25], italics added). Kant *defines* man in terms of this desire, not, to be sure, in so far as he is human, but in so far as he is finite. With this goes his conviction that the inclinations as such are not evil but innocent (*Religion innerhalb* [*Werke*, VI, 58]). Unless it is kept in mind that Kant understands man, in these terms, as a rational *but also finite* being, his doctrine of the *summum bonum* will be seen to be unintelligible.

7 Since Kant is often viewed as some sort of modern Stoic it is necessary to insist that the texts bear out the above interpretation. He frequently charges the 'philosophical sects' with the Stoic 'error,' and contrasts their view with the Christian, which he more or less identifies with his own. See e.g. *Reflection* 6872 (*Werke*, XIX, 187): 'The highest Good of the philosophical sects could be realizable only on the assumption that man could be wholly adequate to the moral law. Thus one was led, either to adopt a presumptuously flattering view of human actions, or a very lax one of the moral law. The Christian, however, is able to recognize the frailty of his personal value and still to hope, even under the conditions of the holy law, to partake of the highest Good.' See also *Reflection* 6876 (*Werke*, XIX, 188ff), *Cr.pr.R.* (*Werke*, V, 85ff, 111ff, and especially 126ff). Kant treats Christian morality 'from its philosophical aspect' only, and credits Christianity with first having recognized the *summum bonum* in its purity (*Cr.pr.R.* [*Werke*, V, 86]). However, he stresses, on the one hand, that the *summum bonum* is intelligible and acceptable on the basis of reason alone, and, on the other, that Christianity alone cannot be wholly reduced to a religion of reason.

8 *Cr.pr.R.* (*Werke*, V, 113)

9 Kuno Fischer's formulation, in his *Immanuel Kant und seine Lehre*, 6th ed. (Heidelberg, 1957), II, 120

10 *Cr.pr.R.* (*Werke*, V, 129ff). This passage ought to be considered as crucial for the whole subject of this essay. Because of its importance we cite it in full, below, note 12.

11 C.D. Broad, *Five Types of Ethical Theory* (London, 1962), 140

12 Cf. e.g. Arthur Schopenhauer, *Grundlage der Moral*, ed. A. Hübscher (Leipzig, 1938), 124: 'This is in the end nothing but a morality aiming at happiness and hence based on selfishness; this eudaimonism which Kant, with much ado, has thrown out of the front door of his system, as being heteronomous, and which now sneaks back in again, through the back door, under the name of the highest Good.' Along the same lines, see also the criticisms of A. Schweitzer, *Die Religionsphilosophie Kants* (Hildesheim, 1974), *passim*; Hermann Cohen (see next note); W. Windelband, *Geschichte der neueren Philosophie* (Leipzig, 1911), II, 131ff; and indeed all the neo-Kantians. Beginning with Fichte, these all attempt to 'purify' Kant's philosophy of its supposed 'eudaemonistic platitudes' (Emanuel Hirsch). This 'purification,' however, involves nothing less than the total dismissal of the Dialectic of *Cr.pr.R.*, which is not only the climax of that work but may be regarded (and is regarded by this writer) as the climax of Kant's whole philosophy. We shall therefore attempt not to purify Kant's doctrine but rather to understand it. It is summarized by Kant himself as follows:

> In this manner, through the concept of the highest Good as the object and final end of pure practical reason, the moral law leads to religion. Religion is the recognition of all duties as divine commands, not as sanctions, i.e., arbitrary and contingent ordinances of a foreign will, but as essential laws of any free will as such. Even as such, they must be regarded as commands of the Supreme Being because we can hope for the highest Good (to strive for which is our duty under the moral law) only from a perfect (holy and beneficent) and omnipotent will; and, therefore, we can hope to attain it only through harmony with this will. But here again everything remains disinterested and based only on duty, without being based on fear or hope as incentives, which if they became principles, would destroy the entire moral worth of the actions. The moral law commands us to make the highest possible good in a world the final object of all our conduct. This I cannot hope to effect except through the agreement of my will with that of a holy and beneficent Author of the world. And although my own happiness is included in the concept of the highest Good as a whole wherein the greatest happiness is thought of as connected in exact proportion to the greatest degree of moral perfection possible to creatures, still it is not happiness but the moral law (which, in fact, sternly places restricting conditions upon my boundless longing for happiness) which is proved to be the ground determining the will to further the highest Good.
>
> Therefore, morals is not really the doctrine of how to make ourselves happy but of how we are to be *worthy* of happiness. Only if religion is added to it can the hope arise of someday participating in happiness in

proportion as we endeavored not to be unworthy of it. (*Cr.pr.R.* [*Werke*, v, 129ff]; *Critique of Practical Reason*, tr. L.W. Beck [New York, 1956], 134)

13 See Hermann Cohen, *Kants Begründung der Ethik* (2nd ed., Berlin, 1910), 348. Prior to Cohen, Schelling had already written: 'The moral law demands as its object the pure will itself' (*Werke* [Stuttgart and Augsburg, 1856–61], I, 429).

14 This is the view of Schleiermacher: see W. Dilthey, *Das Leben Schleiermachers* (Berlin, 1870), Appendix, 13.

15 See e.g. F. Paulsen, *Immanuel Kant* (Stuttgart, 1899), 323.

16 In connection with the view that Kant's ideas of God, immortality, and possibly even freedom are to be understood as necessary fictions it is, of course, especially Vaihinger's work that comes to mind. But whatever may be thought of Vaihinger himself, passages such as *Werke*, VIII, 136–9 are enough to refute the view that this is Kant's doctrine. For Kant himself the *summum bonum* cannot be reduced to a 'mere ideal' (139), and God must somehow *exist.* See further below, note 42.

17 Erich Adickes, the first editor of Kant's *Opus Postumum*, is relieved to discover that in that work 'the whole doctrine of the highest Good, along with the proofs for God and immortality which are based on it, have almost completely disappeared' (*Kantstudien, Ergänzungsheft* 50 [1920], 846). He believes that here at last Kant gets rid of the 'standpoint of mercenariness, which in the doctrine of the highest Good became wholly obvious' (ibid., 720). Other commentators, such as N. Kemp-Smith, follow Adickes' lead.

But it is doubtful whether too much sense can be made of those sporadic passages in the *Opus Postumum* in which Kant attempts to connect God directly with the categorical imperative. More importantly, it would appear to be illegitimate to place the *Opus Postumum* above the three *Critiques* or even to treat it on a par with them. (The work remained a fragment, and its purpose in Kant's own mind is far from clear.) But the doctrine of the *summum bonum* appears in all three *Critiques.*

18 That elements of the old, pre-Kantian metaphysics remain in Kant's writings to the end would seem to be undebatable. But some recent writers surely overreact to the earlier view that Kant brings about a total break with the traditional metaphysics. Thus we can see no justification for G. Martin's assertion that 'Kant is continuing the tradition of Greek and medieval philosophy without a break' (*Kant's Metaphysics and Theory of Science*, tr. P.G. Lucas [Manchester, 1955], 169).

19 *Cr.J.* §91; see also *Cr.p.R.* B395. To suggest that Kant 'takes over' these three doctrines from the enlightenment metaphysics of Wolff and his followers and 'merely gives them a new basis' is no substitute for an exposition. The new basis is not 'mere,' and inevitably affects the doctrines themselves.

20 Man's finitude is constituted for Kant by the fact that, though a rational and

therefore *self-determining* being, he is *not* a *self-making* being. This latter doctrine, essential to Fichte, is so obviously false for Kant as to be disposed of in a subordinate clause (*Grundlegung* [*Werke*, IV, 451]).

21 See e.g. *Cr.pr.R.* (*Werke*, V, 72), *Grundlegung* (*Werke*, IV, 444), *Reflection* 6078 (*Werke*, XVIII, 443).

22 *Grundlegung* (*Werke*, iv, 451)

23 *Cr.pr.R.* (*Werke*, V, 81): 'For man and all other created rational being moral necessity is necessitation, i.e., obligation.' See also *Grundlegung* (*Werke*, IV, 414).

24 Kant criticizes the belief that such a stage can ever be reached, not only as contrary to all our self-knowledge (*Cr.pr.R.* [*Werke*, V, 123]) but also as morally dangerous, not only because 'man is never more easily deceived than in what promotes a good opinion of himself' (*Religion innerhalb* [*Werke*, VI, 75]) but also, still more importantly, because the moment he had *in fact* reached such a stage he would no longer *consider* himself in need of moral constraint. This fear on Kant's part may seem paradoxical. If so, it reflects the condition of a being which is obligated to aim at angelic existence and yet cannot attain it.

25 'A duty to love is an *Unding*' (*Metaphysik der Sitten*, henceforth *M.d.S.* [*Werke*, VI, 401]). Duty requires restraint while love presupposes absence of restraint. Hence we are obligated to do our duty but not to love doing it (*Cr.pr.R.* [*Werke*, V, 83]; *M.d.S.* [*Werke*, VI, 378ff]). Hence also Biblical commandments to love must be interpreted as commandments to act benevolently (*M.d.S.* [*Werke*, VI, 402]; *Cr.pr.R.* [*Werke*, V, 83]).

This is not to say, however, that the categorical imperative does not arouse feeling. But the feeling is respect rather than love, and respect is 'the feeling of our incapacity to attain to an idea that is law for us' (*Cr.J.* §27). Thus on the one hand, because of our *distance* from the moral law, this latter is present to us as obligation, and our feeling toward it is respect. But on the other hand, this distance is not absolute or without degrees; for the greater a person's *sense* of distance the less great is his *actual* distance – and the more respect passes into love. 'Reverential awe changes into affection, respect into love, because of the greater ease in satisfying that which we stand in awe of' (*Cr.pr.R.* [*Werke*, V, 84]). In short, if we consider not only what man ought to do but also what in the 'end' he will do if he does his duty, 'love is an indispensable addition to the incompleteness of human nature' ('Das Ende aller Dinge' [*Werke*, VIII, 338]).

Since man is a creature who has not made himself, he is in principle incapable of wholly reaching the stage of the love of the moral law (*Cr.pr.R.* [*Werke*, V, 842]; *Religion innerhalb* [*Werke*, VI, 145, 160]). How then can he be obligated even to *aim* at 'being holy' when he *cannot reach* this aim? Kant replies: if the mere striving is confined 'to this life' (*M.d.S.* [*Werke*, VI, 446ff]).

The sobriety manifest in this limitation is still further stressed when Kant defines virtue as 'moral strength of the will,' and, since this definition could apply also to a holy or superhuman being, when he qualifies it further as 'moral strength of the will of a *human* being in obeying his *duty*' (*M.d.S.* [*Werke*, VI, 405]; the emphasis is Kant's).

26 *Cr.pr.R.* (*Werke*, V, 84): 'The moral state in which a man can be is virtue, i.e., a moral state of mind in struggle. It is not holiness in a supposed possession of a will in total purity. This latter ... is simply moral *Schwärmerei* and exaggerated self-esteem.'

27 First, man can know only his phenomenal nature (e.g. *Cr.p.R.* B579); second, when passing moral judgment on himself, he is tempted both by pride (*Religion innerhalb* [*Werke*, VI, 68]) and a false, self-deprecating humility (*Religion innerhalb* [*Werke*, VI, 181]; also *M.d.S.* [*Werke*, VI, 441ff]).

28 See *Vorlesungen über die philosophische Religionslehre*, ed. K.H.L. Politz (Leipzig, 1830), 180.

29 Far from holding that the finite moral agent does not aim at ends, Kant teaches that 'there can be no free action unless the agent intends a purpose' (*M.d.S.* [*Werke*, VI, 388ff]; also *Cr.pr.R.* [*Werke*, V, 34]). However, to the extent to which he is moral, this agent aims at ends not because he desires them but because duty directs him (*Cr.pr.R.* [*Werke*, V, 45ff]; *Cr.J.* 91).

Thus, *for purposes of analysis* one may isolate the moral law as the ground of moral will (*Cr.pr.R.* [*Werke*, V, 109]), remaining aware that in so doing one reaches the categorical imperative in a form so abstract as to learn no more than 'what obligation as such implies' (*M.d.S.* [*Werke*, VI, 225]). This must not obscure the fact, however, that any concrete or complete moral willing and acting must include morally commanded purposes. If no such purpose were possible, then, 'since no action can be without purposes, all purposes would only be means to others, and a categorical imperative would be impossible' (*M.d.S.* [*Werke*, VI, 384ff]).

30 Cf. *Gemeinspruch* (*Werke*, VIII, 283): 'Happiness contains all those things (but not more than those things) which nature can give us; virtue, all that which none other than a person himself can give to or take from himself.' Because he holds that we cannot but aim at happiness (*Grundlegung* [*Werke*, IV, 415]; *Cr.pr.R.* [*Werke*, V, 25]), Kant denies that our own happiness can be among the objects of our duty (*M.d.S.* [*Werke*, VI, 385]). Because of a (possibly exaggerated) emphasis on the need for self-acquisition of virtue, he denies that other people's virtue can be among the objects of our duty (*M.d.S.* [*Werke*, VI, 386ff]). See Paton, 'Kant's Idea of the Good,' xxi.

31 H.J. Paton has rightly observed that in asserting that only a good will can be good without qualification Kant does not assert that a good will is the sole good (*The Categorical Imperative* [Chicago, 1948], 43). It must be added that

only if it is geared to a purpose other than itself can the will be good at all. (See e.g. *Grundlegung* [*Werke*, iv, 394].)

32 This possibly somewhat daring interpretation is based on passages in which Kant asserts that even though moral willing-to-act is based on the moral law and not on considerations of success, moral reason 'cannot be indifferent' to such success. (E.g. *Religion innerhalb* [*Werke*, VI, 5], also *Cr.J.* §87.)

33 Kant writes: 'Assume that a person ... persuaded himself that there is no God: he would still consider himself as unworthy if for that reason he considered the laws of duty as imaginary, invalid, unobligatory and decided to violate them unashamedly' (*Cr.J.* §87). Kant proceeds to take Spinoza as an example of a morally decent atheist and to show – since without an implied belief in God and immortality the moral will cannot believe itself to have the potential of success – that the actions of such as Spinoza belie their theories.

34 In our above account of the *summum bonum* we have been careful to exclude from consideration all passages which Schopenhauer and the neo-Kantians might rightly have regarded as lapses into eudaemonism. See, e.g., *Eine Vorlesung Kants über Ethik*, ed. P. Menzer (Berlin, 1924), 102: 'Religion is that which is to give weight to morality, it is meant to be its spring. Here we recognize that the person who acts so as to be worthy of happiness may hope to attain it. ...' Having removed these obstacles, we see the Kantian grounds for hope in a share in the *summum bonum* solely in the duty to further it, together with the conditions without which such furthering cannot be done. There is no further reason to wonder why the *summum bonum* should appear in the *Cr.p.R.* primarily as object of (theoretical) hope and in the *Cr.pr.R.* primarily as an ultimate end to be furthered by our actions. Kant conjoins the theoretical and the practical aspects when he defines his three 'postulates' as 'theoretical but as such unprovable propositions which adhere inseparably to an a priori unconditionally valid practical law' (*Cr.pr.R.* [*Werke*, V, 122]).

35 So far as we know, this contradiction has been noticed only by Hans Urs von Balthasar, *Prometheus* (Heidelberg, 1947), 100.

36 See e.g. *Religion innerhalb* (*Werke*, VI, 133); *Gemeinspruch* (*Werke*, VIII, 278); *Cr.pr.R.* (*Werke*, V, 130). A comparison of these three passages shows a significant wavering which is responsible for our cautious formulation.

37 See e.g. *Religion innerhalb* (*Werke*, VI, 139).

38 See *Prolegomena to a Future Metaphysic* §§57–9; also *Cr.J.*, especially §§88, 59.

39 See 'Von einem neuerdings erhobenem vornehmen Ton. ...' (*Werke*, VIII, 400ff); *Prolegomena* §57.

40 *Prolegomena* §57; also *Cr.J.* §59: 'all our cognition of God is only symbolic. Whoever takes as schematic such attributes as understanding and will ... lapses into anthropomorphism, while to omit everything intuitive is to lapse into Deism.'

41 See *Cr.p.R.* B69; also *Prolegomena* (*Werke*, IV, 290ff).

42 See e.g. 'Von einem neuerdings erhobenem vornehmen Ton ...' (*Werke*, VIII, 401); *Prolegomena* §58; *Cr.J.* §§59, 88; *Religion innerhalb* (*Werke*, VI, 64).

In the case of immortality, the analogical concept is temporal succession. This is symbolic in that we recognize that a 'future' life is future only *for us* (*Cr.p.R.* B839), i.e., a succession which from a hypothetically adopted divine standpoint does not exist (*Cr.pr.R.* [*Werke*, V, 123]). On this point see H. Heimsöth, 'Metaphysische Motive in der Ausbildung des kritischen Idealismus,' *Kantstudien, Ergänzungsheft* 71 (1956), 224.

In the case of God, the analogical concepts needed are 'holiness of a legislator (creator) ... (ii) goodness of a governor ... (iii) justice as a judge ...' (*Religion innerhalb* [*Werke*, VI, 162])

More important than a precise identification of the needed analogical concepts is a precise definition of the analogy required. Here the excesses of the recently fashionable ontological interpretation become fully evident. (See above, note 18.) In criticism of Martin, J. Collins has rightly stressed that Kantian analogy has nothing in common with the Thomistic, if only because Kant rejects any causal inference from nature to God (*Crosscurrents*, 7:1 [1957], 79). Kant himself writes as follows: 'It is in a practical respect alone that an analogy between the divine understanding and will and those of man and his practical reason may be assumed, despite the fact that theoretically there is no analogy at all. Through the moral law which our reason prescribes to us authoritatively, not through the theory of the nature of things in themselves, there arises the concept of God which practical reason compels us to *create for ourselves*' ('Von einem neuerdings erhobenem vornehmen Ton. ...' [*Werke*, VIII, 401], italics added). Passages such as these necessitate the rejection of the 'ontological' interpretation of Kant's doctrine of analogy. They do not necessitate the acceptance of Vaihinger-style fictionalism. In Kant's authoritative view, we are morally certain of the conditions without which the *summum bonum* would be a 'mere ideal' ('Was heisst: sich im denken orientieren?' [*Werke*, VIII, 139]), and we are certain of these conditions while engaged in moral action.

As for the 'what' of these conditions, we can understand them only in anthropomorphic terms, but recognize at the same time that they are *only* such terms. As for the 'that' of the conditions, we are certain that they must *be*, not merely be *believed* to be, and this is all 'existence' can mean in this limiting case. Gerhard Krüger has rightly observed: 'Theoretical cognition is not expanded in that these objects [*Objekte*] become known, but in that the ideas in general acquire objects [*Objekte*]. It is certain that an object [*Gegenstand*] corresponds to them, not what kind' (G. Krüger, *Philosophie und Moral in der Kantischen Kritik* [Tübingen, 1967], 201).

43 See especially the *locus classicus*, *Cr.J.* §76; also the remarkable passage on 'absolute necessity,' *Cr.p.R.* B641.
44 *Cr.J.* §76
45 *Cr.J.* §76
46 *Cr.J.* §87
47 Reflection 6282 [*Werke*, XVIII, 548ff]
48 *Cr.p.R.* B641
49 Ibid.
50 *Op. post.* (*Werke*, XXI, 66)
51 *Ende aller Dinge* (*Werke*, VIII, 355)
52 *Streit der Fakultäten* (*Werke*, VII, 63)
53 'Was heisst ...' (*Werke*, VIII, 142)
54 *Streit der Fakultäten* (*Werke*, VII, 57)
55 'Vorrede zu R.B. Jachmanns Prüfung der Kantischen Religionsphilosophie' (*Werke*, VIII, 441)
56 *Religion innerhalb* (*Werke*, VI, 83)

Chapter 2 Kant and Radical Evil

1 Quoted by K. Vorländer, *Kant-Schiller-Goethe* (2nd ed., Leipzig, 1923), 151
2 *Vorlesungen über die philosophische Religionslehre* (2nd ed., Leipzig, 1930), 150
3 *Kants Gesammelte Schriften*, Prussian Academy ed. (Berlin, 1902–55), VIII, 123. Unless otherwise stated, all quotations refer to this edition, cited as *Werke.*
4 In a letter to G. Körner, dated 28 February 1793, in *Schillers Briefe*, ed. F. Jonas (Stuttgart, n.d.), III, 288
5 In a letter to Herder, dated 7 June 1793, *Werke*, Grossherzogin Sophie von Sachsen ed. (Weimar, 1887), section IV, vol. X, 75
6 Cf. especially Kant's *Streit der Fakultäten*, in particular the preface, *Werke*, VII, 5ff. Cf. also K. Vorländer's edition of *Die Religion innerhalb der Grenzen der blossen Vernunft* (Leipzig 1919), xxxff.
7 The title of Kant's work alone is sufficient proof that he strove to make a sharp distinction between 'natural' or 'philosophical' religion, on the one hand, and 'revealed' religion, on the other. There can be no doubt that Kant was sincere in making this distinction, though it is quite another question (and one well worth asking) whether he managed to preserve it. Nevertheless, one group of critics accused him of seeking to undermine revealed theology, whereas the other group accused him of giving a mere theological apologetic in a pseudo-philosophical form. As far as Kant's intentions are concerned, both accusations are equally unjust. And as regards performance, there may be some justice in the former criticism, but (as this paper seeks to show) there is none whatever in the latter.

8 Kant grants that there is a sense in which love is a duty; but he denies that love, in that sense, is an inclination. Cf. *Werke*, VI, 449: 'However, love is not here understood as feeling (aesthetical), i.e. as delight in the perfection of other people, not as love of pleasure (for no obligation to have feelings can be imposed by others), but rather must be thought as a maxim of goodwill (as practical), which has doing good as a consequence.'

9 *Werke*, IV, 421; *Fundamental Principles of the Metaphysic of Ethics*, tr. T.K. Abbott (10th ed., London, 1926), 46. For an incisive study of the various formulations of the categorical imperative, cf. H.J. Paton, *The Categorical Imperative* (Chicago, 1948), 129ff.

10 *Werke*, IV, 427; Abbott, *Fundamental Principles*, 54

11 *Werke*, V, 72; *Kant's Critique of Practical Reason*, tr. Abbott (6th ed., London, 1923), 164

12 *Werke*, IV, 447; *Fundamental Principles*, 79

13 Reicke, *Lose Blätter aus Kants Nachlass* (c. 1889), II, 139

14 *Werke*, IV, 454ff; *Fundamental Principles*, 89ff

15 *Werke*, V, 60; *Kant's Critique of Practical Reason*, tr. Abbott, 151

16 *Werke*, VI, 19; *Religion within the Limits of Reason Alone*, tr. T.M. Greene and H.H. Hudson (Chicago, 1934), 15. For the most part, we quote from that translation (referred to as *Religion*).

17 *Werke*, VI, 33, 34; *Religion*, 28ff

18 *Werke*, VI, 31; *Religion*, 26

19 *Werke*, VI, 32; *Religion*, 27

20 *Werke*, VI, 20; *Religion*, 16

21 *Werke*, VI, 24; *Religion*, 20

22 *Werke*, VI, 32, 22; *Religion*, 28, 17

23 *Werke*, VI, 41ff; *Religion*, 36ff

24 *Werke*, VI, 45, 41; *Religion*, 40, 36

25 *Werke*, VI, 153, 170; *Religion*, 142, 158

26 *Werke*, VI, 44ff; *Religion*, 40

27 *Werke*, VI, 47ff; *Religion*, 43

28 *Werke*, VI, 41; *Religion*, 36

Chapter 3 Kant's Concept of History

1 Among these we may mention: F. Medicus, 'Kants Philosophie der Geschichte,' *Kantstudien*, 7 (1902), 1–23, 171–229; E. Troeltsch, 'Das Historische in Kants Religionsphilosophie,' *Kantstudien*, 9 (1904), 21–154; P. Menzer, *Kants Lehre von der Entwicklung in Natur und Geschichte* (Berlin, 1911). Cf., however, on some shortcomings of these works, below, note 4. Of treatments in English the following deserve mention: R.G. Collingwood, *The Idea*

of History (Oxford, 1946), 93–104, and W.H. Walsh, *An Introduction to Philosophy of History* (London, 1951), 122–32.

2 When invited to review Herder's *Ideen* Kant replied that he would do so 'zur Probe' (*Werke*, X, 371ff, cf. also *Werke*, VIII, 63). All quotations refer to the Prussian Academy edition of Kant's works, I–XXIII (Berlin, 1900–55).

3 Of Kant's writings which directly bear on history three are, in the opinion of this writer, of the greatest importance. Two of these are: *Idee zu einer allgemeinen Geschichte in weltbürgerlicher Absicht*, published in 1784, and *Mutmaßlicher Anfang der Menschengeschichte*, written in 1785, although published only in 1786 (cf. *Werke*, X, 393) ('Idea for a Universal History from a Cosmopolitan Point of View,' tr. L.W. Beck, and 'Conjectural Beginning of Human History,' tr. E.L. Fackenheim, in I. Kant, *On History*, ed. L.W. Beck [Indianapolis, 1963]). But in 1785 there appeared Kant's *Groundwork of the Metaphysics of Morals*, perhaps his greatest work in the field of ethics! Kant's third main piece on history is chapter 83 of the *Critique of Judgment*, and no careful reader of the third *Critique* needs to be reminded of the crucial systematic importance of that chapter. It is a pity that H. Cassirer's commentary fails to treat chapters 79–91 (the 'Appendix'), a section which contains far more than merely 'interesting observations' (H. Cassirer, *A Commentary on Kant's Critique of Judgment* [London, 1938], VIII).

4 To this writer it seems that even some of the authors mentioned in note 1 have not done Kant full justice. Medicus and Menzer, e.g., explain certain inconsistencies in Kantian doctrine (apparent or real) in terms of a supposed change of mind on the part of Kant. But their account of this change of mind defies belief. In less than fifteen years (all of them in the critical period) Kant's views on history are said to have not merely changed, but wavered back and forth. According to Medicus, Kant in 1784 still understood history as the work of providence, while in 1785 it had become the 'history of freedom'; but in 1795 he had reverted to belief in providence (*Philosophie der Geschichte*, 172, 186, 221). According to Menzer, Kant in 1784 regarded men as the mere tool of providence or 'nature,' a doctrine incompatible with, and abandoned by, the *Critique of Judgment* of 1790; but in 1794 'providence' had won out once more (*Lehre von der Entwicklung*, 276, 285, 291). This wavering is explained by both authors in terms of Kant's historical experience and beginning senility (Medicus, *Philosophie der Geschichte*, 208; Menzer, *Lehre von der Entwicklung*, 299). Undoubtedly Kant's views on history were affected by the turbulent events of his age, and it is a melancholy fact that his intellectual powers waned in the 1790s (cf. *Werke*, xii, 254). Yet reference to these facts, in explanation of Kantian doctrines, is legitimate only after all attempts at systematic explanation have broken down. In the case at hand, this is far from so. For the fact is that Kant never ceased to use the term 'providence,'

and that (at least during the critical period) he always used it with caution. The questions arising for the interpreter are why the critical philosophy is in need of that term, and precisely what it can mean by it. If these questions are satisfactorily answered, the supposed Kantian inconsistencies in this matter may well disappear.

5 *Werke*, IV, 294

6 *Werke*, VIII, 107–23. See my English translation in I. Kant, *On History*, ed. L.W. Beck (Indianapolis, 1963), 53–68.

7 Cf. *Cr.p.R.* A 848ff, B876ff; more explicitly, *Metaphysical Foundations of Natural Science*, *Werke*, IV, 471ff. Of special significance is *Erste Einleitung in die Kritik der Urteilskraft*, ed. G. Lehmann (Leipzig, 1927), 47ff.

8 Cf. *Anthropologie in pragmatischer Hinsicht*, *Werke*, VII, 119ff, and *Metaphysics of Morals*, *Werke*, VI, 214ff, 405ff.

9 This interpretation is subjected to searching criticism by G. Krüger, *Philosophie und Moral in der Kantischen Kritik* (Tübingen, 1931 and 1967), 37ff. Cf. also the perceptive remarks of M. Heidegger, *Vom Wesen des Grundes* (3rd ed., Frankfurt a/M, 1949), 31ff. Krüger makes it clear beyond doubt that a sufficiently profound study of the *Anthropologie* is among the most important *desiderata* of Kant research.

10 This 'should' cannot be a moral should, since the latter would belong to moral anthropology.

11 *Werke*, VII, 119

12 In its Kantian sense, this term covers more territory than in our modern sense. It includes all that which nature (*physis*) has made of man, and which is therefore subject to laws.

13 *Werke*, VII, 119ff, also 136, 176, 189. Cf. also the cited works of Krüger and Heidegger.

14 Kant was, however, aware of some of its problems, cf. e.g. *Werke*, VIII, 29.

15 Our breaking off at this point is motivated (and, we hope, justified) by the systematic exigencies of the present paper.

16 R. Flint seems unable to make this distinction; consequently, he dismisses the *Conjectural Beginning* in a mere half page, as deserving no serious attention (*The Philosophy of History in France and Germany* [Edinburgh and London, 1874], 103ff).

17 *Werke*, VIII, 109ff

18 Cf. especially the *Methodology of Pure Practical Reason*, *Werke*, V, 151ff; also *Werke*, VII, 326ff.

19 *Werke*, VII, 321: 'To allocate a class to man within the system of living nature and so to characterize him, there remains nothing more for us than: that he has a character which he creates himself, since he is capable of perfecting himself according to the ends which he himself has adopted; thereby, as an

animal gifted with the capacity of reason (*animal rationabile*), he can make of himself a rational animal (*animal rationale*). ...'

20 As the quotation in note 19 shows, Kant is not averse to using this term. But strictly speaking, 'rationale' cannot be the differentia of the genus 'animal.' For what is signified by 'animal' belongs to nature while what is signified by 'rationale' transcends nature.

21 We refer in particular to the two-worlds terminology.

22 A new point of departure, that is to say, so far as the systematic development of the present essay is concerned. We are not here interested in the temporal sequence of Kant's writings: the *Idea for a Universal History* ... , to which we shall soon turn, was written one year prior to the *Conjectural Beginning* ... which has occupied our attention in the last two sections, cf. above, note 3.

23 It is tempting to deny that the *Critique of Judgment* has systematic unity, and to regard the work, which treats, among other things, of aesthetics, biology, history, and moral teleology, as a sort of warehouse in which the aging Kant deposited whatever had to be stored somewhere, but could not be given a fitting place. After all, in 1787 he still intended to write merely a 'critique of taste' (*Werke*, x, 488); and in the two years which it took him to complete the third *Critique* he complained about the burden of administrative duties (*Werke*, x, 505) and the beginning weakness of old age (*Werke*, XI, 47). Still, the interpreter must resist this temptation. The work which Schelling could regard as Kant's greatest can hardly be regarded as the product of senility. The interpreter is obligated to take seriously the claim to system which the third *Critique* so manifestly makes. [On this question see John H. Zammito, *The Genesis of Kant's Critique of Judgment* (Chicago, 1992). Ed.]

24 We deliberately use the vague word 'traces' to refer to so divergent manifestations of teleology as the success of scientific method (second introduction, especially chapter 5), beauty (chapter 59), organic nature (chapter 61ff), and history (chapter 83).

25 This will appear to some as a perverse question; and those interested only in Kant's philosophy of science may prefer to ask why he treats anything except biology. But it would appear that if one tries to understand the third *Critique* as one whole (including the 'Appendix'!), and if one takes seriously the two very important introductions, the question we ask is natural and, indeed, inevitable.

26 We cannot here enter into a fuller discussion of Kant's treatment of biology. Cf. especially B. Bauch, *Immanuel Kant* (Berlin and Leipzig 1923), 413ff, and H. Cassirer, *Commentary*, 309ff.

27 *Critique of Judgment*, chapter 82, *Werke*, V, 426ff. The context leaves it doubtful (intentionally, it would seem) how seriously this argument is to be taken.

28 We use the term 'end-in-itself' for Kant's 'Endzweck,' which he carefully dis-

tinguishes from 'final end' ('letzter Zweck'). A 'final end' is the final achievement of nature toward an 'end-in-itself' which latter, if for no other reason than that it *is* an end-in-itself, transcends nature. One is tempted to identify, with Medicus, the 'final end' of nature with the 'animal rationabile,' and the 'end-in-itself' with the 'animal rationale' (cf. above, note 19, Medicus, *Philosophie der Geschichte*, 193). But as we shall see, the core of Kant's construction of history lies in the attempt to create, *from the side of 'nature,'* a link between mere 'potential' rationability (which may be regarded as the work of 'nature') and 'actual' rationality (which can only be the work of man himself); and it is this link which must be regarded as 'nature's' final end. Cf. chapters 82–4 of the *Critique of Judgment*, *Werke*, V, 425ff.

29 It must be clearly understood that Kant's construction of the historical process cannot be regarded as a corollary of the doctrine of the *summum bonum*, expounded in the second *Critique*. Such an interpretation may at first sight seem plausible. But passages such as *Werke*, V, 122, 129ff, 132ff, 144 make it clear that this is mistaken, for at least two reasons: (i) As we have already asserted, the doctrine of the *summum bonum* postulates a link between morality and nature, but is not at all concerned with seeking evidence of such a link in nature. But Kant's construction of the historical process can be understood only as part (the crucial part) of an attempt to find such evidence. (ii) The teleological construction of history cannot solve the problem which the doctrine of the *summum bonum* is designed to solve. For the former implies that, in some sense, some human beings are means to others; indeed, that all generations are means to the last. This implication Kant recognizes with the utmost clarity. He writes: 'It remains strange that the earlier generations appear to carry through their toilsome labor only for the sake of the later, to prepare for them a foundation on which the later generations could erect the higher edifice which was Nature's goal, and yet that only the latest of the generations should have the good fortune to inhabit the building on which a long line of their ancestors had (unintentionally) labored without being permitted to partake of the fortune that they had prepared' (*Werke*, VIII, 20; *On History*, 14). As we shall see, Kant can accept this 'perplexing' implication, so long as it is not in a moral sense that 'nature' uses some beings as means to others (cf. below, 48). But this makes it all the more clear that the doctrine of progress in history is not a corollary of the doctrine of the *summum bonum*.

30 Troeltsch justly accuses Medicus of distorting the teaching of the third *Critique*, by the undue stress he lays on the 'as-if' concept (Troeltsch, 'Das Historische ...' 121ff). This stress not only distorts the Kantian teaching; it also makes some of it unintelligible. The 'as-if' interpretation may seem plausible in the case of biology because biological phenomena, and biological science,

require the teleological as a heuristic concept. The same (according to both Kant and Medicus!) cannot be said for empirical history. As we shall see, teleology is needed in history, not in order to explain historical events, but to show that they have value. Hence if the teleological concept in history is a fiction, it must be a fiction necessary, not theoretically but morally. But what is this necessity? Medicus writes: 'The theme of the philosophy of history is ... the *sense of* history, not history itself. ... Further, it is not so much a question of deriving this sense of history from history – in this way as well would the philosophy of history as a theoretical science be under threat – but rather of establishing a priori "from a practical perspective" that the historical being of humanity may be, indeed must be, seen as something full of sense and value' (*Philosophie der Geschichte*, 10). But Medicus does nothing to show that the fiction of the moral meaning in history is 'permissible,' much less that it is 'necessary'; nor is it possible to show this. It is true, of course, that Kant frequently asserts that his historical construction is justified only 'for practical purposes'; but this means, not that it is a fiction, but that it is theoretically insufficient, and morally relevant (but not necessary!). E. Lask correctly credits Kant with having drawn, implicitly, the distinction between an 'explanatory' and an 'evaluating' method of approach. But since he seems mainly concerned with Kant's contribution to later modes of thought he fails to ask why, *for Kant*, the 'evaluating' method of study is necessary, and how it is possible. (Cf. E. Lask, *Fichtes Idealismus und die Geschichte* [Tübingen, 1902]), 1ff.)

31 Kant writes: 'Even if we are too blind to see the secret mechanism of its (i.e., of "nature's") workings, this Idea (i.e., of an intention of "nature") may still serve as a guiding thread for presenting as a system, at least in broad outlines, what would otherwise be a planless conglomerate of human actions' (*Werke*, VIII, 29; *On History*, 24). For Kant, the 'idea' of such a 'system' is, to be sure, a 'mere' idea, sufficient only for 'practical purposes.' But it is not therefore a fiction. It is mere idea only because of our 'shortsightedness.'

32 Kant can write: 'For what is the good of esteeming the majesty and wisdom of Creation in the realm of brute nature and of recommending that we contemplate it, if that part of the great stage of supreme wisdom which contains the purpose of all others – the history of mankind – must remain an unceasing reproach to it?' (*Werke*, VIII, 30; *On History*, 25).

33 All three must be involved. Mechanism and teleology, without freedom, would reduce history to a mere part of nature. Mechanism and freedom, without teleology, would deprive history of purposiveness, beyond the purposes of individuals and groups. Teleology and freedom, without mechanism, would enable the philosopher to evaluate history, but not to explain it.

34 *Werke,* VIII, 22, Walsh's translation, in *Introduction,* 126
35 *Critique of Judgment,* chapter 83, *Werke,* V, 432, English tr. by J.H. Bernard (New York, 1951), 282
36 *Critique of Judgment,* chapter 83, *Werke,* V, 431; tr. Bernard, 281
37 *Werke,* VIII, 21, 311; VII, 328ff
38 E.g., *Werke,* VIII, 365, perhaps 312ff
39 *Werke,* VIII, 355, 366
40 *Werke,* V, 432; VII, 26
41 *Werke,* VIII, 366
42 Cf. Krüger, *Philosophie und Moral,* 55ff. Cf. also the quite different doctrine of part I of *Religion within the Limits of Reason Alone.* On that doctrine, cf. chapter 2: 'Kant and Radical Evil.'
43 Cf. above, note 29
44 *Werke,* VIII, 30
45 Kant writes: 'What is the use, one might well complain, of placing at the basis of all these arrangements a great understanding incommensurable by us and supposing it to govern the world according to design if nature does not and cannot tell us anything of the final design? For without this we cannot refer all these natural purposes to any common point, nor can be form any teleological principle. ...' (*Critique of Judgment,* chapter 85; *Werke,* V, 440; tr. Bernard, 291)

Chapter 4 Schelling in 1800–1801: Art as Revelation

1 In *Lectures on the History of Philosophy,* tr. Haldane and Simson (London, 1895), III, 513. This comment is not contained in the new edition of the 1825/6 lectures.
2 *Sämmtliche Werke* (Stuttgart and Augsburg, 1856–61), I, 3.327–634 (henceforth referred to as *Werke*); *System of Transcendental Idealism (1800),* tr. P. Heath (Charlottesville, 1978)
3 A reproduction of this photograph can be found on the cover of A. Bowie, *Schelling and Modern European Philosophy* (London, 1993).
4 Schelling, *Werke,* I, 8.268; *The Ages of the World,* tr. F. Bolman (New York, 1942), 156
5 Schelling, *Werke,* I, 3.618; *System,* 223
6 J.G. Fichte, *Sämmtliche Werke,* ed. I.H. Fichte (Berlin, 1845–6), V, 9–174; *Attempt at a Critique of All Revelation,* tr. G. Green (Cambridge, 1978)
7 Fichte, *Werke,* I, 83–328; *Science of Knowledge,* tr. P. Heath and J. Lachs (New York, 1970)
8 See my *Encounters between Judaism and Modern Philosophy* (New York, 1973; Northvale, 1994), 39ff.

9 Kant comes close to this view in a few jottings in his *opus posthumus*, but not in his published works, which latter must be considered authoritative.

10 The chief Fichtean theses relevant to his concept of religion – nature as the material of duty rendered sensuous, God as the moral order of the world, religion as the joy implicit in moral action – are all found in the essay which provoked the atheism controversy, 'Über den Grund unseres Glaubens an eine göttliche Weltregierung' (Fichte, *Werke* [Berlin, 1845], v, 175–90; 'On the Basis of Our Belief in a Divine Governance of the World,' *Introductions to the Wissenschaftslehre and Other Writings (1797–1800)*, tr. D. Breazeale [Indianapolis, 1994], 141–54).

In the course of the controversy Fichte kept returning to one or another of his basic theses, perhaps most tersely as follows: 'Morality and religion are absolutely identical: each is a grasp of the supersensuous, the one as action, the other as faith' (*Werke*, v, 209). The major contributions to the atheism controversy are collected in *Die Schriften zu J.G. Fichte's Atheismus-Streit*, ed. Hans Lindau (Munich, 1912).

11 *Über die Religion, Reden an die Gebildeten unter ihren Verächtern* (Berlin, 1799); *On Religion: Speeches to Its Cultured Despisers*, tr. J. Oman (New York, 1958)

12 *Über die Religion*, 121–2; *On Religion*, 91

13 Schleiermacher, *The Christian Faith* (Edinburgh, 1928), §4

14 *Über die Religion*, 54; *On Religion*, 40

15 G.W.F. Hegel, Foreword to H.F.W. Hinrichs, *Die Religion im inneren Verhältnisse zur Wissenschaft* (Heidelberg, 1822), xviii–xix; G.W.F Hegel, *Gesammelte Werke*, xv (Hamburg, 1990), 137; English tr. in E. von der Luft, *Hegel, Hinrichs and Schleiermacher on Feeling and Reason in Religion* (Lewiston-Queenston, 1987), 260

16 *Werke*, I, 10.96; *On the History of Modern Philosophy*, tr. A. Bowie (Cambridge, 1994), 111. The following interpretation relies heavily on this text, containing as it does Schelling's retroactive self-interpretation. It differs from the conventional. According to this latter, Schelling, a 'subjective idealist' prior to 1797, embraces 'objective idealism' in his philosophy of nature in 1797 – 'objective' because requiring a realistic epistemology, and 'idealism' because nature is seen as struggling toward mind – becomes 'subjective idealist' again in his 1800 *System of Transcendental Idealism*, and, finally, in his *My System of Philosophy* of 1801, adopts a standpoint of indifference in which subjective and objective are synthesized. While having a basis in a few texts (mainly the prefaces of the 1800 and 1801 works), the conventional account is shallow, hackneyed, and, accusing as it does Schelling of an unprincipled swinging back and forth, incredible. My own account owes a debt to Kurt Schilling, *Natur und Wahrheit* (Munich, 1934).

17 I confine myself to two poems by the greatest of German poets:

Was wär' ein Gott, der nur von aussen stiesse,
Im Kreis das All am Finger laufen liesse!
Ihm ziehmt's, die Welt im Innern zu bewegen,
Natur in Sich, Sich in Natur zu hegen,
So dass, was in Ihm lebt und webt und ist
Nie Seine Kraft, nie Seinen Geist vermisst.

Wär nicht das Auge sonnenhaft,
Die Sonne könnt es nie erblicken.
Läg nicht in uns des Gottes eigne Kraft,
Wie könnt uns Göttliches entzücken?

Goethe, *Werke* [Hamburg, 1956], I, 357, 367)

I resist the temptation to translate Goethe, who can only with difficulty be called a romantic and at any rate transcends the limits of romanticism. Goethe was fervently admired by all German idealists after Kant.

18 In the *Systemfragment*, first published, analysed, and attributed to Schelling by Franz Rosenzweig, *Zweistromland* (Berlin, 1926), 126. [This text has been attributed to Hegel and Hölderlin as well as Schelling in subsequent scholarly debates. An English translation can be found in H.S. Harris, *Hegel's Development: Toward the Sunlight, 1770–1801* (Oxford, 1972), 510ff. Ed.]

19 Names coming to mind include Henri Bergson and Alfred North Whitehead.

20 *Werke*, I, 10.90; *Modern Philosophy*, 106

21 *Werke*, I, 10.93–4; *Modern Philosophy*, 109

22 *Werke*, I, 10.107; *Modern Philosophy*, 120

23 As early as 1795 Schelling writes: 'It has been said that it is the fault or weakness of human reason ... that we do not have knowledge of things in themselves. It would be better to say that the weakness lies in this, that we have knowledge of objects at all' (*Werke*, I, 1, 211; English tr. by F. Marti in *The Unconditional in Human Knowledge* [Lewisburg, Pa., 1980], 106).

24 In the above-quoted key passage Schelling writes that there is nothing to prevent him from 'assuming' a 'region below the now existing consciousness.' This assumption clearly requires justification.

25 *Werke*, I, 3.619; *Transcendental Idealism*, 225

26 *Werke*, I, 10.97; *Modern Philosophy*, 112

27 *Werke*, I, 3.369; *Transcendental Idealism*, 27. This is, of course, Schelling's intellectual intuition, introduced by us at this late point only in order that it should not be misunderstood. It is not the passive intuition of an object, which would be subject to Kant's famous criticism, but rather an activity, at once a doing and a knowing. This kind of intuition is, in Fichte, limited to what the finite or human Ego produces, namely, itself. But in Schelling's uni-

versal or absolute Ego it accompanies all its reproducing of what both nature and consciousness have already produced.

28 *Werke*, I, 1.383; 'Treatise Explicatory of the Idealism in the *Science of Knowledge*,' in *Idealism and the Endgame of Theory*, tr. T. Pfau (Albany, 1994), 90

29 *Werke*, I, 3.627; *Transcendental Idealism*, 231

30 *Werke*, I, 3.587–606; *Transcendental Idealism*, 199–214

31 *Werke*, I, 3.597, 596; *Transcendental Idealism*, 206

32 *Werke*, I, 3.597; *Transcendental Idealism*, 206

33 *Werke*, I, 3.601; *Transcendental Idealism*, 209

34 Ibid.

35 *Werke*, I, 3.602, 603; *Transcendental Idealism*, 210, 211

36 The ancient saying is attributed to Seneca.

37 *Werke*, I, 3.604; *Transcendental Idealism*, 212. Schelling's division of history into three periods is much too brief – less than two pages! – to allow for a clear exposition. Also, his projected last period gives rise to a problem: if only when God *is* Providence will be fully revealed, will not then religion-as-belief-in-Providence be transcended by the ultimate religion of art? (On this, see further below.) But then, Schelling also historicizes art and in particular poetry, through a prognosis of a 'new mythology' which will not be 'the invention of an individual poet' but only of a 'whole generation, representing, as it were, One Poet.' He seems certain of this, but adds: 'how such a new mythology can arise – that is a problem the solution of which can be expected only from ... the future course of history' (*Werke*, I, 3.629; *Transcendental Idealism*, 232f).

The role of history in Schelling's thought requires a separate investigation.

38 *Werke*, I, 3.605; *Transcendental Idealism*, 213

39 *Werke*, I, 3.630; *Transcendental Idealism*, 233. In contrast, 'philosophy may reach the Highest, but carries to this point only, as it were, a fragment of man' (ibid.).

40 *Werke*, I, 3, 618; *Transcendental Idealism*, 223

41 The two major ones are *On Freedom* (*Werke*, I, 7.331–416; *Of Human Freedom*, tr. J. Gutmann [Chicago, 1936]) and *The Ages of the World* (*Werke*, I, 8.195–344; *The Ages of the World*, tr. F.W. Bolman [New York, 1942]). Of the latter work no less a thinker than Franz Rosenzweig has said that, were it not for the two facts that it remained a fragment, and that it contained nothing on Judaism, it would have made his own *Star of Redemption* superfluous.

42 *Werke*, I, 6.131–214

Chapter 5 Schelling's Philosophy of the Literary Arts

In a letter dated 3 September 1802. See *Aus Schellings Leben in Briefen*, ed.

G.L. Plitt (Leipzig 1869), I, 398. For evidence of careful study of Schlegel's manuscript, cf. 427ff.

2 The section on the figurative arts is influenced in particular by A.W. Schlegel, that on the literary arts by Friedrich Schlegel's *Geschichte der Poesie der Griechen und Römer*. R. Zimmermann rightly observes: 'None of his other works bears so clearly the mark of his dependence with regard to material on his romantic contacts with the stars' (*Sitzungsberichte*, phil. hist. Klasse, Wiener Akademie, 80, 1875, 674).

3 For this distinction, cf. also *Sämmtliche* (Stuttgart and Augsburg, 1856–61), I, 5.350ff, 368; F.W.J. Schelling, *On University Studies*, tr. E.S. Morgan and ed. N. Guterman (Athens, Ohio, 1966), 149ff, and F.W.J. Schelling, *The Philosophy of Art*, tr. D.W. Stott (Minneapolis, 1989) 15–16.

4 Cf. *Werke*, I, 5.363; *Philosophy of Art*, 12f.

5 *Werke*, I, 5.361ff; *Philosophy of Art*, 11f

6 *Werke*, I, 3.627; *System of Transcendental Idealism (1800)* tr. P. Heath (Charlottesville, 1978), 231

7 Cf. e.g. that most romantic of German romantics, Novalis: 'The separation of poet and thinker is only apparent and to the detriment of both. It is a sign of illness and a sickly constitution' (fr. 1907). Cf. also note 8.

8 This treatment is an oversimplification. On the one hand, Schelling arrived at his aesthetic idealism under the influence of Kant and Hölderlin rather than Fichte. In 1795 he considered writing an interpretation of the *Critique of Judgment* (cf. *Schellings Briefwechsel mit Niethammer*, ed. Dammköhler [Leipzig, 1913], 19). And an early fragment of his, making art the highest act of reason, may well have been influenced by Hölderlin (cf. F. Rosenzweig, 'Das älteste Systemprogramm des deutschen Idealismus,' *Zweistromland* [Berlin, 1926], 123ff; E. Cassirer, *Idee und Gestalt* [Berlin, 1924], 130ff). On 4 September 1795 Hölderlin wrote to Schiller: 'I am striving to develop for myself the idea of an infinite progress in philosophy; I am endeavouring to show that the unremitting demand (which must be made of every system) of uniting subject and object in an absolute – ego or whatever one wants to call it – is possible aesthetically to be sure in intellectual intuition, but theoretically only through an infinite approximation.' Hölderlin expressed similar opinions as early as 10 October 1794. On the other hand, Fichte too turned, in his later years, to the idea of art as highest synthesis. He wrote: 'Fine art does not cultivate, as does the scholar, only the understanding, nor as the popular moral instructor, only the heart, but rather the whole integrated person' (*Werke*, ed. I.H. Fichte [Berlin, 1845–6], IV, 353; cf. also II, 315ff). However, Fichte's later thought had no historical influence, and Schelling's relations to Hölderlin – let alone to the *Critique of Judgment*! – are far too complicated to be considered here.

9 This is, of course, an implicit criticism of excessive romantic *Schwärmerei*.

10 Schelling uses 'Kunst' to signify the conscious and planned, 'Poesie' to signify the unconscious aspect of aesthetic creation.
11 *Werke*, I, 3.616; *Transcendental Idealism*, 222
12 *Werke*, I, 3.619; *Transcendental Idealism*, 225
13 *Werke*, I, 3.624, cf. also 628; *Transcendental Idealism*, 228 and 321f
14 *Werke*, I, 3.618; *Transcendental Idealism*, 223
15 *Werke*, I, 3.627 (*Transcendental Idealism*, 231) makes art the organon of philosophy, but *Werke*, I, 3.349 (*Transcendental Idealism*, 12) gives the same designation to the *philosophy* of art (cf. also *Werke*, I, 3.612; *Transcendental Idealism*, 219). But Schelling asserts that art is 'an incomprehensible, but nevertheless undeniable fact' (*Werke*, I, 3.617ff; *Transcendental Idealism*, 223ff), and this can only mean that art is superior to philosophy. True, Schelling seeks to qualify this by saying that art is incomprehensible only to mere reflection (ibid.). But to make intelligible how philosophy can do more than mere reflection he is compelled to turn philosophy itself into a form of aesthetic intuition. (Cf., on this whole point, R. Kroner, *Von Kant bis Hegel* [Tübingen, 1921–4], II, 56ff, also K. Schilling, *Natur und Wahrheit* [Munich, 1934], 133ff.)
16 *Werke*, I, 3.630; *Transcendental Idealism*, 233
17 *Werke*, I, 5.348ff; *On University Studies*, 147
18 In the work of 1800 Schelling uses the term 'Absolute' once; but he hastens to correct this into 'absolute self' (*Werke*, I, 3.615; *Transcendental Idealism*, 221).
19 The work which draws this distinction most sharply is the *Bruno* of 1803. (The English translation is F.W.J. Schelling, *Bruno, or On the Natural and the Divine Principle of Things*, tr. M.G. Vater [Albany, 1984].)
20 Cf. above, note 3.
21 Cf. e.g. *Werke*, I, 4.305; *Bruno*, 201: 'If you could find the right words for expressing an activity that is as motionless as the deepest rest, and for a rest that is as energetic as the peak of activity, you would manage to some extent to approximate in concepts the nature of that most perfect being.'
22 *Werke*, I, 5.419; *Philosophy of Art*, 54. On the two possible approaches to the Absolute, cf. also *Werke*, I, 4.140: 'All construction works out from a relative identity. The absolute is not constructed; rather it simply *is*.'
23 E.g. *Werke*, I, 5.363; *Philosophy of Art*, 128
24 Schelling expresses the relationship between the Absolute in itself, and the Absolute in the form of art, by means of the untranslatable terms 'Urbild' and 'Gegenbild.' The *Urbild* is in a sense logically and metaphysically prior to the *Gegenbild*. Nevertheless, the *Gegenbild* is not inferior: it is explicitly contrasted with a mere Platonic *Abdruck* (*Werke*, I, 5.369; *Philosophy of Art*, 16).
25 *Werke*, I, 5.369, 381; *Philosophy of Art*, 16f, 28f
26 Cf. *Werke*, I, 5.381; *Philosophy of Art*, 28: 'Philosophy is ... within the phenome-

nal ideal world just as much the resolution of all particularity as God is in the archetypal world.'

27 *Werke*, I, 5.357; *Philosophy of Art*, 3. The organic unity of all art is, of course, a quite general romantic idea. Schelling attempts to provide it with a metaphysical justification.

28 *Werke*, I, 5.484; *Philosophy of Art*, 101

29 *Werke*, I, 5.502; *Philosophy of Art*, 116

30 The epic is temporally prior to the lyric. Also (as we shall see) it would seem to be logically prior in that it represents an identity from which difference has not yet broken loose. Nevertheless, Schelling is inclined to give the lyric dialectical priority: apparently because this makes possible the analogy of the series lyric-epic-drama to the series music-painting-sculpture (*Werke*, I, 5.639ff, 649ff; *Philosophy of Art*, 207ff, 214ff), on the one hand; to the series science-morality-art (*Werke*, I, 5.645ff; *Philosophy of Art*, 211ff), on the other.

31 *Werke*, I, 5.641; *Philosophy of Art*, 208–9

32 *Werke*, I, 5.646, 651; *Philosophy of Art*, 212, 215

33 *Werke*, I, 5.647; *Philosophy of Art*, 213

34 *Werke*, I, 5.646; *Philosophy of Art*, 212

35 *Werke*, I, 5.650; *Philosophy of Art*, 214

36 *Werke*, I, 5.652ff; *Philosophy of Art*, 216

37 *Werke*, I, 5.652; *Philosophy of Art*, 216

38 Cf. above, note 13.

39 We are alluding to the famous passage in the preface to Hegel's *Phenomenology*.

40 Notably the eighth lecture of the *Vorlesungen über die Methode des akademischen Studiums* of 1803, *Werke*, I, 5.286ff; *On University Studies*, 82ff

41 *Werke*, I, 5.288; *On University Studies*, 84

42 *Vorlesungen über dramatische Kunst und Literatur* (Leipzig, 1846), 16

43 *Werke*, I, 5.154ff. This remark is found in the celebrated essay *Über Dante in philosophischer Beziehung*. Schelling regarded Dante as uniquely expressing the condition of modern poetry, and his work as *sui generis*, requiring separate treatment (*Werke*, I, 5.686; *Philosophy of Art*, 239).

44 Schelling is prepared, however, to permit exceptions which prove the rule. Cf. e.g. his remarks on *Hermann und Dorothea*, *Werke*, I, 5.657; *Philosophy of Art*, 219f.

45 As a result of this historization, the Greek period – the period of absolute harmony – turns out to be the tragic period of mankind (*Werke*, I, 5.290; *On University Studies*, 86): its harmony was a relative, not an absolute harmony after all, and it was therefore subject to dialectical destruction.

46 It is interesting to note that R. Wagner thought of himself as doing more or less exactly what Schelling prophesied the future artist would and should be

doing! Schelling also speaks of a future epic to which he ascribes a similar synthesizing function (*Werke*, I, 5.153ff).

47 *Werke*, I, 5.350ff; *On University Studies*, 149ff

48 Notably the section on tragedy, cf. *Werke*, I, 5.xvii

49 Despite popular misconceptions to the contrary, Schelling had a healthy respect for the variegations of empirical fact, at least in fields with which he was reasonably well acquainted. He wrote: 'I hate nothing more than the inane attempt to eradicate the multiplicity of natural causes with a fabricated identity' (*Werke*, I, 2.347). On the other hand, the desire to do justice to empirical fact frequently conflicted with the metaphysical requirements of the Absolute. A contemporary astutely observed how Schelling was apt to escape such conflicts: 'As a friend of mine quite correctly commented, Schelling helps himself out by throwing into Remarks and Notes what he cannot situate in the absolute' (letter of A.L. Hülsen to A.W. Schlegel, *Briefe deutscher Romantiker*, ed. W.A. Koch [Leipzig, 1938], 192).

50 For Schelling's later development, cf. 'Schelling's Philosophy of Religion,' below.

51 Schelling died in 1854, and this essay is published in honour of the centenary of this event.

Chapter 6 Schelling's Philosophy of Religion

1 *Entwicklungsgeschichte der neuesten deutschen Philosophie* (Berlin, 1843), 130

2 *Schelling* (Danzig, 1843), xxxiv

3 Schelling's behaviour is in part responsible for the treatment he received by the historians. Consider the following testimony of a famous eye-witness: 'Hegel's philosophy became dominant ... and poor Schelling became a mediated philosopher, wandering about sadly in Munich, among all the other mediated philosophers. There I saw him once and almost shed tears at the miserable spectacle. Most miserable of all were his words: envious abuse of Hegel, the man who had supplanted him. Like a cobbler accusing another cobbler of having stolen his leather ... thus I heard Schelling talk about Hegel. ... 'He has taken my ideas' ... , the poor man repeated again and again. Once the cobbler Jacob Boehme talked like a philosopher; now the philosopher Schelling talks like a cobbler.' Heinrich Heine, *Die romantische Schule*, in *Sämtliche Werke*, ed. E. Elster (Leipzig and Wien, n.d.), V, 294. Heine was, of course, hardly an unbiased observer. See his *Religion and Philosophy in Germany* (London, 1891), 155. Michelet – not a wholly unbiased reporter either – contrasts Schelling's behaviour with Hegel's reaction to it: 'when informed of Schelling's hostile utterances, Hegel shook his head incredulously and observed tactful reserve' (*Entwicklungsgeschichte*, 220).

4 *Die Religion innerhalb der Grenzen der blossen Vernunft*, ed. C. Vorländer (Leipzig, 1919), 197
5 *Nachgelassene Werke*, ed. I.H. Fichte (Bonn, 1835), III, 114
6 *Werke*, I, 7.351. Unless otherwise stated, all quotations refer to the complete edition of Schelling's works, published under the editorship of Schelling's son (Stuttgart and Augsburg, 1856–61). There are competent English translations of Schelling's *Of Human Freedom*, by J. Gutmann (Chicago, 1936), and of *The Ages of the World*, by F. Bolman (New York, 1942), both from this period.
7 *Werke*, I, 1.306; *Philosophical Letters on Dogmatism and Criticism* in *The Unconditional in Human Knowledge*, tr. F. Marti (Lewisburg, Pa., 1980), 172
8 *Werke*, I, 7.352; *Of Human Freedom*, 26
9 *Werke*, II, 3.114
10 'Either real evil is admitted, in which case it is unavoidable to include evil itself in the infinite Substance or in the Primal Will, and thus totally disrupt the conception of an all-perfect Being; or the reality of evil must in some way or other be denied, in which case the real conception of freedom disappears at the same time' (*Werke*, I, 7.353; *Of Human Freedom*, 26).
11 *Werke*, I, 7.368; *Of Human Freedom*, 44
12 Goethe, *Faust*, tr. B. Taylor (New York, n.d.), 77
13 *Werke*, I, 7.372; *Of Human Freedom*, 48
14 *Werke*, I, 7.354; *Of Human Freedom*, 28
15 *Werke*, II, 1.460
16 *Werke*, II, 1.485
17 *Werke*, I, 8.268; *The Ages of the World*, 156
18 *Faust*, 88
19 *Werke*, II, 3.154
20 *Werke*, II, 3.171
21 *Werke*, II, 1.560
22 *Werke*, II, 1.566
23 *Werke*, II, 3.195

Chapter 7 Schelling's Conception of Positive Philosophy

1 See Manfred Schröter's edition of the 1811 and 1813 versions of the *Weltalter* (Munich, 1946), Horst Fuhrmans' editions of *Initia Philosophiae Universae*, Lectures from Erlangen, 1820–1 (Bonn, 1969), and *Zur Grundlegung der positiven Philosophie*, Lectures from Munich, 1832–3 (Turin, 1972), and Miklos Vetö's edition of the *Stuttgarter Privatvorlesungen* of 1810 (Turin, 1972) (English translation in *Idealism and the Endgame of Theory*, tr. T. Pfau [Albany, 1994], 195–243). The Bavarian Academy of Sciences is publishing an

Historisch-kritische Ausgabe, under the editorship of H.M. Baumgartner, W.G. Jacobs, H. Krings, and H. Zeltner (Stuttgart–Bad Cannstatt, 1976–).

2 For an attempt to understand one aspect of Schelling's thought as a continuous development, see Chapter 6, 'Schelling's Philosophy of Religion,' above.

3 We must stress, however, that the Schelling revival has already produced a number of substantial studies. See e.g.: Paul Tillich, *Mystik und Schuldbewusstsein in Schellings philosophischer Entwicklung* (Gütersloh 1912) [English tr. Lewisburg, Pa., 1974. Ed.]; G.J. Dekker, *Die Rückwendung zum Mythos: Schellings letzte Wandlung* (Munich and Berlin, 1930); H. Schelsky, 'Schellings Philosophie des Willens und der Existenz,' *Christliche Metaphysik und das Schicksal des modernen Bewusstseins* (Leipzig, 1937), 47–108. The most substantial work on Schelling's last phase is H. Fuhrmans, *Schellings letzte Philosophie. Die negative und positive Philosophie im Einsatz des Spätidealismus* (Berlin, 1945). For Schelling bibliographies available in English see *Schelling: On Human Freedom*, tr. with introduction and notes by J. Gutmann (Chicago, 1936), and *The Ages of the World*, tr. with introduction and notes by F. de Wolfe Bolman (New York, 1942). These two works belong to earlier phases in Schelling's development, but they contribute to making the last intelligible. Of the *Philosophie der Mythologie und Offenbarung*, no part has as yet been translated into English. [This note was written in 1954. For a more recent bibliography, see *Idealism and the Endgame of Theory: Three Essays by F.W.J. Schelling*, tr. T. Pfau (Albany 1994) Ed.]

4 For an excellent account of this collapse, see K. Löwith, *Von Hegel bis Nietzsche* (Zurich–New York, 1941), English tr. by D. Green (Garden City, 1967).

5 In the case of Kierkegaard, this fact is too well known to require documentation. Heidegger appears to have struggled with Hegel early in his career (see Löwith, *Von Hegel bis Nietzsche*, 159), and has more recently written on him (see 'Hegels Begriff der Erfahrung,' *Holzwege* [Frankfurt a/M, 1950], 105–92). F. Rosenzweig's *Stern der Erlösung* (Frankfurt a/M, 1921) [English tr. by W.W. Hallo, New York, 1970] is a running fight against Hegel, and it was written after his *Hegel und der Staat* (Munich and Berlin, 1920). Tillich's thought is clearly related to his early Schelling studies (see, in addition to his above-quoted work, *Die religionsgeschichtliche Konstruktion in Schellings positiver Philosophie* ... [Breslau, 1910]), and thus indirectly to Hegel. It would be easy to give further examples.

6 According to Schelling's own testimony, the 'positive philosophy' was completed as early as 1831; see *Werke*, II, 4.231. All quotations refer to the complete edition of Schelling's works, published under the editorship of Schelling's son (Stuttgart and Augsburg, 1856–61).

7 *Werke*, II, 4.366

8 Gans' comment was made as early as 1833, and based on hearsay; cf. Hegel,

Werke, ed. Gans et al. (2nd ed., Berlin, 1845ff), VIII, xii–xiv. Schelling took Gans' remark very seriously, and regarded it as typical enough to comment on it in his inaugural lecture (*Werke*, II, 4.364).

9 He wrote as follows: 'I am so pleased to have heard Schelling's second lecture – indescribably. I have sighed for long enough and my thoughts have sighed within me; when he mentioned the word "reality" in connection with the relation of philosophy to reality the fruit of my thought leapt for joy within me as in Elizabeth. I remember almost every word he said from that moment on. Here perhaps is the dawning of truth. ... Now I have put all hopes in Schelling. ...' (*Journals*, ed. and tr. A. Dru [London–New York–Toronto, 1938], 102).

10 Kierkegaard, *Journals*, 104

11 *Werke*, II, 3.128

12 *Werke*, II, 3.76

13 *Werke*, I, 4.129. Nicolai Hartmann rightly comments: 'The Schellingian is distinguished from all other forms of philosophical monism in that here not only is everything one "in the final analysis," but already in concrete singularity' (*Die Philosophie des deutschen Idealismus* [Berlin, 1923], I, 160). Schelling wrote in the same work: 'The basic error in all philosophy is the presupposition that the absolute Identity has actually externalized itself' (*Werke*, I, 4.119). Now the positive philosophy turns to this very 'error'!

14 Schelling argues this point on many occasions, perhaps most clearly in his critique of Descartes (*Werke*, I, 10.15ff; *Modern Philosophy*, 50ff).

15 *Was ist Metaphysik?* (Frankfurt a/M, 1949), 38

16 *Werke*, II, 3.7, also II, 3.242

17 Dialectic is capable of 'no actual cognition'; it is dependent on something beyond itself (*Werke*, II, 3.152ff). Since this 'beyond' is, at all levels save the last, experience, the negative philosophy may be called 'a priori empiricism.' For it concerns itself with the a priori aspects of a knowledge which is otherwise empirical (*Werke*, II, 3.130). Cf. below, note 43.

18 The positive philosophy raises further, derivative, questions. In answering these derivative questions, it becomes philosophy of history and speculative theology. But since we are here merely concerned with Schelling's concept of a positive philosophy we may ignore the derivative questions which determine parts, and concentrate on the primary questions which determine the principles of the positive philosophy. For although Schelling never succeeded in working out any except the historical and theological parts of the positive philosophy, he firmly maintained that that philosophy was one whole, of which history and theology were merely parts. And he rejected sharply any suggestion that the positive philosophy was not metaphysics at all, but dogmatic theology or even apologetics (cf. *Werke*, II, 3.174).

19 Schelling has occasional words of praise for empiricism, but only in so far as it is a 'mere, and partly blind, protestation ... against a one-sided rationalism' (*Werke*, I, 10.216).

20 Cf., e.g, *Werke*, II, 1.565. In this passage Schelling states clearly that there are two elements in this crisis, one theoretical and one that he calls 'practical'; cf. below, note 28.

21 Schelling does not actually use the term 'leap' in this connection, although it had made its appearance in his writings as early as 1804 (*Werke*, I, 6:38). Cf. also in this connection Schelling's assertion that there is a 'wide, nasty moat' ('ein garstiger, breiter Graben') between Hegel's *Logic* and his *Philosophy of Nature* (*Werke*, I, 10.154; *Modern Philosophy*, 155 and *Werke*, I, 10.213). It is most probable that Schelling writes with Lessing in mind. Lessing uses exactly the same expression when considering the relation between 'necessary truths of reason' and 'contingent truths of history' (Lessing, *Werke*, ed. Bornmüller [Leipzig and Vienna, n.d.], V, 494–5). And Schelling had earlier used this expression with explicit reference to Lessing (Schelling, *Werke*, I, 5.250; *On University Studies*, 44). Kierkegaard, too, comments on the Lessing passage, quoting Lessing's words: 'That, that is the wide, nasty *moat*, over which I have not been able to go, however often and earnestly I have attempted the *leap*.' (*Concluding Unscientific Postscript*, tr. Swenson and Lowrie [Princeton, 1941], 90, my translation; my italics)

22 See *Werke*, II, 1.413. That this is the aim is evident throughout the entire negative philosophy. The aim is reached when finally the 'self declares itself as not-principle and subordinates itself to God' (*Werke*, II, 1.560).

23 *Werke*, II, 3.163

24 *Werke*, II, 1.560

25 *Werke*, II, 3.171

26 See, e.g., this remarkable passage: 'Only now does the individual recognize the abyss between God and himself. ... Hence he now yearns for God Himself. Him, Him he wants, the God who acts ... , who, as a factual God, can alone deal with the factual fall, in short, the God who is the Lord of all Being' (*Werke*, II, 1.566).

27 Schelling makes it perfectly clear that the issue is not rationalism vs. irrationalism. The issue is between a philosophy asserting a gap between man and God, and the system of identity, whether in the rationalist version of Hegel or the irrationalist of Schleiermacher. Thus Schelling does not exalt feeling at the expense of reason; for it is open to the same (and worse) objections. Irrationalist idealism implies the deification of feeling rather than reason; and an irrationalism which abandons the doctrine of identity leads to the view that 'God is only the creature of our feeling ... , each religious idea has merely psychological significance' (*Werke*, II, 3.154). Because there is a gap

between man and God, a leap is required to bridge it; and this Schelling finds in will and decision. 'A free action is not a gradual transition, but absolute beginning, pure positing ... , decision and deed' (*Werke*, II, 3.114). It is significant to note in this connection that Schelling does not equate faith with religious feeling, but asserts that it involves an act of will (*Werke*, I, 10.183; *Modern Philosophy*, 177ff); and we may observe in passing that contemporary existentialist theologians tend to speak of the 'decision of faith,' whereas idealists are apt to speak of 'religious experience.' It would seem that the issue between these two schools is not dissimilar to the issue between Schelling and the philosophy of identity.

28 More precisely, Schelling means the condition of man, not qua man, but qua individual or existing man. See *Werke*, II, 1.569: 'We have seen that the self's need to possess God as external to his reason (as other than mere thinking or idea) is practical. But this is not an arbitrary will; it is a will of spirit which, by an inner necessity, and because of its yearning for liberation, cannot remain satisfied with the mere God-idea. This demand for the existing God cannot arise from theory. But neither can it be a postulate of practical reason. Not, as Kant wants it, this latter, but only the individual as such leads to God. For not the universal in man, but only the individual desires beatitude.'

29 *Werke*, II, 3.132

30 *Werke*, II, 1.579

31 *Werke*, II, 4.11

32 Exodus 3:14

33 *Werke*, II, 1.171, II, 3.269ff. See also, and especially, the searching discussion in the *Ages of the World*, *Werke*, I, 8.263ff, Bolman tr., 151ff.

34 E.g., *Werke*, II, 3.113ff, 129ff, and numerous other passages. See below, note 43.

35 E.g., *Werke*, II, 1.565: 'With the pure That ... one can do nothing. In order that there should be science, the Universal, the What, must enter, but now as consequent, not antecedent to the That.'

36 *Werke*, I, 10.252; II, 3.247ff

37 Negative philosophy concerns itself, not with what exists, but with what can exist. At its culminating point (which is at the same time its crisis) it asks how the Ultimate can exist. And it becomes ecstatic in answering this question because the Ultimate must be pure Existence beyond all possibility. The positive philosophy is the inversion of the negative; for here pure Existence is primary, possibility secondary (*Werke*, II, 3.155ff). For the problems implicit in the transition from Existence to possibility, see further *Werke*, II, 1.565.

38 *Werke*, II, 3.256

39 *Werke*, II, 3.248

40 *Werke*, II, 3.244ff

41 This is Schelling's explicit teaching in his earlier *Ages of the World* (*Werke*, I, 8.310, Bolman tr., 200).

42 Cf. section III in the previous chapter.

43 See above, note 34. Cf. the following summary: 'Not the absolute Prius itself is to be proved; (this is beyond all proof, the absolute Beginning which is in itself certain). ... But we must prove, as a fact, what derives from it, and thus the Godhood of that Prius. We must prove that it is God and that God exists' (*Werke*, II, 3.129). See also this summary of the characteristics of negative and positive philosophy: 'Negative philosophy is a priori empiricism, i.e., the a priori of empiricism, and for that reason itself not empiricism. ... Positive philosophy is empirical apriorism, i.e., the empiricism of the a priori, inasmuch as it reveals the Prius, via the Posterius, as God' (*Werke*, II, 3.130).

44 *Werke*, II, 1.573–90. The problem is also raised elsewhere; cf., e.g., *Werke*, II, 1.331.

45 *Werke*, II, 1.586

46 *Werke*, II, 1.589; cf. also II, 1.314, 331

47 *Werke*, II, 1.587

Chapter 8 Metaphysics and Historicity

1 *The Aquinas Lecture, 1961*. I wish to thank the Oxford University Press, for permission to quote a lengthy passage from Erich Frank, *Philosophical Understanding and Religious Truth* (New York, 1945); and the Princeton University Press, for permission to quote an even lengthier passage from Walter Lowrie's translation of S. Kierkegaard's *Either/Or* (Princeton, 1944).

2 For the development of modern Western historical consciousness, cf. especially F. Meinecke, *Die Entstehung des Historismus* (Munich, 1936).

Gerhard Krüger describes the predicament of history as follows: 'We are able to inquire into history only while being part of it. We seek permanent truths about history; yet we ourselves, our whole thinking included, are nothing permanent. This is the predicament of history, radically stated: that we are so changeable and yet are in such need of the permanent' (*Grundfragen der Philosophie* [Frankfurt, 1958], 49). Krüger describes the development of Western awareness of this predicament as follows. The Greeks had not yet discovered it. Thinkers such as St Augustine coped with it in terms of the Christian doctrine of Providence. The Enlightenment dealt with it in terms of the belief in progress. Because it was first to abandon the belief in the superiority of the present over the past, Romanticism was first to discover the predicament of history; but both Romanticism and German Idealism sought to resolve it by rising above history into timelessness. Because the belief in the possibility of such a rise is no longer acceptable in the present age, this age is 'an age of total historicity,' one of 'mutually incompatible standpoints' (ibid. 8). This chapter will make clear that we do not wholly agree with Krüger's account; we have summarized it here because it is profoundly challenging.

3 The first great warning against the possible ill effects of a strongly developed historical self-consciousness was given in 1874, in Nietzsche's *Use and Abuse of History*. The most famous literary document which illustrates these effects is Oswald Spengler's *The Decline of the West* (London, 1926–8).

4 Contemporary manifestations of pragmatic make-believe are so common as to leave one at a loss which to cite as an example. As apt as any is the current North American search for a purpose, when what is wanted is not a truth which commands dedication, but merely an effective tool in the struggle against neurosis, juvenile delinquency, or cold war foes. Such a tool, if it is merely a tool, is foredoomed to ineffectiveness.

Commenting on pragmatic make-believe in its religious application, Erich Frank writes: 'If we believe in ... God not because He is the truth, but assume His truth only because we believe in Him, then there are as many gods and as many truths and values as there are beliefs. In that case, pluralism is the inescapable consequence, and it remains for the individual and his liking to choose his own truth and his own God. ... This subjective concept of belief is a contradiction in itself. A belief that believes only in itself is no longer a belief. For true belief transcends itself; it is a belief in something – in a truth which is not determined by faith but which, on the contrary, determines faith' (*Philosophical Understanding and Religious Truth* [London–New York–Toronto, 1945], 42–3).

The pragmatic is by no means to be confused with the existentialist concept of religious truth. The latter does not assert that commitment *makes* a belief true. It asserts that only in commitment can a person discover whether a belief *is* true, and hence – since commitment is 'subjective' whereas the truth to which it commits itself is 'objective' (if it is truth at all) – that all religious commitment is shot through with risk. Thus Abraham's predicament, as expounded in Kierkegaard's *Fear and Trembling* (Garden City, N.Y. 1954), is that *if* God commands him to sacrifice Isaac, then this commandment is 'objective,' i.e., valid quite independently of Abraham's belief or lack of belief; but that, at the same time, Abraham has no standards other than his own 'subjective' belief in terms of which to decide whether the commandment is objective and divine, or the mere product of his own imagination.

5 So long as 'belief which believes only in itself' (cf. note 4) still believes in *one* thing beyond itself – democratic tolerance – it will tolerate a pluralism of beliefs. It is when the overwhelming need for certainty and absoluteness destroys this one remaining belief that 'belief which believes only in itself'

turns into ideological fanaticism. On the connection between scepticism and fanaticism, cf. Karl Jaspers, *Philosophie* (Berlin, 1948), 208. On the most demonic form of contemporary ideological fanaticism, cf. Hermann Rauschning, *The Revolution of Nihilism* (New York, 1939).

Perhaps the most arresting account of totalitarianism is Hannah Arendt's *The Origins of Totalitarianism* (New York, 1958). Among the countless insights offered in this brilliant work is the close and indeed inseparable connection, in totalitarianism, between nihilism, ideology, fanaticism, and the perpetuity of 'movement.' It was an essential part of Nazism to assert 'the futility of everything that is an end in itself' (ibid., 323); for only then could the deified 'movement of history' be absolute and all-embracing. Yet this 'movement' was itself devoid of definable ends toward which it was directed; for only thus could the 'Führer's' authority have the kind of absoluteness which included the defining and arbitrary redefining of every 'program' as whim dictated. It was therefore not at all out of character that men such at Hitler and Goebbels should, in the end, have expressed ghoulish satisfaction at the prospect that their downfall might carry in train the doom, not only – or even at all – of their enemies, but of the 'master-race.'

6 For a contemporary example of metaphysical argument across the ages in St Thomas' behalf, cf. E. Gilson, *Being and Some Philosophers* (Toronto, 1949).

7 Cf. especially *The Joyful Wisdom*, §125; cf. M. Heidegger, 'Nietzsche's Wort "Gott is tot,"' *Holzwege* (Frankfurt, 1950), 222: 'Der Name Wahrheit bedeutet jetzt weder die Unverborgenheit des Seienden, noch die Übereinstimmung einer Erkenntnis mit dem Gegenstand, noch die Gewissheit als das einsichtige Zu- und Sicherstellen des Vorgestellten. Wahrheit ist jetzt, und zwar in einer wesensgeschichtlichen Herkunft aus den genannten Weisen ihres Wesens, die beständigende Bestandsicherung des Umkreises, aus dem her der Wille zur Macht sich selbst will.' We cannot agree that truth, for Nietzsche, is 'will-to-power willing itself.' Rather, it would seem to be will-to-power willing something *beyond* itself which will itself creates. Even so, Heidegger clearly sees not only that but also how Nietzsche historicizes metaphysical truth.

8 Cf. *An Essay on Metaphysics* (Oxford, 1940). Cf., however, below, note 34.

9 For Dilthey, cf., e.g., *Briefwechsel Zwischen Wilhelm Dilthey und dem Grafen Paul York von Wartenburg, 1877–1897* (Halle, 1923) (e.g., York's statement, p. 251: 'Hence there is no genuine philosophizing which is not historical. The distinction between systematic philosophy and history of philosophy is in principle false'). On Dilthey and York, cf. Heidegger, *Sein und Zeit* (Halle, 1935), 397ff. For Croce, cf. his *History as the Story of Liberty* (New York, 1941). For Dewey, cf. his doctrine, appearing in many of his works, of a natural and a social matrix, constituting a situation limiting all human activities, philosophy included. For Heidegger, cf. below, note 45.

10 Thus Dilthey's statement 'only history brings to light the potentialities of human being [*Dasein*]' (*Schriften*, V [Berlin and Leipzig, 1924], xci) is a metaphysical thesis, not an empirical generalization. Any Aristotelian would agree that potentialities are disclosed only by their actualization. But he would not concede that our knowledge of essential human potentialities is subject to perpetual revision as history causes new actualities to come into view; nor would the study of history extract this admission from him. Conceivably man's essential potentialities have long been disclosed; and if subsequent history *does* bring novel potentialities to light, it is because man has unessential as well as essential potentialities, and because his essential potentialities can be perverted in countless ways. On Dilthey's views on human nature and human history, cf. Collingwood, *The Idea of History* (Oxford, 1946), 171ff.

Karl Löwith has made this astute observation: 'The historical variations in the manifold interpretations of being human ... do not prove that human nature has essentially altered; they refer only to a change in the self-understanding of man. No more than there is a modern nature, albeit a modern natural science, is there a modern human nature and to that extent a "modern man," albeit up-to-date and antiquated anthropologies' (*Wesen und Wirklichkeit des Menschen, Festschrift für H. Plessner*, ed. K. Ziegler [Göttingen, 1957], 64). Löwith's distinction serves to corroborate our point that empirical history does not, by itself, suffice to establish the doctrine of historicity. On the other hand, his distinction does not, by itself, refute the doctrine of historicity. If there is a human nature, then the historical changes of human self-understanding are as irrelevant to that nature as are the changes in the physical sciences to physical nature. But if human being is an historically situated self-making, then the historical changes in human self-understanding (itself a form of human self-making) must necessarily affect human being.

On the point made in this note, cf. also below, note 35.

11 As a rule, non-metaphysicians cannot even recognize this task, let alone perform it. The psychologist W. McDougall writes: 'The impossibility of banishing altogether the notion of substance is even clearer in the case of psychological than of physical science. My consciousness is a stream of consciousness which has a certain unique unity; it is a multiplicity of distinguishable parts or features which, although they are perpetually changing, yet hang together as a continuous whole within which the change goes on' (*Body and Mind* [London, 1911], 162). What 'unique unity' or 'hanging together' must be accounted for, and how does 'substance' account for it? Is 'substance' the source of identity? And is *self*-identity a mere species of the genus identity?

12 Collingwood, *The Idea of History*, 213ff *et passim*.

13 It is an assumption because it can, with some plausibility, be denied. Positiv-

ists will seek to explain the sequence 'x entertains an objective,' 'x decides upon an action calculated to realize this objective,' and 'x performs the action,' in terms of laws which cover this sequence, rather than in terms of x's own categories which involve no reference to such laws. At the same time, the assumption of free action is one which manifestly even a positivist will make in practice, i.e., while he himself is the deciding and acting x.

14 It is not, however, forgotten by all modern philosophers of history. Among those who remember it are Schelling and Heidegger.

Does belief in divine action in history *ipso facto* commit the believer to the doctrine of historicity? The study of mediaeval philosophy shows that this is far from the case. A thinker such as St Augustine, though believing that 'the fundamental principle for the pursuit of this religion [i.e., Christianity] is history' (*De Vera Religione*, VII, 3), can nevertheless credit pagan Platonists with having perceived *some* truth. And a thinker such as St Thomas Aquinas, while maintaining that revealed doctrine is the highest truth, nevertheless insists that unaided philosophical effort can achieve *some* knowledge (*Summa Theologica*, I, q.1 a.1). Both thinkers affirm a human nature which, however affected by the fall on the one hand, by divine salvation on the other, nevertheless *is* a nature.

15 Divine action in history, as understood in the Bible, does not rule out freedom. Thus God's use of Nebuchadnezzar for His purposes does not rule out the reality of Nebuchadnezzar's own purposes, which are, to be sure, very different from those of God. Further, the divine purpose in this case – the meting out of just punishment – presupposes freedom on the part of those who are to be punished.

In the context of secularistic interpretations of history, human freedom is sometimes denied because of the 'well-known fact that in history the results of our willed actions reach beyond the mark of their intended goal, thus revealing an inner logic which overrules the will of man' (Frank, *Philosophical Understanding*, 137). The fact here referred to is real enough. But it does not prove (and Frank does not think it proves) the unreality of human freedom: that history is sheer fate. It suggests, on the contrary (as Hegel, for example, well knew), that freedom in history is real enough to give rise to the most momentous consequences; although, because human freedom is finite, these consequences are always partly, and often wholly, other than those intended. History is never fate. But it is true enough that history often *looks* like fate: when the consequences of human acting have become at once so powerful and so alien to human purposes as to seem to leave, or even in fact to leave, men wholly at their mercy. When this happens history assumes a degree of tragedy which no vain fight against nature can ever match. The latter is merely contradiction. In history there is self-contradiction: when the circumstances in which men find themselves – alien, unwilled, and even heroically though vainly fought against – are nevertheless the product of human action. Tragic self-contradiction in history reaches its climax when the alien and unwilled consequences flow from the actions of the same men who later vainly fight against them, shaken to the core by the monstrous consequences of their actions.

16 *Poetics*, IX, 1451b6

17 S. Alexander, 'The Historicity of Things,' in *Philosophy and History: Essays Presented to Ernst Cassirer*, ed. H.J. Paton and R. Klibanski (Oxford, 1936), 11ff

18 *The Idea of History*, 210ff

19 In this section, 'human being is a self-constituting process' has merely been identified as the hypothesis without which the doctrine of historicity cannot arise. For a sketch of the reasons which have made philosophers accept that hypothesis, see the 'Conclusion,' below.

20 *Über die Vierfache Wurzel des Satzes vom Zureichenden Grunde*, chap. 2 §8

21 For the principle *operatio sequitur esse*, cf., e.g., St Thomas Aquinas, *Summa Theologica*, I, q. 75 (which, treating of the human soul, treats first 'ea quae pertinent ad essentiam animae' [that which pertains to the essence of the soul], then 'ea quae pertinent ad virtutem sive potentias eius' [that which pertains to its virtues and powers], and finally 'ea quae pertinent ad operationem eius' [that which pertains to its operations]), and *Summa Contra Gentiles*, II, 21 and III, 42 ('sicut enim operatio substantiam sequitur, ita operationis perfectio perfectionem substantiae') [for just as operation follows substance, so the perfection of the operation follows the perfection of the substance].

For the principle *esse sequitur operationem* one can cite only with hesitation John Scotus Eriugena, *De Divisione Naturae*, I, 72: 'Therefore God was not, before he made all things'; 'when we hear that God made all things we ought to understand that God is in all things, that is, that the essence at all subsists.' But one can cite without any hesitation Jacob Boehme, *Werke*, ed. K.W. Schiebler (Leipzig, 1831–46), IV, 429: 'Freedom, as the Nothing, has in itself no essence'; and VI, 413: 'The "unground" [*Ungrund*] is an eternal Nothing and yet makes an eternal beginning as a craving; for the Nothing is a craving after something; ... the craving is itself the giving of that which is yet nothing other than merely a craving desire'; Schelling, *On Human Freedom*, tr. Gutmann (Chicago, 1936); and Berdyaev (for Boehme as well as Berdyaev himself), 'Jacob Boehmes Lehre von Ungrund und Freiheit,' *Blätter für Deutsche Philosophie* (1932–3), VI, especially 325: 'As perhaps the first in the history of human thought, Boehme has recognized that the fundament of being and, prior to being, groundless freedom is the passionate desire of Nothing to become something,' and also *The Beginning and the End* (New York, 1957). Cf.

also Hegel, *Logic*, tr. W. Wallace (London and Oxford, 1904), §87: 'The supreme form of Nought as a separate principle would be Freedom.' For Schelling's use of the term *μὴ ὀν*, as distinct from *ὀυκ ὀν*, cf. *Werke* (Stuttgart and Augsburg, 1856–61), II, 1.288ff, 306ff.

If the doctrine of the four causes is granted, then St Thomas' argument against a *causa sui* as required by meontological metaphysics is incontrovertible; cf. *Summa Theologica*, I, q.2 a.3: 'nothing is found, nor is it possible that anything be, the efficient cause of itself; since then it would be prior to itself, which is impossible.' But can meontological metaphysics grant the doctrine of the four causes? The cited passages suffice to show that its *Nihil* must be at once material and efficient cause, and be creative of the formal and final, all of which is, in terms of the doctrine of the four causes, unintelligible.

22 We do not deny, of course, that *some* 'metaphysical assertions' are radically unintelligible, and hence neither metaphysical nor assertions.

23 It may be observed in passing, however, that the greatest attempt to explicate this kind of logic is beyond all doubt Hegel's work by that name.

24 Cf., e.g., Hegel, *Werke* (Berlin, 1847), VII, 1, 60: 'In the positive meaning of time one can say: only the present is; before and after is not. Yet the concrete present is the result of the past and it is pregnant with the future. The true present is thus eternity' (*Philosophy of Nature*, §259, *Zus.*).

25 What distinguishes the meontological concept of eternity from that of such thinkers as Boethius (*De Consolatione Philosophiae*, V: 'nunc stans,' 'interminabilis vitae tota simul et perfecta possessio') and Plotinus (*Enneads*, III, 7.3: '*ζωὴ μένουσα ἐν τῷ αὐτῷ ἀεὶ παρὸν τὸ πᾶν ἔχουσα*' [a life remaining in sameness, always possessing the whole as present]) is that here *direction*, even though sublated in eternity, is also preserved in it. Thus Schelling can describe eternity as a 'self-renewing movement' (*Werke*, I, 8.230, tr. Bolman, *The Ages of the World* [New York, 1942], 116). Thus also the Hegelian Idea, at the end of the *Logic*, is a return to Being, which is at its beginning; and yet the process from Being to Idea has a direction which remains preserved. And Hegelian Absolute Spirit, arising after and on the basis of both Nature and History, is a return to the realm of Logic which is prior to both Nature and History; and yet in this return both Nature and History are preserved.

It ought to be added, however, that Hegel's synthesis of history and eternity caused a split among his followers between 'left-wingers' who retained historical direction but abandoned eternity, and 'right-wingers' who retained eternity but abandoned historical direction; and that this split among Hegelians has remained until this day. The most fascinating contemporary 'left-wing' and 'right-wing' interpretations are, respectively, Alexandre Kojève, *Introduction à la Lecture de Hegel* (Paris, 1947), and I. Iljin, *Die Philosophie Hegels als Kontemplative Gotteslehre* (Bern, 1946). Cf. also below, note 42.

Dissatisfied with the Hegelian synthesis, Schelling in his old age produced a profound and revolutionary synthesis of his own. But significantly, Schelling's synthesis remained a fragment. Cf. *The Ages of the World* and chapter 7 in this volume.

26 Both Collingwood and Heidegger recognize that the historical past is truly historical only because it can be appropriated and re-enacted in the present. But whereas Collingwood, concentrating attention on the epistemology of historiography, seems to regard such a re-enactment as mostly, if not entirely, an affair of the present historian, Heidegger considers all such re-enactment of the past to be mediated by the anticipating of the future which is cast back on the past. Cf., e.g., *Einführung in die Metaphysik* (Tübingen, 1953), 34: 'Geschichte als Geschehen ist das aus der Zukunft bestimmte, das Gewesene übernehmende Hindurchhandeln und Hindurchleiden durch die Gegenwart.' ['History as event is the acting and suffering throughout the present that is determined out of the future and that appropriates what has been.'] Cf. also *Sein und Zeit*, especially §74. While it is not necessary for the present purpose to enter into a discussion of this issue, it may be said in passing that of the two, Heidegger's would appear to be the profounder conception, if only because he squarely faces up to what Collingwood notes only occasionally and in passing: that if human being is qua being and qua human historical, there can be no ontological divorce between the historical consciousness of the historian and the consciousness of the historical agent who is involved in history, and geared to the future.

27 Idealists such as Schelling and Hegel recognize, as much as any naturalist, that history remains dependent on nature so long as it is history at all. If they disagree with naturalism in this matter, it is in attributing a direction to history, and in claiming that its aim is emancipation from dependence on nature, and hence transcendence of history itself. This view is already contained in one strain of Kantian thought, cf. chapter 3, above. Cf. further on this issue, below, note 28.

28 If Fichte's idealism regards the world – the 'non-self' – as the self's own self-limitation, however, it is not so much because he ignores or underestimates its aspect of otherness. It is rather because his belief in the absolute ontological primacy of morality leads him to consider the world as the mere 'material of our duty rendered sensuous' (*Werke* [Berlin, 1845], V, 185), incapable of giving absolute resistance to the moral will. Dewey, while qua metaphysician describing human being as a self-making-in-a-situation, abandons this concept whenever he falls prey to naturalistic or positivistic ways of thinking.

Unlike Fichte, Schelling and Hegel regard the human self as limited by a nature genuinely other-than-self. If they nevertheless arrive at idealistic conclusions, it is because they hold the human self to be capable of transcending not only dependence on nature but also all finiteness and hence humanity and selfhood itself. If and when such transcendence occurs, natural limitations such as temporality and death still exist, of course; but because they no longer structure the self – itself now more than self – they have become 'unessential.' Cf. also below, note 32.

It is existential philosophy which denies transcendence-of-situation, such as is asserted by Schelling and Hegel; and this denial has brought fully to light the dialectical relation between situation and situated self-making. Cf. further below, 'The Concept of Human Situation,' in this chapter.

29 This is the precise reason why Hegel, inquiring into human being qua being and qua human, must inquire into history; for man *is* what he has *become*, or rather, what he has freely *made* of himself.

It is a commonly held view that Hegel asserted 'laws' of history, which imply at once the denial of human freedom and the possibility of predicting the future. But Hegel never made predictions. And he regarded history, not as governed by patterns of recurrence, but as a single plot. Further, his historical dialectic, far from denying human freedom, on the contrary presupposes it. Cf. further below, note 35.

30 It is for this reason that man's 'present situation,' once considered irrelevant for metaphysics, has preoccupied modern metaphysicians, from Hegel (cf., e.g., the Preface to his *Phenomenology of Mind*, tr. J.B. Baillie [London, 1931]) to Jaspers (cf., e.g., his *Man in the Modern Age* [Garden City, N.Y., 1957]) and Heidegger (cf. virtually all his later writings).

31 This is true only so long as the natural is artificially isolated from the historical situation – an isolation which is artificial because it nowhere exists. Man-in-civilization obviously transforms nature. But man qua civilized is both naturally and historically situated. Cf. also below, note 33.

32 According to Schelling and Hegel, such a rise in fact occurs when human being – no longer historical – rises to Absolute Spirit. Reaching this stage it still differs, however, from the quasi-historical eternity of the meontological God. For while the latter is beyond all situatedness the former transcends a situatedness which this transcendence presupposes. Moreover, natural otherness has not vanished, and even historical otherness has not wholly done so; everything that remains other has merely become 'unessential.' Cf. also above, note 28.

33 Cf. above, note 31. It would seem that Fichte was the first to attempt a radical historization of nature, although certain strains in Kant already point in that direction. (Cf. chapter 3 above.) Kant regards natural inclinations as simply given, and hence as both unalterable and innocent. Fichte, in sharp contrast, regards such inclinations as neither unalterable nor innocent, and hence their gradual elimination through cultural and moral effort as a task to be

performed by man in history. Consequently, while both thinkers affirm a *summum bonum*, understood as 'the correspondence of the will of a rational being with the idea of an eternally valid will (moral goodness) and correspondence of the things outside us with our will (happiness)' – the formulation is Fichte's, *Werke*, VI, 299 – Kant means by the latter correspondence the satisfaction of unalterably given and hence morally innocent inclinations (*Werke*, Prussian Academy edition, V, 107ff), while Fichte means their gradual elimination through culture.

34 This is the position adopted, for example, by Collingwood in *An Essay on Metaphysics*. It is instructive to note, however, that he is much too subtle a thinker simply to remain with that position. Rather he considers the belief that metaphysics consists of historically changing *Weltanschauungen* itself to spring from a metaphysical thesis of a different order; the thesis being that mind changes through history because it is its own self-constituted functions. Cf., e.g., *The Idea of History*, 288, 292, and *Speculum Mentis* (Oxford, 1924), 207. This latter thesis is neither history nor one *Weltanschauung* among others but rather what Germans would call a *Weltanschauungslehre*.

35 Leo Strauss, *What Is Political Philosophy?* (Glencoe, Ill., 1959), 57

Karl Popper has given his private definition of historicism: 'the doctrine that there is a developmental law which can be discovered, and upon which predictions regarding the future of mankind can be based' (*The Open Society and Its Enemies* [London, 1945], 7 and elsewhere). But this is highly confusing. Hegel – supposedly an historicist in Popper's sense – never made predictions; indeed, precisely because he held that man's very being changes in history he could not believe in 'laws ... upon which predictions regarding the future of mankind can be based.' On Popper's account of Hegel, cf. W. Kaufmann, 'The Hegel Myth and Its Method,' *Philosophical Review*, 60, (1951), 459ff and especially 473ff. On the other hand, a thinker might well be an historicist in Popper's sense precisely because he is not a historicist in the accepted sense – because he considers human being to have enough permanence to justify predictions based on laws.

The reader who agrees that the doctrine of historicity, if developed to a certain point, leads to historicism may nevertheless wonder whether there are not other roads to historicism. What, for example, of a simple distinction between the natural sciences, understood as disciplines discovering laws, and historiography, understood as a discipline incapable of discovering laws? But a mere insistence on the unpredictable in history is not enough to justify historicism. Why should it be assumed that the historical changes to which man is subject affect him so profoundly as to make tomorrow's philosophical truth unpredictable today? This assumption, as was shown above (note 10), is a metaphysical thesis, not an empirical generalization. And it can be none other than that developed in the course of this chapter. For if human being consists of a permanent human nature we never come anywhere near historicism; and if human being is a simple rather than a self-constituting process, the process in question is not distinctively historical.

36 Cf. above, note 10.

37 Cf., e.g., Strauss' remarks on Dewey, *What Is Political Philosophy?* 72.

Our above refutation of historicism may seem to differ but slightly, if at all, from the standard refutation of relativism in general. But the difference is, nevertheless, important. Conceivably the standard refutation may be met by a doctrine which asserts that statements such as 'all truth is relative' differ in logical type from statements such as 'the statement "all truth is relative" is true.' But our above refutation of historicism cannot be met by this doctrine, at least if it is granted that historicism springs from the doctrine of historicity. For historicism asserts, in that case, not only that all metaphysical assertions are historically relative; it adds that this is so because these assertions are part of an historically situated process of self-making. And it is then forced to concede that the assertion 'historicism is true' is also part of this process of self-making. But the crux is that both statements, no matter how different in type, must be part of one and the same self-constituting process; and it is precisely this that historicism cannot account for without collapsing in self-contradiction.

38 This is among the chief questions inspiring Kierkegaard's protest against the historicist thinking of his time. Kant, though anticipating historicist thinking in one strain of his thought, in the end repudiates it precisely because it seems to historicize man's free decision, including the decision for a conversion. (In Kant's case, the conversion is moral rather than religious.) Cf. especially *Werke*, VI, 19ff, *Religion within the Limits of Reason Alone*, tr. Greene and Hudson (Chicago, 1934), 15ff, and chapter 2, above. Cf. also chapter 3, above.

39 Such a response can be given only in terms of the doctrine of historicity – which understands the grounds for historicism – restated in a form which both recognizes and avoids the inconsistencies of historicism. It is such a response alone which can refute historicism *ab intra*. Mere refutations *ab extra* may no doubt be sound enough; but they do not provide an understanding of the full challenge of historicism, a challenge which has far deeper roots than historicism, taken by itself.

40 *Werke* (Berlin, 1840), XI, 64; *Lectures on the Philosophy of Religion*, tr. Speirs and Sanderson (London, 1895), I, 65. Compare *Vorlesungen: Ausgewählte Nachschriften und Manuskripte*, III, 120; *Lectures on the Philosophy of Religion*, tr. P. Hodgson et al. (Berkeley, Los Angeles, London, 1984), I, 212; and G.W.F. Hegel, *Gesammelte Werke* (Hamburg, 1987), XVII, 52:8ff.

41 Hegel's ultimate sublation of man's finite in his infinite aspect results not only from philosophical considerations such as those here referred to. It also results from his Christian convictions. But this is too complex a matter to be dealt with here.

On whether the doctrine of man-as-unresolved-struggle must in fact lead back to historicism, cf. the whole remainder of this chapter.

42 There are two opposite attempts to save Hegel's *Philosophy of History*. In the one, stress is laid on Hegel's refusal to predict the future. But this is here taken to include not only future history but also future philosophical interpretations of history. Hegel's work, which concludes with the modest remark 'to this point has consciousness reached' (*Werke*, IX [Berlin, 1848], 546), is viewed as an interpretation of history, not from an absolute standpoint but merely from the standpoint of the early nineteenth- century. But this interpretation not only leads back to historicism; it is also contrary to Hegel's explicit intentions. For he holds that history manifests a synthesis of political realities and absolute religious truth: a synthesis which his own age had at least in principle achieved.

The opposite attempt to save Hegel's *Philosophy of History* lays proper stress on Hegel's concept of the transhistoricity of religious and philosophical truth. But it views history as essential only so long as religious and philosophical truth are still in the process of development, and no longer once these truths are fully disclosed. But this ignores Hegel's belief that religious truth, to be fully actual, must be embodied in history, an embodiment which includes political realities.

Of the two attempts, the second is more defensible. But in order to be tenable, it would have to show that the events of nineteenth- and twentieth-century history can be understood in the terms in which Hegel understood history until his time. And it is more than doubtful that such an attempt could succeed.

43 The correlation between 'attempt-at-transcendence,' 'border situation,' and 'foundering' is fully developed in Jaspers, *Philosophie*, especially 467ff. Perhaps the best-known and most succinct account is Heidegger's 'What Is Metaphysics?' in *Existence and Being*, tr. Brock (London, 1949), 353ff.

Helmut Kuhn has made a useful distinction between 'critical' and 'social' existentialism, the former emphasizing 'crisis' in the attempt at radical self-transcendence, the latter, 'social' existential possibilities falling short of radical self-transcendence, such as what Martin Buber calls an I-Thou relationship ('Existentialism,' in V. Ferm, *A History of Philosophical Systems* [New York, 1950], 405ff). If in the present context we refer only to 'critical' existentialism, it is because the issue under discussion is the possibility of metaphysical transcendence.

It is true that Buber asserts the possibility not only of inter-human but also of human-divine dialogue. But it must be remembered that the latter is beyond the realm of unaided human effort, and possible only by virtue of divine incursions into time and history.

Kuhn's distinction, while useful, cannot be considered absolute. It would seem that, if Buber could not accept the reality of a divine address to man, he too would be driven to the conclusion that man's unaided effort at transcendence culminates in crisis (cf. below, note 50). And Kierkegaard is the 'father' of both emphases, stressing the foundering of man's unaided attempts at transcendence, and at the same time committed to belief in divine Grace.

44 Only if two points are perpetually kept in mind can the existential concept of human situation be understood. First, it is not an objective fact laid out before a detached knower, but a situation which situates the knower, and which is understood by him as such only when he faces up to it as his own. The human situation is not an anthropological fact. But neither, secondly, is it a mere part of an individual's autobiography. For though discovered by each for himself, the human situation, when recognized as such, is understood to be universally human. Thus death is part of the human situation, and yet distorted when viewed as a mere objective fact. 'All men must die' is a mere objectification. The existential truth is 'each man must die for himself,' when faced up to by an individual as a truth which applies to himself.

45 Heidegger explicitly repudiates historicism (*Sein und Zeit*, 396), by means of achieving a radical grasp of historicity, as characterizing the human situation – a step in part anticipated by Dilthey, who writes: 'the historical [*historische*] consciousness of the finitude of each historical [*geschichtlichen*] appearance, ... of the relativity of each type of faith is the final step in freeing man for his sovereignty' in *Schriften*, VII, 290).

It is a noteworthy fact that in his later works Heidegger becomes once more involved in historicism, at a deeper level. Thus in *Was ist das – die Philosophie?* (Pfullingen, 1956), he makes these assertions: (i) philosophy is wholly bound up with language, and language is historical; (ii) philosophy is essentially Greek, and hence the term 'European philosophy' is a mere tautology; (iii) not only philosophy but also Heidegger's own inquiry into it is historical; (iv) the identity of philosophy is not that of a timeless, transhistorical essence but merely an identity of continuity over a limited period, albeit one long enough to have lasted from Plato to Nietzsche; (v) hence every philosophical inquiry into the 'essence' of philosophy can be no more than a confrontation between two ages. Otto Pöggeler comments as follows (in *Philosophischer Literaturanzeiger*, 12 [1959], 194ff): *Sein und Zeit* had described *Existenzialien*, or the structure of human existence, but it had left unanswered whether or not these *Existenzialien* are universal categories. For in that work human existence had been understood only preliminarily; its ultimate understanding was to be achieved in terms of Being which was as yet not understood. But Heidegger's later works do seek to understand Being, and they understand it historically. That is, Being is understood as manifesting itself differently in different periods of *Seinsgeschichte*. Consequently, the *Existenzialien* which structure human existence must, in the end, be understood historically as well.

But we must insist that while many – in particular, theologians – might sympathize with the thesis 'Being manifests itself differently in different periods,' the *total* historization of philosophy toward which the later Heidegger seems to be moving is open to the same objections as the crudest forms of historicism. The very thesis 'Being manifests itself differently in different periods' cannot without self-contradiction be historicized.

It is noteworthy in this connection that, like Nietzsche before him, the later Heidegger seems to take refuge more and more in poetry. But such a refuge is surely an escape from the responsibilities proper to philosophy. Qua poet, Nietzsche may be entitled to proclaim that 'God is dead.' But why should anyone accept this proclamation even if he is moved by Nietzsche's poetry and shares his sense of alienation? Why should he not instead lament, with the Psalmist, that 'God hides His face'? In the total absence of philosophical argument, the choice is made entirely on authority. But while philosophy assuredly cannot remove this need for choice it cannot escape from its own responsibilities by becoming itself an authority. At least part of the task of philosophy – existential philosophy included – must consist of argument, however inconclusive, such as the systematic elaboration of presuppositions and implications.

On the role of speculative discourse in existential philosophy, cf. further below, note 54.

46 Heidegger, 'What Is Metaphysics?' 369ff

If Heidegger's later historicism is accepted – of which, however, 'What Is Metaphysics' would seem to show no signs – existential anxiety discloses, not a transhistorical limit of human being, but merely an historical limit of an age for which 'God is dead.' (Cf. Heidegger, *Holzwege*, 193ff and especially 202.)

47 Cf. J.P. Sartre, *Existentialism* (New York, 1947), 19ff.

Our analysis of the dialectical relation between situation and situated self-making, in its application to the human situation, is enough to refute the widespread view that existential philosophy is fatalistic – a view which implies that human being is the mere product of what situates it. 'Existential limitation' and 'existential freedom,' 'standing-out-into-Nothingness' and 'being challenged to act authentically' are correlative, not mutually exclusive terms.

48 The following passage deserves to be quoted in full: 'But what is it I choose? Is it this thing or that? No, for I choose absolutely, and the absoluteness of my choice is expressed precisely by the fact that I have not chosen this or that. I choose the absolute. But what is the absolute? It is myself in my eternal validity. ... But what, then, is this self of mine? If I were required to define this, my first answer would be: it is the most abstract of all things, and yet at the same time it is the most concrete – it is freedom. ... He chooses himself, not in a finite sense (for then this "self" would be something finite along with other things finite), but in an absolute sense; and yet, in fact, he chooses himself and not another. This self which he then chooses is infinitely concrete, for it is in fact himself, and yet it is absolutely distinct from his former self, for he has chosen it absolutely. This self did not exist previously, for it came into existence by means of the choice, and yet it did exist, for it was in fact "himself." *In this case choice performs at one and the same time two dialectical movements: that which is chosen does not exist and comes into existence with the choice; that which is chosen exists, otherwise there would not be a choice.* For in case what I chose did not exist but absolutely came into existence with the choice, I would not be choosing, I would be creating; but I do not create myself, I choose myself. Therefore, while nature is created out of nothing, while I myself as immediate personality am created out of nothing, as a free spirit I am born out of the principle of contradiction, or born by the fact that I choose myself.' Kierkegaard, *Either/Or*, tr. Lowrie (Princeton, 1944), II, 179ff (my italics). Cf. also Jaspers, *Philosophie*, 463ff.

It must be noted that the 'absolute' to which the Kierkegaard passage refers is not Hegel's Absolute; and that whenever he refers to human being as a synthesis of finiteness and infinitude his meaning is different from that of Hegel, whose terminology he is apt to borrow. Because, unlike Hegel, he regards human being as existentially limited by its human situation, his human 'infinitude' consists, not of identification with the Hegelian Absolute, but merely of recognition and free acceptance of its own finitude, which, if authentically performed, is its 'absolute.'

Confusion with the traditional terms 'essence' and 'existence' has given rise to the view that 'existence,' as understood in existential philosophy, is wholly unstructured, 'essence' consisting of any structure which an individual may arbitrarily choose to adopt. Sartre's 'existence precedes essence' (*Existentialism*, 18), quoted out of context and used as a slogan, may have furthered this view. But it is wholly mistaken. A wholly unstructured existence would not be a self at all; and a choice of self made on this basis would make the distinction between authentic and unauthentic choice wholly groundless. Yet this distinction is insisted on by every existential thinker, Sartre included. Unless all human existence had qua human a common structure, how could Sartre insist, barely two pages after stating that 'existence precedes essence,' that in an authentic choice an individual must assume responsibility for all men?

Existential 'existence,' then, differs from traditional 'existence' not merely in referring to human existence only. This is generally recognized. It also differs in having a structure of its own. If 'existence' is nevertheless distinguished from 'essence,' it is because the structure of existence cannot be an object of cognition apart from acts of choosing, and because these latter acts have a structure of their own. Because they do have such a structure, all attempts to understand the structure of existence must in some way alter that structure. But there is a 'true' and a 'false' altering. The former authentically faces up to existence instead of being in unauthentic flight from it. That is, the 'true' altering must be one which is not an altering – a conclusion which leads back to the dialectic of self-choice.

Kierkegaard's 'altering which is not an altering' does not entail the absurdities that our formulation may seem to suggest. It does not deny, for example, that my historical opportunities remain unrealized unless I myself realize them; that free historical acting is an 'altering which *is* an altering.' But if I am humanly as well as historically situated, such free acting, radically considered, is part of an altering which is *not* an altering. For the historical opportunities which I realize were mine before my realization of them; and only if I choose them *as* mine is my realization of them part of an authentic act of self-choice, rather than, to use Kierkegaard's language, a mere choice of this or that.

For much of the foregoing, cf. Heidegger, 'Über den Humanismus,' in *Platons Lehre von der Wahrheit* (Bern, 1947), 70ff, especially 71: 'Das deutet an, dass sich jetzt das "Wesen" weder aus dem esse essentiae, noch aus dem esse existentiae, sondern aus dem Ek-statischen des Daseins bestimmt. *Als der Ek-sistierende steht der Mensch das Da-sein aus, indem er das Da als die Lichtung des Seins in die "Sorge" nimmt. Das Da-sein selbst aber ist das "geworfene." Es west im Wurf des Seins als des schickend Geschicklichen*' (my italics). Because of the many plays on German terms, this passage has been left untranslated.

Because of the misunderstanding that existential 'existence' is structureless, existential ethics is often regarded as nihilistic. But existential ethics never denies objective right and wrong; it merely insists that these can be discovered only in the existential situation, and hence that their discovery is shot through with risk. Franz Kafka tells the story of an individual who, though desiring to find his road to the moral law, yet fails to do so until the end of his life, both because he cannot know the right road before embarking on it, and because there is no one else to join him. It is only at the end of his life – when there is no longer time for choosing either right or wrong –

that he discovers that no one else could have joined him on his road because the road was for him alone (*Vor Dem Gesetz* [Berlin, 1934], 8ff). What gives poignancy to Kafka's story is precisely these two factors, taken in conjunction: that there is only one right road for a man, and that he cannot know whether it is right except by embarking on it.

49 This possibility is fully explored by Hegel, for whom philosophy is both the realization and part of the self-realization of the Absolute.

50 It must be borne in mind, however, that pointing-to-the-Other, the last achievement of unaided philosophical thought, need not be regarded in existential thought as necessarily the last achievement of man: if the Other is God who reveals Himself. On this point, cf., e.g., Schelling's distinction between 'negative' and 'positive' philosophy (cf. chapter 7), and Buber, *Eclipse of God* (New York, 1952), 50.

51 Kant's case against Hume is too well known to require documentation. (For a clear statement of Kantian 'self-identity,' cf. H.J. Paton, 'Self-identity,' in *In Defence of Reason* [London, 1951], 99ff, especially 102.) For the case against the reduction of 'being-for-itself' to 'being-in-itself,' cf. Fichte, *Werke*, I, 435ff, English tr., *Science of Knowledge*, ed. P. Heath and J. Lachs (New York, 1970), 16ff.

Kant, though inspiring the doctrine of human self-making in his successors, did not himself accept it. 'Even as to himself, a man cannot pretend to know what he is in himself from the knowledge he has by internal sensation. For *as he does not as it were create himself*, and does not come by the conception of himself a priori but empirically, it naturally follows that he can obtain his knowledge even of himself only by inner sense, and consequently only through the appearance of his nature and the way in which his consciousness is affected' (*Werke*, iv, 451, tr. Abbott, *Kant's Theory of Ethics* [London, 1889], 70ff, my italics).

Then why did Fichte accept the doctrine of human self-making, the first post-Kantian philosopher to do so? Three reasons may be cited for Kant's refusal to accept it, and of these the third is decisive. First, he regards natural inclinations as *ultimately* given, and hence as morally innocent. Secondly, he regards moral law too as ultimately given, and merely appropriated in human acts of self-legislation. (This interpretation is controversial, but we cannot here pause to defend it.) Thirdly, he regards the metaphysical knowledge of man as a task which transcends human power. If he is left with two human 'natures' – the empirical and the intelligible – despite the fact that there can ultimately be only one man viewed from two perspectives (e.g., Abbott, *Kant's Theory of Ethics*, 69ff), it is because of the impossibility of rising to an absolute standpoint in which the two perspectives are synthesized.

Fichte disagrees with Kant on all three points, although he is not fully aware of the fact of disagreement. First, natural inclinations are not ultimately given; for they are not innocent, and they are destined to moral transformation and eventual elimination. (Cf. above, note 33.) Secondly, moral law is produced by the self-legislating self who, in moral action, has a share in the creation of the intelligible world. Thirdly, metaphysical cognition of the self by the self is not impossible, although it is knowledge of a kind quite different from that asserted in pre-Kantian metaphysics. In intellectual intuition 'I know something because I do it.' Without this creative intuition there would be no awareness of self-identity, and without the awareness, no self-identity; but without self-identity the self would not be a self at all (*Werke*, I, 460ff, *Science of Knowledge*, 35ff).

It must be added, however, that for Fichte it is one thing to assert the indispensability of an intellectual intuition which at once knows and creates, quite another to explain the conditions of its possibility (*Werke*, I, 465, *Science of Knowledge*, 39ff). Fichte accepts idealism as the only theory capable of explaining that possibility. But subsequent developments, down to existentialism, show that the doctrine of human self-making is not necessarily bound up with idealism.

52 Cf., e.g., Fichte's 'Über den Grund unseres Glaubens an eine göttliche Weltregierung' (*Werke*, V, 177ff; English tr. by D. Breazeale, 'On the Basis of Our Belief in a Divine Governance of the World,' in J.G. Fichte, *Introductions to the Wissenschaftslehre and Other Writings* [Indianapolis, 1994], 141–54), an essay which became famous because it unleashed the famous 'atheism controversy.' While defending belief in Providence, Fichte assails the doctrine of a created self: 'Nothing other than the self may be assumed as the ground in terms of which it is to be explained. ... For how can the self explain itself – nay, even just wish to explain itself – without thereby going beyond itself and thus ceasing to be a self? Wherever we even just ask for an explanation there can no longer be a pure (absolutely free and self-dependent) self; for all explanation makes dependent' (*Werke*, V, 180, 'Basis of Our Belief,' 145).

53 These forms are art, religion, and philosophy. In these manifestations of spiritual life the self transcends selfhood itself. This implies that, so long as the self remains a self at all, it remains dependent on a natural background which is other-than-self.

54 It need hardly be said that this whole chapter has moved in the realm of speculative discourse; and that, unless it is to cease to be philosophy, all existential philosophy must in part move in that realm. But this gives rise to two questions: can existential philosophy justify its own movement in this realm; and precisely how must speculative discourse be related to what is *not* speculative discourse but immediate existential commitment – 'foundering,' 'encounter with Nothingness,' 'existential decision,' and the like? It is no

exaggeration to say that the future of existential philosophy *as philosophy* depends on its ability to answer these questions.

55 *Schriften* (Landshut, 1809), 9, *Werke*, I, 168

Chapter 9 The Historicity and Transcendence of Philosophic Truth

1 In the argument of the first part of the paper, in which reference is made to linguistic philosophy, Kant, Hegel, Marx and Nietzsche, it will be impossible to give full enough interpretations, let alone to justify the interpretations offered. Under these circumstances, no purpose is served by documentation. Only the sections dealing with Heidegger will be documented.

2 *Kant und das Problem der Metaphysik* (Frankfurt a/M, 1929; 2nd ed., 1951); *Kant and the Problem of Metaphysics*, tr. J.S. Churchill (Bloomington, 1966)

3 Already in *Sein und Zeit* (Halle, 1927) (subsequently referred to as *SZ*) Heidegger writes of Kant: 'Even if the theoretical is built into the practical reason, the *existenzial*-ontological problem of the self remains not only unsolved but even unraised' (320). I cannot agree with this Kant-interpretation, but am obviously unable here to give my own, except to say that the inadequacies of Heidegger's interpretation have in part been remedied by G. Krüger, *Philosophie und Moral in der Kantischen Kritik* (Tübingen, 1931 and 1967). (Since the page numbering of *SZ* is incorporated in its English translation, *Being and Time*, tr. J. Macquarrie and E. Robinson [New York, 1962], it will suffice to cite only the German text.)

4 Throughout this paper I use the term *ratio* to designate a thought which seeks a radically universal, and hence transhistorical, truth. I avoid the term *logos*, not because I agree with Heidegger's very special interpretation, but in order to avoid unnecessary complications.

5 On Schelling, cf. chapter 7, above.

6 Cf. *What Is Philosophy?*, bilingual edition, tr. W. Kluback and J.T. Wilde (New York, 1958).

7 *Einführung in die Metaphysik* (Tübingen, 1963), 32; *Introduction to Metaphysics*, tr. R. Manheim (New York, 1961), 35

8 Chapter 8, above

9 Chapter 8, note 45, pp 227f above

10 *SZ*, 229

11 Provided one ignores or rejects the view that nature, its laws included, is itself ultimately subject to 'historical' change; cf. e.g. S. Alexander, 'The Historicity of Things,' in *Philosophy and History*, ed. H.J. Paton and R. Klibanski (New York, 1963), 11ff. Cf. chapter 8, p 127.

12 R.G. Collingwood, *The Idea of History* (Oxford, 1946) argues this case at length, against the doctrine of a permanent human 'nature.'

13 Not accidentally this term (by now common and watered down) begins to appear, with a precise meaning, in the writings of the post-Kantian idealists. Cf. e.g. J.G. Fichte, *Werke* (Berlin, 1845), V, 184; cf. 'On the Basis of our Belief' in *Introductions to the Wissenschaftslehre*, tr. D. Breazeale (Indianapolis, 1994) 149; F.W.J. Schelling, *Werke* (Stuttgart, 1856–61), IV, 395; D.F. Schleiermacher, *Über die Religion* (Berlin, 1799), 55ff, 118ff; cf. *On Religion*, tr. J. Oman (New York, 1958), 278ff, 89ff. Hegel reduces the Kantian moral philosophy to the reflection of what he calls *die moralische Weltanschauung*, which is an historically limited *Lebenswelt*; cf. *Phänomenologie des Geistes*, ed. J. Hoffmeister (Hamburg, 1952), 424ff.

14 This view is already prepared, but not reached, by Fichte, who writes 'one must know the specific stage of culture reached by that society of which one is a member' (*Werke*, VI, 327).

15 A secondary, but of course very important difference between Marx and Nietzsche is that whereas the future post-historical classless society is inevitable (at least according to standard interpretations) the future post-historical overman is only one of two possibilities. The other is 'the last man' – the extreme form of decadence.

16 *This* 'universal,' however, is – to use Hegelian language – 'concrete' rather than 'abstract,' i.e., not an unhistorical possibility of all men but an historical actuality of world-historical significance.

17 *SZ*, 226–30

18 This term has by now become so much part of English philosophical usage as to require neither translation nor explanation.

19 Heidegger's 'temporality' is not natural, and the distinction between it and 'historicity,' though important, may be ignored for the purposes of the present paper.

20 *SZ*, 310

21 Cf., e.g. *SZ*, 12ff, 199, 248.

22 *SZ*, 312

23 Cf. e.g. *SZ*, 196: 'The explication of the being of *Dasein* as care does not force this latter under a fabricated idea, but merely brings into the form of an *existenzial* concept what is already disclosed *existenziell*-ontically.' Also *SZ*, 309: 'The question of the ability-to-be-whole is one of *existenziell* facticity. *Dasein* answers the question by being decisive.' (In some respects 'resolution' is a rendition of *Entschlossenheit* superior to 'decisiveness.' We choose the latter to preserve the contact with 'decision' [*Entschluss*]. Again, 'disclosure' is in some respects preferable to 'openness,' for *Erschlossenheit*, for it has objective rather than subjective connotations. Heidegger's term has both, cf. *SZ*, 364ff: 'In the *Erschlossenheit* of the *Da* the world is disclosed as well [*miterschlossen*].')

24 *SZ*, 260, also 266
25 *SZ*, 312
26 *SZ*, 314ff
27 *SZ*, 311
28 *SZ*, 315
29 *SZ*, 280. Karl Löwith has rightly asserted a resemblance between Heidegger's *Entschlossenheit* and Kant's categorical imperative (*Gesammelte Abhandlungen* [Stuttgart, 1960], 81; cf. above, section V).
30 *SZ*, 343
31 Cf. *SZ*, 298: 'But in what direction does *Dasein* open itself up in decisiveness? What shall it decide? The answer can be given only by the actual decision. ... Nevertheless, the *existenziell* indeterminacy of decisiveness, which can determine itself only in the decision, has its own *existenzial* determinateness.' On this latter, cf. further below, section VII.
32 The call, made in the beginning of this section, for a doctrine which shows how the *Lebenswelt* can provide a *Sitz both* for the historically situated *Weltanschauungen and* the philosophical insight into their historicity has now been given its Heideggerian answer. *Decision* gives rise to every particular 'ontisch-weltanschauliche Daseinsauslegung' (*SZ*, 200). *Decisiveness* makes these particular decisions possible. The *existenzial* interpretation of the relation between decision and decisiveness both incorporates historicism and transcends it. The question whether that interpretation, once achieved, destroys the possibility of still deciding on a *Weltanschauung* is tantamount to the question whether *Sein und Zeit* leads to nihilistic conclusions. This question transcends the scope of the present paper.
33 *SZ*, 261ff. Cf. Löwith, *Gesammelte Abhandlungen*, 81ff.
34 Heidegger virtually ignores the prophets. Of what little he says Martin Buber remarks: 'I have never in our time encountered on a high philosophical plane such a far-reaching misunderstanding of the prophets of Israel' (*Eclipse of God* [New York, 1952], 97).
35 This is true at least if we accept at face value Heidegger's own claim that his later thought is a continuation and development of *SZ*, not, as some critics have strongly argued, a repudiation of it. Cf. Karl Löwith, *Heidegger. Denker in dürftiger Zeit* (Frankfurt a/M, 1953).
36 Heidegger's later thought is best summed up in his *Letter on Humanism*, on which, for the sake of convenience, we rely heavily in the following (*Platons Lehre von der Wahrheit: mit einem Brief über den Humanismus* [Bern, 1947], henceforth referred to as *H*).
37 *H*, 53, 79; *What Is Philosophy?* 94ff
38 *Was ist Metaphysik?* (5th ed., Frankfurt a/M, 1949), 33, 9; *Existence and Being*, tr. W. Brock (London, 1949), 372; 'The Way Back into the Ground of Meta-

physics,' in W. Kaufmann, *Existentialism from Dostoievsky to Sartre* (New York, 1956), 209

39 *H*, 82

40 *H*, 54; *Was ist Metaphysik?* 9; Kaufmann, *Existentialism*, 209

41 *Identität und Differenz* (Pfullingen, 1957), 10; *Essays in Metaphysics*, tr. K.F. Leidecker (New York, 1960), 10; *Aus der Erfahrung des Denkens* (Pfullingen, 1954), 7

42 Buber writes: 'The light of the Truth which inheres in Being fragments itself in the human spirit, and achieves worldly manifestation in this fragmentedness, hence specifically *as* non-adequate. Man denies this reality proper to him when he declares himself to be the 'clearing' of Being' (*Nachlese* [Heidelberg, 1965], 137ff).

43 *What Is Philosophy?* 24ff

44 *H*, 53

45 Heidegger admits that '*to begin with*, every quest for Being, including that for the Truth of Being, must introduce itself as metaphysical' (*H*, 64, my italics). But he fails to say whether this 'to begin with' applies to all future recalling thinking, or merely to the present recalling thinking, which latter exists in an 'indigent' age, is immediately post-metaphysical, and 'too early for Being.' If the first is the case, the *ratio* is not subject either to destruction or to indefinite transformation. If the second, the quest for Being dissolves into poetry the moment it has destroyed the metaphysical 'to begin with.' For it has lost then the interpreting power by which it relates itself to, and distinguishes itself from, poetry.

Chapter 10 Hegel on the Actuality of the Rational and the Rationality of the Actual

1 Many of the points which in this brief chapter can only be stated are developed in their appropriate context in my *The Religious Dimension in Hegel's Thought* (Bloomington, 1968).

2 Hildesheim (Olms, 1962), photomechanical reproduction of the original 1857 edition. See in particular 367–8.

3 Sidney Hook, 'Hegel and the Perspective of Liberalism,' *A Hegel Symposium*, ed. C.D. Travis (Austin, 1962), 51

4 *Hegel und der Staat* (Munich and Berlin, 1920), II, 79

5 Cf., e.g., Hook, 'Hegel ... ,' 45. Hook's case is instructive because, obviously relying on memory, he is well enough served by it to quote the German text accurately – but not its order.

6 Hook, 'Hegel ... ,' 53

7 See below, section VII.

8 *Vorlesungen über die Philosophie der Religion, Werke* (Berlin, 1840–7), XI, 222ff; cf. G.W.F. Hegel, *Vorlesungen: Ausgewählte Nachschriften und Manuskripte* (Hamburg, 1983), III, 249f; *Lectures on the Philosophy of Religion*, tr. Hodgson et al. (Berkeley, Los Angeles, and London, 1984), I, 349f)

9 Ibid. *Werke*, XII, 336; cf. *Vorlesungen* (1984), V, 260; *Lectures* (1985), III, 337

Epilogue Holocaust and *Weltanschauung*

1 See my 'Holocaust and Philosophy,' *Journal of Philosophy*, 82:10 (1985), 505–14.

2 The prize surely goes to Treblinka Kommandant Franz Stangl. When asked why they had murdered the Jews, Stangl replied that they wanted their money – as if the victims had not already been stripped naked! When asked about the point of all the humiliation and cruelty, if murder was to follow anyway, he replied that it was to condition the murderers – as if these needed conditioning! Gitta Sereny, *Into That Darkness* (London, 1974), 101. See also my *To Mend the World* (New York, 1982), 214, henceforth cited as *TMW*.

3 Since this document is published and cited in many places, no reference is needed. For the meaning of the German word *das Judentum*, see below, note 20.

4 The best brief account of this theory is C.G. Hempel, 'The Function of General Laws in History,' conveniently available in *Readings in Philosophical Analysis*, ed. H. Feigl and W. Sellars (New York, 1949), 459–71.

5 I have little doubt that, as the decades wear on, the 'why' of the Holocaust will become less rather than more intelligible, with the consequence that the 'madness' 'explanation' may keep gaining ground. But since a twelve-year-long collective madness is plainly absurd, the belief may also gain ground that the Holocaust did not happen because it could not have happened.

6 See especially William Dray, *Laws and Explanation in History* (London, 1957).

7 See R.G. Collingwood, *The Idea of History* (London, 1946), part V.

8 David Irving's thesis in *Hitler's War* (New York, 1977), to the effect that Hitler ordered the deportation of Jews but not their mass murder, was never to be taken seriously. (See *TMW*, 245.) It is now refuted by Gerald Fleming's *Hitler and the Final Solution* (Berkeley, 1984). In Nazi Germany a direct *Führerbefehl* superseded all else, Hitler-inspired laws included.

9 No further reference is needed than to the 'secret' (but now well known) Himmler address to the SS murderers, in which he praises them for having done the deed, while yet remaining *anständig* ('decent'). See *TMW*, 185ff.

10 See *TMW*, 270ff.

11 See note 9, above.

12 Autonomy, as defined by Kant, does not require a person to legislate to him-

self but only, in the case where a law is given by another, to approve of it as though he himself were the legislator. Hence only the robots and sadists among the murderers can be dismissed as persons lacking in autonomy. The case of the 'idealists' among the SS, such as Eichmann and Himmler until he became *treulos* (also dismissed on these grounds as such by Bruno Bettelheim), is more complex than is fancied in the textbooks of pre-Nazi Vienna. See *TMW*, 226–30.

13 See below, note 17.

14 The thesis, put forward in Rauschning's 1938 *Die Revolution als Nihilismus* as well as his 1940 *Gespräche mit Hitler*, is ably discussed in Eberhard Jäckel, *Hitlers Weltanschauung* (Tübingen, 1969), 13ff.

15 Any notion to the contrary is a fabrication or, more correctly, 'nice' propaganda spread by people who (fairly enough) feel uncomfortable about the singled-out condition of Jews in Nazi Germany. That condition, however, was a fact. The Nazis viewed Slavs as *Menschentiere*, to be decimated and, when opportune, worked to death. But there is still a difference between these 'human animals' and Jewish 'vermin' fit only for 'extermination.'

16 In Jäckel, *Hitlers Weltanschauung*

17 Adolf Hitler, *Mein Kampf*, tr. Ralph Manheim (Boston, 1943), 22. (The German *Weltanschauung* is translated incorrectly as 'philosophy.') When throughout this essay I speak of the 'extremity that showed forth the truth' of the 'why' of the Holocaust – indeed, I would claim, of Nazism as a whole – I do no more than put Hitler's claim to a 'granite-like' *Weltanschauung* to the pragmatic test.

18 *Mein Kampf*, 55ff

19 In the book virtually every aspect of the *Weltanschauung* turns out to be subject to opportunistic modification or even abrogation – except *das Judentum*, treated in chapter 3.

20 In Hegel this German term denotes an honest (if debatable) philosophical definition of the 'essence' of the Jewish religion. A perversion already sets in with Marx, for whom this 'essence' is meant to encompass the 'existence' of the 'real' Jew, whose 'God' is 'money.' (Marx sees no need for gathering data about either the financial or mental condition of the poverty-ridden Jews of Czarist Russia.) The perversion is complete when *das Judentum* becomes the inborn character of the 'real' Jew. With Marx that Jew can still escape *das Judentum*, as was done by Marx himself. This is cut off by the Nazi *Weltanschauung* for young and old, rich and poor, the most as well as the least religious.

21 Saul Friedländer quotes Albert Speer as follows: 'New York in a hurricane of fire. He described the skyscrapers being turned into gigantic burning torches, collapsing upon one another, the glow of the exploding city illumi-

nating the dark sky.' One page later Friedländer quotes Ernst Jünger, a right-wing, militaristic, but anti-Nazi writer reacting as follows to applause given to an 18 December 1944 Hitler speech: 'The frenetic applause that accompanied his appearance was the agreement for self-destruction, a highly nihilistic act' (*Reflections of Nazism* [New York, 1984], 70–1).

22 See Dietrich Eckart, *Der Bolschewismus von Moses bis Lenin: Zwiegespräch zwischen Adolf Hitler und Mir* (Munich, 1924).

23 *Mein Kampf*, 65

24 See *Religion in Geschichte und Gegenwart*, 2nd ed., V, 1845.

25 'The all-shatterer' – a nickname given to Kant by those who understand him as shattering not only this or that metaphysical doctrine but the whole discipline of metaphysics, as harking back to the Greeks.

26 In his *Phänomenologie des Geistes*; *Phenomenology of Spirit*, chapter 6, C, a

27 In his *Erste Einleitung in die Wissenschaftslehre* (see *Introductions to the Wissenschaftslehre and Other Writings*, tr. D. Breazeale [Indianapolis, 1994], 7–35). Fichte was a rabid antisemite, but this does not enter into our present reflections.

28 In his *Reden über die Religion*; *On Religion: Speeches to Its Cultured Despisers*, tr. J. Oman (New York, 1958)

29 In his *System des Transcendentalen Idealismus*; *System of Transcendental Idealism (1800)*, tr. P. Heath (Charlottesville, 1978)

30 For a brief account of this important but complex subject see Robert G.L. Waite's excellect *Adolf Hitler – The Psychopathic God* (New York, 1977), 99ff.

31 This is a vast subject in its own right, the exploration of which is not attempted here. A small but insufficient attempt is my 'Philosophical Reflections on Antisemitism,' in *Antisemitism*, ed. Michael Curtis (Boulder, 1986), 21–38.

32 This Waite believes about Hitler: *Adolf Hitler*, 85.

33 See e.g. Alvin Rosenfeld, *Imagining Hitler* (Bloomington, 1985).

34 The furthest Martin Heidegger ever came in his *Denken* about Nazism was to dissipate it into a flattened-out loss of Being. (See *TMW*, 147–90.) The furthest Ernst Nolte comes in his *Denken* is to dissipate it into but one of three 'faces' of fascism, and fascism itself into a flattened-out revolt against transcendence. (See E. Nolte, *Three Faces of Fascism* [New York, 1965].) As for the Holocaust, this is acknowledged by Nolte but viewed as of no philosophical significance. In Heidegger's *Denken* it does not appear at all.

Permissions and Acknowledgments

The author, editor, and publisher express their appreciation to the following for permission to republish articles in this volume: Cambridge University Press, for 'Kant's Philosophy of Religion,' originally published as 'Immanuel Kant,' in *Nineteenth Century Religious Thought in the West*, edited by Ninian Smart, John Clayton, Stephen Katz, and Patrick Sherry (1985), 1:17–40; University of Toronto Press, for 'Kant and Radical Evil,' from the *University of Toronto Quarterly*, 23 (1953), 339–53, and for 'Schelling's Philosophy of Religion,' from the *University of Toronto Quarterly*, 22 (1952), 1–17; Walter de Gruyter & Co, for 'Kant's Concept of History,' from *Kantstudien*, 58:3 (1956–7), 381–98; Blackwell Publishers, for 'Schelling's Philosophy of the Literary Arts,' from *Philosophical Quarterly*, 4 (1954), 310–26; *Review of Metaphysics*, for 'Schelling's Conception of Positive Philosophy,' from 7:4 (1954), 563–82, and 'On the Actuality of the Rational and the Rationality of the Actual,' from volume 23:4 (1970), 690–8; Marquette University Press, for *Metaphysics and Historicity* (1961); Oxford University Press and Indiana University Press, for 'Holocaust and *Weltanschauung*: Philosophical Reflections on Why They Did It,' originally published in *Holocaust and Genocide Studies* 3(2): 197–208 (1988), and reprinted in *Jewish Philosophers and Jewish Philosophy*, edited by M. Morgan (Bloomington, 1995). 'The Historicity and Transcendence of Philosophical Truth' first appeared in the Proceedings of the Seventh Inter-American Congress of Philosophy, held at Laval University, Quebec, in 1967.

Index

www.ingramcontent.com/pod-product-compliance
Lightning Source LLC
LaVergne TN
LVHW082158080826
844660LV00046B/1265

9781487587215